The Rainbow Language:

The Sight, Sound & Color of the Holy Tongue

by
David Mathews

CCB Publishing
British Columbia, Canada

The Rainbow Language:
The Sight, Sound & Color of the Holy Tongue

Copyright ©2015 by David Mathews
ISBN-13   978-1-77143-239-9
Third Edition

Library and Archives Canada Cataloguing in Publication
Mathews, David, 1958-, author
The rainbow language : the sight, sound & color of the holy tongue
/ written by David Mathews. -- Third edition.
Issued in print and electronic formats.
ISBN 978-1-77143-239-9 (pbk.).--ISBN 978-1-77143-240-5(pdf)
Additional cataloguing data available from Library and Archives Canada

All Scriptural quotes are from the 1987 version of the KJV Bible and are in the Public Domain.

All other Authors or Authors' materials quoted herein are quoted by permission.

All images contained within are in the Public Domain with the exception of those that the author personally designed and those used with permission; specifically the works of Eric Bissell and William Sanford, to whom permission is gratefully acknowledged.

The Hebrew fonts contained within are from BibleWorks.
"BWHEBB, BWHEBL, BWTRANSH [Hebrew]; BWGRKL, BWGRKN, and BWGRKI [Greek] PostScript® Type 1 and TrueType fonts Copyright ©1994-2013 BibleWorks, LLC. All rights reserved. These Biblical Greek and Hebrew fonts are used with permission and are from BibleWorks (www.bibleworks.com).

Extreme care has been taken by the author to ensure that all information presented in this book is accurate and up to date at the time of publishing. Neither the author nor the publisher can be held responsible for any errors or omissions. Additionally, neither is any liability assumed for damages resulting from the use of the information contained herein.

For information regarding written permission or for author interviews please contact:
Manna from Heaven Ministries
7488 Mt. Angel Hwy NE
Silverton, OR   97381
www.livingmanna.net

Publisher: CCB Publishing
                  British Columbia, Canada
                  www.ccbpublishing.com

Dedication

To my wife Brenda who alone stood with me through the years of transition. Her stalwart heart and prayerful lifestyle have been a constant source of strength. I can't imagine this journey without her. We have truly walked together. This book is a small sample of the fruit of our labors. May you enjoy.

Acknowledgements

Where do I begin, so many have contributed to this endeavor? My children more than most, by sharing me with so many others, unselfishly gave themselves while bringing me the daily love and encouragement every daddy needs. Though I would gain the whole world, what profit would there be without my own family? B.J. Joy, (you two were there every day) Bryanna, Brandy, Candace, Rebecca, Renisa – thank you.

Brittney Scott, you challenged me to dig deeper, walk further, climb higher. You endured the task-master that I often am. I have not said thank you enough.

The Manna Crew! You followed me on the Oregon Trail! Sometimes we felt like 'Oregon or bust', yet, we're seeing the fruit of our obedience as He demonstrates His Plan.

Manuel, you and Ada 'Se ha Ganado mi Corazon y mi familia.'

Gen. Cameron Crawford U.S. Army (Ret.) Thank you sir for the honor you bestowed in helping to edit this book.

Hank and Jean Floyd. Wow! It takes resources to propagate the Kingdom! You guys have supported us on this journey more than anyone. Sis, hopefully, you'll agree your efforts were worth it. (You guys just thought I was on vacation in the Bahamas☺)

There are many others. Though I may forget to add your names here, please accept my gratitude for making this book possible.

Disclaimer

This book is designed to provide what I believe to be an exhaustive source for anyone looking at the origin of the Language of Creation. Though I am not a Linguist, I have gone to great lengths to extract a preponderance of Scriptural and extra-Biblical evidence in order to support my opinion: the language of Creation was/is Hebrew! There will be many who would argue for a literal interpretation of the text and cite my excess as one engaged in adding to or taking away from that text. In doing so, many will limit their exegesis to its traditional narrow boundaries. I do not claim to be an expert in any of the fields I have called upon as a material source to support the statements that I have made within this book, including those Scriptural texts that I have studied for more than 30–years. I am merely a student attempting to become a Disciple of that Greatest and most Infinite Teacher whose mind cannot be limited to the conventional wisdom of a single Theologian or the Doctrinal Imperative of a particular organization. Though I believe I have received personal revelation for much of what I have written, I cannot assume credit for its origin, which alone belongs to His Spirit; I have been allowed the pen.

David Mathews

Contents

Foreword

After the appearing of the diversity of languages as a model of separation of nations; a promise has been latent in the heart of the Creator for the last days, as a preamble to the total restoration of all things. That promise is a common language of unity that brings a standardized criterion of worship within the margins of what holiness represents.

Hebrew is the eternal language and heritage of the people of Israel that has been prophesied to be constituted as the vector of the promised restoration which has been waiting to be awakened through the eternal rain of His teaching, such that, like in the times of Noach, it would be manifested as a banner among all the nations.

The analogy of this revelation as the multicolored language, represented as an arch between the clouds will manifest profound truths of its own nature and is prophesied to take place before the promised coming of the Messiah. The same, as in ancient times though not obvious to the natural sight, will allow us to see these truths through a prism that will make us dig deep; far and beyond what our own natural eyes can perceive.

The effort of David to show us the relevance of the language in which the Creator expresses himself is immeasurable, taking us to seek answers that have been waiting to be revealed to all those honest seekers of the truth. It is now that the journey (which will enable us to visit all possible routes in the search of resolution) begins; from its' inception, through the Scriptures, we will travel like pilgrims to a land of promises; there we will find answers to all those matters waiting to be revealed.

Manuel Chavarria
Emet en la Torah

Preface

This journey began 30 years ago. However, a major event happened along the way just over 15 years ago, exposing the fallacy of many of the bricks in the foundation of my religious beliefs. I found myself broken, angry and frankly, my dear wife Brenda and I on the verge of quitting ministry altogether. At our wits end we had what can only be described as a Divine Encounter – though I knew Him, I did not understand intimacy with Him. What happened introduced us to the Word of the King and forever changed our lives. The journey seems only to have just begun and I find myself at this writing with an appetite for His Word more insatiable than ever! Throughout the journey we've taken turns that I couldn't anticipate and as a result, I've learned to expect the unexpected, to relish the cutting edge of new concepts and the forbidden areas that many, because of our traditions, have been afraid to explore. It hasn't been easy, but, as with every worthwhile endeavor, it has been worth the effort.

We've fought against accusations of "adding to or taking away from" His Word. How can our feeble, finite minds limit the thoughts of the Creator to only what we think He says? We've been told "it's too hard", or, "it's not necessary". Frankly, those excuses flow from a fleshly, carnal, lazy attitude that causes us to limit the amount of revelation available to those who would seek Him. Don't succumb to limitations, rather, rise to the occasion that will find you becoming the Man or Woman you've been called to be!

It is my hope to bring you, the reader to the precipice of your Faith and to provoke you to leap into an area that has been hidden from you for millennia. I encourage you to let the pages of this book do what they're designed to do –let them stretch you, challenge you and finally, conform you into His Image by confirming to you, the plan of Yahweh from the beginning - His plan for this final generation – to restore the DNA of Creation (The Living Word Himself encapsulated in the petroglyphs of Mt. Sinai who confirms the Covenant Promises of the Eternal Husband) to His Bride.

You will more than likely read things here you have never heard before. A word of caution; do not take my word for the Truth, examine it yourself. His word can stand your tests and when the dust settles, my prayer is that you will have begun your own journey into the unfathomable depths of The Rainbow Language!

Furthermore, you may be asking why I consider it necessary to learn the Hebrew language. Let me be as succinct as possible. In the days ahead we are going to be facing catastrophic events that will impact the Universe as we know it. There will be climatic upheaval as the Earths' magnetic poles change, and other weather related anomalies that are born out of conflict between Nations in which weapons capable of weather modification will be used to inflict carnage at a level destroying millions. In addition, we will be introduced to genetically modified monsters and Fallen Angelic Beings who, upon being cast down to the Earth with Satan will vent their rage upon humanity. There will be wars manifested in the natural among the armies of the Nations in direct proportion to the Spiritual conflict raging in the heavens. At the same time, terrifying signs of apocalyptic proportions will cause the hearts of many to fail them. Across the Nations, multitudes will awaken to the hard facts of the lies inherited from their fathers, in particular the most heinous of all, the idea that these end-time events are somehow reserved for the Jews, while a "get out of Jail free" card gets issued to the Christian Church. Friend, pooh-pooh this if you will. The fact remains it will not allow you to escape the reckoning that is the legal cause of YHVH. In order to not only survive, but become the true Ambassadors of the King, we must be able to stand against the machinations of the Counterfeit One – The Anti-Messiah, who will appear with 'lying signs and wonders'. How can we resist such physical much less, spiritual, supernatural forces? It is my contention, that we must familiarize ourselves with the Weapon of Choice, used by the likes of Noah, Abraham, Moshe, King David and finally – Yahshua. That weapon is His Word!

We will endeavor to prove that His word when first spoken became light. This 'Light' became the essence of all Creation, the crowning achievement of which was Man. This essence provided an aura, a covering. It became the amniotic sac of Eden, allowing Adam to function as the Regent of the Earth in the face of the arch-enemy of YHVH – Lucifer. Adam breathed in this Word – Light and exhaled it in kind as he functioned as 'creator' in a limited fashion after his Father. This light became Life. In the account of the Fall in Genesis 3 we see a transformation occurring. Adam is now mortal, death works in him. The Plan of Creation cannot be stopped, the Light – Word must now take on a different form as well in order to provide redemption for Adam. The Light takes on the Flesh of Adam. In the same fashion, light as we know it, infused the flesh in the form of congealed light known as blood! This light can be seen, felt and heard. It transcends the limits of time and space, binding the two – mortal and immortality – heavenly and earthly through the Union of Faith. Its power has not been lost. Only the knowledge suppressed by those who would keep the Union from occurring! We hope through this book to open the doorway to the restoration of the Light, Sound and Color of this Lingua Franca and thereby, see the Last Adam – the generation co-regent with Messiah, bedecked with the splendor and power due those who would once again oppose the Great Counterfeit, Satan himself!

Throughout the Ages, every attempt has been made to water-down, or otherwise obfuscate the Purity of this Word, by manipulating the Language of the Word's origin – Hebrew! It is my belief that with the advent of today's technology there is no excuse for anyone who desires, to become familiar with and intimately handle this creative power wielding it in such a way, as to become a force the Enemy must reckon with! Hebrew alone is able to reveal the thoughts and intents of the Father's heart. It is the encapsulation of His DNA! It will change you, change your circumstance and render your enemy impotent. You have asked yourself and God – Where are the miracles, where is the power, where are the men like those of old? Friend herein lays your answer! As you read this book you will begin to hear "Rise up O Mighty Man of Valor"! You're the One, you've been called. Now's the time!

I have endeavored to provide you a launching point: The Revelation contained within, He alone supplied. You must provide the will to implement it. It won't be easy. Hence, the reason we've exhausted the boundaries of conventional thinking and worked to provide you with material, references, links and our personal commitment to support you. You must learn to think outside the box. You may find much of what you read new. Don't despair. You will learn no matter you're previous level of understanding. You don't have to be a Hebrew Scholar to begin, nor a genius to decipher the code. You just need to supply the vessel – let Him fill it! Take your time, take copious notes. I hope to have made it easy for you to track down and confirm much of the content of this book, by inserting definitions, and numerous other reference materials. Some of what you will find included within. There are numerous references to Numeric Values or Gematria. These terms used to describe the number value assigned to the Hebrew letters. Hebrew is an Alpha-Numeric language, and therefore, the letters and their equivalent numbers are interchangeable. To enable your efforts at deciphering these number/letter combinations I am including a chart at the back of the book to help you work through this code source! Many people have a difficult time with the numeric values contained in this teaching. Frankly, evidence is occurring daily that reveals the restoration of the veracity, not only of His language – Hebrew – but the numbers embedded within the text. We should be careful to dismiss anything without properly doing our own research. Manna From Heaven Ministries will help you should you desire further study in this area.

Let me remind you: Numbers do not have personal feelings. They have no philosophical or theological bias. Gematria or numeric values are something that either exists, or else it does not exist. (There is no such thing as a woman being 50% or partially pregnant) Either YHVH placed an additional secret code to support the Hebrew letters in the Bible and it can be seen in every letter, word and phrase of the Bible from top to bottom, or else the pursuit is a waste of time and contains no merit whatsoever.

The presence of the numeric values is valid, else my trying to find spiritual significance in the numerical values of the Hebrew words of the Bible, would have no more merit than seeing the Face of YHVH in a Jelly Roll. What I have found is that the only criticism of this subject you will ever hear (on the Web or anywhere), will only come from people who give these notes a cursory review from an uninformed, 'biased by traditions' – analysis. When confronted they deny their own cynicism. As with the points made throughout regarding the association of His word with light, sound, color, musical notes, and vibrational frequencies no one will be able to delve into the mountain of evidence and come up with any credible statistical evidence that will cast doubt on the overall validity. This subject contains no fatal flaws. It is only this poor authors' limitation in conveying them.

In addition to letter/number charts I have also taken the liberty of supplying the Hebrew definition of countless words with their Strong's Numbers. This is for cross-referencing your definition to the Strong's Exhaustive Concordance, an invaluable aid to help you toward understanding the significance of the Hebrew origin of the Scripture. You will see those listed in the following manner: H#3701 (random number choice). To find this number, refer to the Hebrew section of the Strong's concordance where that numeral is listed for the definition. You may find several online sources that will aid you in a much quicker fashion.

I have also chosen to use the Hebrew Names of God the Father. How I have the name listed is my personal choice. I prefer: Yahweh or the Tetragrammatons': YHVH. I have also taken the liberty of using the Hebrew name of our Messiah: Yahshua. Please understand these are my opinion and I have no desire to offend those who may choose otherwise. I value the opinion of my brothers who feel the Name should not be made 'common'. However, He has made it very plain that He intends to restore His name: Zechariah 14:9:

And the YHVH shall be king over all the earth:
in that day shall there be one LORD, and his name one.

A Prayer for Understanding:

Before we begin, I want to ask you to indulge me a moment as I share a prayer of petition to the Father. It is my opinion, that should you find things difficult for you to normally grasp (As Scripture so often presents) if you have prefaced your efforts by asking for an anointing specific to understanding what He would divulge to you it would be a huge advantage. The following template has been an invaluable aid as my petition. I am taking the gist of this prayer from the New Testament book of Colossians chapter 1: 9 – 14. The Apostle Paul voiced this prayer on behalf of those hearing the Truth. It is my hope for you as well:

Father, let this Reader be filled with the knowledge of
Your will in all wisdom and spiritual understanding; That
he or she might walk worthy of Messiah unto all pleasing,
being fruitful in every good work, and increasing in the
knowledge of YHVH: Strengthen them with all might, ac-
cording to His glorious power, unto all patience and
longsuffering with joyfulness; We give thanks in advance

unto you Father, which hath made us able to be partakers of the inheritance of the saints in LIGHT: You have delivered us from the power of darkness, and translated us into the Kingdom of your dear Son: In whom, we have redemption through His blood, even the forgiveness of sins:

Finally, let me make you aware of Matthew 5:8:

Blessed are the pure in heart: for they shall see God.

For those who are skeptical in reading this book I applaud you! You should be careful and weigh everything. You will be challenged. The rest is a heart issue. If you look for Him, you will see Him.

Now, my dear Reader, may your efforts lead you into a Divine Encounter with the King of Creation! Please consider throughout your journey that my efforts are bent toward blessing you. Should you discover something that you're not comfortable with, measure it against His Word and remember specifically - my frailties and limitations as an author. Shalom!

Unleash the Hounds!

David Mathews

Chapter 1

Back to the Beginning

Our culture teaches us that the future is in front of us, yet because the Creator transcends time as we know it, He sees both the beginning and the end. Notwithstanding, our myopic viewpoint hinders a proper Eschatological (End times) understanding simply because we never look back at the patterns of Prophecy that have been cleverly hidden from the casual seeker; especially those found in the Book of Beginnings – Genesis. This poses problem #1 for the critical thinker – alienating the source that has the answers! When in doubt, consult the 'Owners' Manual! What a novel idea! (No pun intended) Genesis is that *'Owner's Manual'*. In fact, Yahweh plainly states the same in Isaiah 46:10. Let's examine it carefully in order to put this book into proper perspective. For the sake of simplicity most of the Scripture quoted in this work will be from the King James Version (KJV hereafter) however, we will break that apart by looking at the Original Text in the Hebrew. Before we're finished you will know why!

> ***Isaiah 46:10*** *Declaring the end from the beginning, and from ancient times the things that are not yet done, saying, My counsel shall stand, and I will do all my pleasure.*

One translation says, "Only I can tell you the future before it even happens." With our collective breath held, deciphering the Authors' intent here is titillating. Yet, the picture language of Hebrew probes even deeper: If you're ready for this adventure then let's examine the key words here.

♦ Declaring, H#5046   נָגַד   *nagad*

Translated as meaning 'to be conspicuous, to publish, to avow, to announce'. The individual Hebrew letters add greater understanding with their own word pictures. The Nun (נ) indicates life and all that pertains to it. The Gimmel (ג) the One lifting or lifted up, while the Dalet (ד) represents the Door. It would seem then the word picture has to do with the Life of the One who would be lifted up and thus become, the Door.

♦ End, H#319,   אַחֲרִית   *'achariyth,*

Meaning the latter part, the end. Latter time (prophetic for future time) posterity.

♦ Beginning, H#7225,   רֵאשִׁית   *re'shiyth,*

The first, beginning.

Reasonable deduction would conclude the Creator is stating His original intent was to make conspicuous (obvious) the purpose of lifting up the Word – Messiah, the Life or DNA of Yahweh – that He (The Word) would become the Door (for understanding the Creator?) This would be prophetically declared from the inception of Creation indicating that those at the Latter Time would be able to 'See or Know' The Word and thus, Him. This was in fact, declared from the Book of Beginnings – Genesis or B're'shiyth – 'In the Beginning'.

This should help put into perspective the words of Yahshua in John 12: 31 & 32, which see:

Now is the judgment of this world: now shall the prince of this world be cast out. And I, if I be lifted up from the earth, will draw all men unto me.

This follows the Audible Voice of YHVH being heard! It seems a legal judgment is being rendered regarding 'the prince of this world who is being cast out' and Yahshua being 'lifted up'. We understand the connection here to the method of His execution upon the crucifixion stake, but, there's more – far more than meets the eye! Yahshua is the WORD! To lift up the Word, indicates to bring attention, to restore, to vocalize it! It is my opinion that the legal judgment rendered upon the execution of Yahshua opened the way for the Living Word to be interjected into the Fleshly Lives of Adam's descendants rejuvenating – making them alive! Sure, this speaks of spiritual resurrection, but, how much more, the physical restoration of the Sons of YHVH that Romans 8 speaks of? Those for whom Creation awaits are the Sons able to take over the affairs of the Fathers' business. Hence, the unabated longing for the visible manifestation of those individuals whose spoken Words will break the bonds of the curse and set free Creation!

Am I wrong or can we surmise that the WORD (Who became flesh) of YHVH is the key to understanding the Creator Himself and any and all communication between He and creation? If so, then we must learn all we can about this 'Word' - 'Language'. We'll begin by linking words that are synonymous, as well as, those used metaphorically to describe this 'light infused, word-language' throughout Scripture. This should help us see the different 'facets' or faces of the Word. By becoming more aware, you'll learn to recognize the subtleties expressed in each distinctive use. You will see Him captioned in the pictograph that is the Hebrew language like no other source. You will learn to 'handle the Word of YHVH with a reverence, fear and respect due only the King of Creation!

The first place we'll look is Psalm 119 which *just happens to be divided* into 22 stanzas of 8 verses each, one stanza for each Hebrew letter, which will begin each verse in the stanza. For an example in verse 105 the stanza begins with the letter Nun – life. Here the Word is compared to a Lamp and a Light. Verse 130 is part of stanza Pey – the mouth, that which is spoken or breathed, and again links Light and Word. (According to the Psalmist this revelation gives understanding to the simple, the Hebrew word is H#6612 פְּתִי pĕthiy rendered simple, but also 'open-minded'; one who is able to think outside the box of tradition) In the Gospel of Mark, chapter 4 tells us the Word is Seed, the book of Hebrews and that of Ephesians, liken the Word unto a Sword. We see in Gen. 3 the Voice of YHVH is metaphorically used to represent the Word. Additionally, throughout the description of the Tabernacle the Menorah or Lampstand, the Fire of YHVH can also be seen as another dimensional revelation of the Word representing the Character or DNA, life or Presence of YHVH.

These are some of the more familiar adjectives and where either is used one of the others could be substituted and not detract from the hidden meaning in the text. Thus, *voice-sound, light, seed, fire* and *sword* can each, interchangeably, represent the Word. Yet, which word, which language? Was it just any known language? We are told the 'whole earth was of one language, and of one speech' in Gen. 11:1, 6 and that 'nothing will be restrained from them which they imagined to do'. If their tongues were confounded at Babel in Gen. 11 is it possible that a language yet exists that exhibits each of the above descriptions - without the compromise of Babylon, one perhaps that has been hidden, protected – waiting to be restored for this last generation? If so, the possibilities for those who learn it are limitless!

Before you answer, gather all the information contained here forward and process it through the lens of Scripture. If what I postulate is true (I believe Zephaniah 3:9 confirms it) you are about to embark on a journey of discovery that will leave you breathless in anticipation of the potential of His Word in your mouth! By the way, the Hebrew word Zephaniah, H#6846 צְפַנְיָה

though commonly rendered "Jehovah has treasured", is derived from the root tsefan meaning, to hide, store up, to hide from discovery [until the time of the unsealing or unveiling perhaps?]. Chapter 3 verse 9 tells us that He will 'turn (The Hebrew word here means to transform, to change, to turn) to the people a pure – shining, polished, bright – word that will enable them to worship Him with one consent! It is my opinion this word or language is the Lashon Qodesh – The Holy Tongue. Some may argue, but I am convinced it's Hebrew, the language of Creation! I do acknowledge that the current Chaldean Flame letters are probably not the original letters, rather the Paleo-Hebrew. The Consensus is that all languages that exist are learned, *Hebrew alone is the language that is studied!*

I also believe all languages past and present were confounded at Babel (Gen. 11) with the exception of this Holy Tongue, Hebrew; it alone left in the charge of the Shem-ite lineage. Where's my proof?

> **Genesis 10:30** *And their dwelling was from Mesha, as thou goest unto Sephar a mount of the east.*

♦ Mesha, H#4852,   מֵשָׁא   *Mesha'*

Though defined as 'freedom', it is spelled the same as H#4853, massa, a masculine noun meaning a burden or load, by extension, a burden in the form of a prophetic utterance or oracle.

♦ Sephar, H#5611,   סְפָר   *Cĕphar,*

Rendered 'a numbering' it is the same word for BOOK – Sefer!

♦ Mount, H#2022, הַר *har*,

Translated as mountain, it euphemistically can indicate the abode or authority of YHVH.

♦ East, H#6924, קֶדֶם *qedem*

Defined as 'east', antiquity, that which is before, *the beginning*!

Our extrapolated definition is eye-popping:

The House of Shem carried the burden of the prophetic utterance – THE LANGUAGE – which was contained in the Book or Sefer of YHVH - the authority from the Beginning!

Please remember that Sefer can also indicate to NUMBER – and the Hebrew language demonstrates the use of the letters as numerals. The letters and numbers are interchangeable and one enhances the understanding gleaned from the other!

Furthermore, I contend that Shem passed this language on to Abraham in Genesis 14: 20 where we see what is normally said to be the place where Abraham pays tithes to the King of Salem, Melchisedek. However, when I read the text in Hebrew I see:

וַיִּתֶּן־לוֹ מַעֲשֵׂר מִכֹּל:

Vayitten-lo maser mikol.

The sentence structure and use of pronouns here makes it plain that Melchisedek is the subject of this sentence *and in my opinion the one who pays tithes to Abraham*, again, in my opinion, we're witnessing a transference of the Priestly lineage and the charge of the Language of the Priesthood!

Abraham was first called 'the Hebrew' in Gen. 14: 13 where I believe the encounter with Shem (As Melchisedek) would also occur. Further investigation of this words' origin (Hebrew - from which the language takes its' name) is intriguing.

♦ Hebrew, H#5680   עִבְרִי   *'Ibriy,*

"One from beyond". This common definition doesn't do justice to the word. The 3-letter root Ayin-Bet-Resh is first seen in Gen. 10:21: *Unto Shem also, the father of all the children of Eber, the brother of Japheth the elder, even to him were children born.*

This verse presents a conundrum. Shem was not the father of Eber, nor his children; rather, he was the grandfather, with Arphaxad being the Father. Now let's set the stage for context: *Remember this is during the time that the Tower of Babel event occurs. The Principal antagonist of the Shemites would be the leader of the Babylonian rebellion – Nimrod. Now, looking at the literal translation of Eber, עֵבֶר 'Eber while it can indicate the 'region beyond', across, the other or opposite side, *it does also infer to stand in opposition to.*

In other words, it would seem Eber is standing in opposition to Nimrod. How? Again, look at Gen. 10:25, where we're told Eber 'names' – or prophesies over – his son, calling him Peleg, *'for in his days was the earth divided.'* Though, like many, I agree the land masses could have been divided in his day, I'm convinced a sharp *spiritual division* occurred regarding the profanation of the Lashon - Qodesh - Holy Tongue by Nimrod, leading to the confounding of the language(s) and subsequent dispersion of the Nations by the division of the land masses! The word Babel can be translated 'confusion by mixing' as in mixing the tongues. We've already discussed how word and seed can be synonymous. In this instance, we have Nimrod attempting to profane the seed-line (Serpent Seed vs. Woman's Seed Gen. 3: 15) again by verbal in-

7

tercourse, which causes a proliferation of spiritual children to be born! This pattern can be seen in the physical realm as well from Gen. 3 through Gen. 6!

It is my opinion that the Language of Creation was Hebrew, the Word of YHVH, i.e. His Seed. In order to propagate His lineage, the word or seed, must remain pure. An Heirloom Seed, so to speak. To counterfeit that word or seed, the enemy must in some way manipulate the gene pool or language. A GMO (genetically modified) hybrid would be his answer.

Some of you may be unfamiliar with the possibility of two competing seed lines or lineages: One through which the 'dark side' or Serpent's race could be propagated, the other the lineage through which Messiah would come. Various opinions abound, including some that have heinous racial implications. We will not lend credence to that lie within this work, but, we will concentrate a few moments on a short explanation of these two opposing lineages, whose offspring have been and still are, locked in mortal (Immortal is more appropriate) combat!

The Two Distinct Seed Lines

To begin with, what possible link could there be between these opposing seed lines and the Language of Creation? Much more than meets the casual eye I might say. Perhaps you will also, as we delve into the realm that has been forbidden to anyone but the 'diligent seeker'.

For arguments sake, without subjecting ourselves to 'thinking outside the box' the premise that there would even be a need for a Holy Tongue in what should have been a perfect world is nonsensical. The mere consideration of a mixed or confounded lingua franca is quite an awful taste to the refined palate that has become todays' Bible Student. Yet, none-the-less, it points us backward to the encounter in Genesis 3 where the conflict regarding the proper interpretation of the Creator's Word originated. If one looks in the Hebrew text, there are clues much further backward (Genesis 1 to be exact), revealing how the line of demarcation between Light and Darkness - Good and Bad Seed - forced the initial separation.

Following that separation, whose boundary lines were not to be compromised upon penalty of death, we can see the telling results of how a choice that is made out of rebellion may impact each successive generation who also failed to heed the warning; much like the aftereffect following the original declaration of YHVH to Adam:

> **Genesis 2:16-17** *Of every tree of the garden thou mayest freely eat: But of the tree of the knowledge of good and evil, thou shalt not eat of it: for in the day that thou eatest thereof thou shalt surely die.*

The Law of Genesis states that each tree yields fruit, whose seed [was] in itself, after his kind: We don't have a problem understanding the physical application, yet, to contemplate a *Spiritual Being* likened unto a tree and releasing fruit with seed in it takes us into a different dimension. [Here's where my readers usually begin to hyper-ventilate]

Genesis 3 begins to reveal exactly what occurred between Adam, Eve (Chavah) and the Serpent! This was not just your common Apple (Whose Seed was in Himself) being passed around. It could not have been good fruit anyway, because a good tree brings forth good fruit while an evil one produces just that, evil seed. So, what does happen? The Hebrew language makes it very apparent that more than just a casual 'tete-a-tete' occurs between the three individuals. It is my opinion that strong evidence exists to prove a sexual tryst taking place. If one takes the time to break apart the Hebrew words, particularly in Gen. 3: 6 you find words like 'pleasant', H#8378, אַוָה ta'avah, which carries the idea of a lustful desire, and its connection to the eyes, H#5869, Ayin, which can infer the Eye, while euphemistically indicating a spring or well, the womb as a spring or well, thus, the sensual tone is unmistakable. Biting a simple apple seems rather hard to swallow (Pun intended) particularly when the result of doing so would cause YHVH to curse an entire specie simply because of tasting a literal piece of fruit. There had to be much more, far more; it becomes obvious when we note how this passage follows the dissertation of Gen. 2 where Adam is seen being charged with naming the animals that have been brought before him to be examined for suitability as *HIS help mates.* (Gen. 2: 20) The phrase 'help meet' is interesting. The Hebrew has it: עֵזֶר כְּנֶגְדּוֹ. Ezer K'negdo. The word Ezer simply translated indicates a helper, in particular a 'female'. Adam is a male, with seed, remember that. The letter Kaf (K) appended at the front K'negdo suggests, 'like or as, or toward'. This leaves us with the root word neged, H#5048, נֶגֶד, meaning what is in front, before your face, in or for your purpose. It is a cognate (Relative of) H#5046, nagad, spelled with the same consonants, yet indicating to make something or someone known, to manifest, and [Brace yourself for this] To Bring someone/something to the light – to make it conspicuous! This same word is also used in Daniel 7:10 to describe the fiery stream that issues forth out of the Ancient of Days! There was no way that just any vessel could 'house the seed' and bring One to the Light! This is a confirmation that Marriage is between One Man and One Woman for the express purpose of releasing seed-light and receiving seed-light, thereby producing Godly SEED!

> *Malachi 2:15 And did not he make one? Yet had he the residue of the spirit. And wherefore one? <u>That he might seek a godly seed.</u> Therefore take heed to your spirit, and let none deal treacherously against the wife of his youth.*

Any attempt at sexual intimacy outside this framework becomes a direct example of insurrection against the Creator! Hence, the reason Adam is tested with the animals above, and later, tested with the Serpent – Lucifer, whose method of operation was exactly that – cross the boundary, pervert the seed.

Again, this is a stretch for some, but, Ancient documents indicate that part of the Luciferic Rebellion and subsequent debauchery engaged in by the Fallen Ones of Gen. 6 would have included sexual perversion with animals. It follows that Adam would have been tested as well. If this was an attempt to compromise the Seed Line ...then surely you're beginning to understand how those Ancient 'myths' regarding monstrous Beings, hybrid creations like the Cyclops, Centaurs, and many others had their roots in truth! You should expect nothing less in our day! In fact, Science is, as we speak, attempting to create the same hybrid, chimera seed line, producing 'cloned' species, spliced gene-modified mutations the end result of which is to seduce you into the mindless acceptance of a perverted gene pool, where no true Children of YHVH can be found!

I'm sorry Toto; you're not in Kansas anymore! Brace yourself for the Wizard – he's coming!

As we look at the Genesis tryst of Adam, Eve (Chavah) and the Serpent and our outlandish claim is examined, then where is the result of that 'encounter'? Seed gets planted, naturally, there must be offspring right? Else, this becomes the ranting of an eccentric author who has been exposed to one too many "Close Encounters of the 3rd Kind". Let's look a bit further:

Genesis 4: 1 – 3 is our destined place: The KJV reads in a way that makes these events separate from Gen. 3. However, in the Hebrew there are no punctuations, no italicized words, and no chapter divisions. So, in context this chapter has to be included in the prior one. Yet, the chronology doesn't fit in the KJV either.

What we have is a past-tense explanation. Adam knew – was intimate with – Eve - Period. The next statements regarding Cain are quite interesting. She remarks "I have gotten a man from YHVH". The sentence structure indicates it could easily have read, "I have gotten a man against – YHVH". Cain is the son of the Serpent and Eve, while Abel is the Seed of Adam and Eve. They were, without doubt (in my opinion) twins in the womb! Ouch! Don't choke on me!

There is a well-known medical term today used to describe this very issue: Hetero-paternal superfecundation - which is defined as two different eggs fertilized by the sperm of two different men, i.e. twins in the womb from two different fathers. Now, time doesn't permit in this work to dig much deeper but, we've a number of teachings to add further insight should you desire. (*See the contact info at this books' end) I only wanted to establish a bit of a foundation simply because we use the term 'Two Seed lines' quite extensively! Hopefully, this will help you to understand why the language, which we contend, is word or seed, becomes such a focal point of contention throughout recorded history. YHVH considered it so relevant that He Himself came down to get involved in the confounding of the tongue – seed of those who would oppose Him! He has proven to respond to the Enemy's efforts at genetically modifying the Hebrew language, by physically revealing Himself to all as the Manifest Presence or Living Word. He did in the Garden, at Babel and he did so again at the Mt. Sinai encounter where the Manifest Presence Himself descended on the mountain to 'vocalize' the terms of the Betrothal contract to Israel. It is at this encounter that we see the Mountain literally become emblazoned with the Fire and Light of His Word! Look at this one verse:

> ***Exodus 20:18*** *And all the people saw the thunderings, and the lightnings, and the noise of the trumpet, and the mountain smoking: and when the people saw it, they removed, and stood afar off.*

Though rendered 'all the people saw the thunderings and lightnings' Jewish Scholars have always known that a more literal translation of the Hebrew would say that "all the people saw the voices and the flames."

Philo, the first-century Jewish philosopher, describes the scene as follows (quoted in [5, p. 29]): "Then from the midst of the fire that streamed from heaven there sounded forth to their utter amazement a voice, for the flame became articulate speech in the language familiar to the audience, and so clearly and distinctly were the words formed by it that they seemed to see them rather than hear them."

Another parallel rabbinic tradition, recorded in the Babylonian Talmud (Tractate Shabbat 88b), answers the second question by saying that the flames of God's words divided into smaller sparks that traveled in all directions, proclaiming Torah (The first 5 books of the Bible according to the Jewish Sages. However, this author views all Scripture as inspired and future references will indicate such unless noted) in all the languages of the world [3, p. 135; 5, p. 28]. Two other scriptures were advanced in support of this scenario:

> **Psalm 68:11** *The Lord gave the word: great was the company of those that published it.*

According to this interpretation, the "great company" of Ps. 68:11 was the sparks that spread the word in many languages.

> **Jeremiah 23:29** *Is not my word like as a fire? Saith the Lord; and like a hammer that breaketh the rock in pieces?*

These references were seen as an indicator of God's words splitting into smaller pieces.

A further tradition asserted that when God's word was announced in the languages of the world, Torah was being offered in some sense to all nations. However, only Israel was willing at that time to say [http://graceandknowledge.faithweb.com/tongues.html]:

> **Exodus 24:7** *All that the Lord hath said will we do, and be obedient.*

The above tradition has caused many Jewish Scholars to view the account of the Day of Pentecost in Acts with regard, though denying the 'Messiah' connection.

It is my opinion the Tower of Babel confrontation sets into motion a vivid view of the contrast between the Language of YHVH and that of His Enemy who speaks with a 'forked tongue' (☺).

Shall we get back to the Tower of Babel incident?

Once again, if we confine our study to what is understandable through the lens of the KJV, we're stymied here. For instance, if we read Gen. 11:1 it would seem that no division over the Lashon Qodesh – Holy Tongue ever existed as I contend in the above paragraph. Such predicaments serve only to reinforce my opinion that without a fundamental understanding of the Hebrew language we cannot hope to grasp what the Creator is trying to convey to us. It is as if we're looking at a coded message and are unaware of it. However, if one has access to the Cipher itself, the code becomes a means of keeping the true intent of the text from others! Incidentally, the word 'cipher' comes from the Hebrew word Cepher – meaning to number, tally, to record, to etch with a mark, while also meaning 'a book'. Without that coded cipher we're left to assume that as of Gen. 11 and the Babel incident, all the earth's people spoke one language. *This means the Hebrew would have also been corrupted!* Well, what do you think? Hmmm? Come on, let's step outside the box of conventional thinking and see if perhaps something else is being said.

First, I'll rattle your cage of comfort by explaining that Hebrew is read from right to left, while English is read left to right. (Of course you knew that) This by itself doesn't seem a problem, yet English is one of, if not the, hardest languages to learn and I'm convinced it is so by design. Why? To begin with let's discuss a developmental language disorder most prevalent in English speaking nations called Dyslexia. Research suggests that phonological processing skills are crucial in the translation of symbols to sounds, and the development of rapid and automatic decoding skills. There are studies whose research indicates children, whose phonological processing skills are compromised in some way, are at risk of experiencing difficulties in the acquisition of literacy; it supports the suggestion that dyslexia can be viewed as lying on the continuum of developmental language disorders. This impairment according to new research suggests the phonetic system (System of sounds of a particular language) may be to blame! [http://journals.plos.org/plosone/article?id=10.1371/journal.pone.0044875]

The English language, in all honesty, hinders us from proper understanding of Torah! So, how can we really understand Scripture when our English way of thinking and reading is backwards? For an example of how skewed our perceptions may be, we'll take a look at the Tower of Babel incident once again, to hopefully, prove a point! ☺

To begin, I'll place Gen. 11:1 here in the counterfeit, backward, Kings' English:

And the whole earth was of one language, and of one speech.

Next, we'll review it in the Real King's Language: (The King of Creation - Hebrew)

וַיְהִי כָל־הָאָרֶץ שָׂפָה אֶחָת וּדְבָרִים אֲחָדִים׃

Vayehi Kol – haaretz saphah echat udevarim echadim.

15

Some translators render the verse: "The entire world had one language and one way of speaking". But, I don't think that's the case here! Granted, I am an opinionated individual, though not ignorantly so!

In Hebrew the phrase 'Kol haaretz saphah echat' is in the singular form – 'The Whole Earth spoke one language', while the phrase 'udevarim echadim' is in the plural. The Ancient Sage Ibn Ezra accepted the words literally by explaining that some would have had a more extensive knowledge of this language, while others would have a limited vocabulary – though the same language.

However, there are other more intriguing views that seem to allow for a broader perspective. For example: though the word echadim is rendered 'One', it is hard to pluralize 'One'. On the other hand, if we look at the root of echad, H#259, אֶחָד 'echad, one, once, etc. the cipher of the code kicks in. The two letter root –stem is the Chet-Dalet, H#2297 & H#2298. The latter definition meaning 'sharp' and used metaphorically, as in the sharp tongues of those opposed to YHVH. It also describes the deadly seductive tongue of an adulteress. The plural form echadim above, though contextually out of place as the plural of 'One', according to some translators, can be defined as 'two beings or people', as well as, indicating 'One plan against the One God' (Rashi and Pseudo-Jonathan) This has led some Ancient Sages to form the opinion that this verse could expose the conflict broiling between Shem and Nimrod – Once again, those two opposing Seed lines. I have looked at the same, and here lies my 'extrapolated' definition, you decide:

The entire earth had the sharp tongue of the Adulteress standing in opposition to (Two People – Shem and Abraham who were charged with keeping the language perhaps?) the Plan of YHVH!

What plan was this? The same as that of Adam – to ensure that Noah's generation and offspring would become fruitful, multiply and replenish, subdue and have dominion! Shem who as the *lan-*

guage guardian passes the language across the flood to Abraham (Abraham who is 48 years old at Babel) will become High Priest in Shem's stead and the first "Hebrew" - one identified as a carrier - born after the flood! By fulfilling the role of High Priest and Firstborn, we see how both were instrumental in the propagation of the earth with/through the Seed/Word/Light known as the Lashon Qodesh – Holy Tongue, Hebrew!

Abraham is a type of YHVH. The example of his two wives, Sarah & Hagar, is a striking picture of the Covenant wife contrasted with the wife of the Flesh! Curiously, Hagar, H#1904 is not defined in the Strong's Concordance, so you have to do some digging. The word is a cousin to H#1898, hagah, meaning to remove, to take away, and to separate, as in removing dross or impurities from silver. It refers to YHVH driving away the rebellious. [*Abarim Publications defines Hagar: To take flight, a sojourner, the dragged away one*] She was from Egypt – typifying sin! Thus, she pictures a future Israel – 10 northern tribes who are separated from the Bridal Company – While Judah remains in Covenant! It is this separated Bride – the Lost Sheep – ewe, H#7354, לרח the Rachel that Messiah came for.

Perhaps we'll look later in this work at how Abraham passes the language to his descendants. For the time being it is evident that something strikingly powerful seems to reside within this Tongue! What hidden force resonates in each letter waiting to be unveiled to the Generation who will search for it? Before we go let's work on this tangled web surrounding the Tower of Babel just a tad more, shall we?

After gleaning the kernels of truth left behind from our earlier extrapolation of Genesis 11: 1, it's not hard to see the conflict arising between the two camps. We find them segregated by an obedience toward or rebellious stance against, the Great Suzerain King and the language of His Covenant. It would seem a juxtaposition of the genuine bride versus her harlot sister, who is seduced by the anti-Messiah of that day – Nimrod. This conflict rages throughout history culminating in a final battle between the arch foes: Messiah – Yahshua, guardian of the Covenant Language and the coming Anti-Messiah who will raise great words against this Covenant. By looking here, we can see why it was necessary for the first appearance of Yahshua and His assignment to gather the Lost Sheep of the House of Israel, who, following the above pattern had been scattered among the nations again. It would seem that He is willing to offer Himself for those within the camp of the wicked if they will avail themselves of His sacrificial efforts. Rev. 18: 4 echoes this same plaintive admonition to those still in Babylon at His next appearing: "Come out of her my people..." We can follow the same script in the New Testament account of Mark 16: 9 where we see Yahshua appearing after His resurrection to Mary Magdalene, the former harlot, out of whom, He had cast seven devils. Most just skip past this verse never seeing the Gen. 11 connection, but you will! Let's examine her name:

♦ Mary, H#4813, מִרְיָם, *Miryam*

Translated 'Miriam', and meaning "Rebellion". By breaking the word apart, we see the Mem-Resh (rm) root which indicates bitterness, rebellion and the Yod-Mem (יָם) which reveals 'seas or great waters'. This sounds like the bitter waters of jealousy test for the Adulterous bride! (Read Numbers chapter 5) Indeed! Mary was a harlot!

♦ *Magdalene*, G#3094, translated 'a tower'. It is from the same Hebrew word translated as tower, H#4026, מִגְדָּל migdal, in Gen. 11: 4! You're looking at the rescue of the Adulterous Bride because Yahshua paid the penalty for her by drinking the bitter cup of jealousy meant for her. Now you know why He makes this famous declaration while in Gethsemane:

Matthew 26:39 *And he went a little further, and fell on his face, and prayed, saying, O my Father, if it be pos-*

sible, let this cup pass from me: nevertheless not as I will, but as thou wilt.

If she comes out of Babylon at the Last Days, she will not have to drink of that Cup. However, Babylon will drink doubly from it!

No matter the effort of the enemy to destroy the Language and thus, the Seed or Lineage of YHVH, He – YHVH - always has *The Plan*. It will not fail! You should learn the language of that plan and make provisions to exercise your option as one rescued from Babylon. Take a look at the powerful declaration of the Great King concerning His word below!

Isaiah 55:11 *So shall My word be that goeth forth out of My mouth: it shall not return unto me void, but it shall accomplish that which I please, and it shall prosper in the thing whereto I sent it.*

Doesn't this sound remarkably like the concern of Yahweh written in Gen. 11: 6! If the wicked of Nimrods' day had access to the Rainbow – Hebrew language, nothing they aspired toward would have been withheld. There's power in His Spoken – Written Word! It amazes me that the occult realm understands and strives for the control of that power, far better than many who call themselves 'Believers'!

Furthermore (*Note how verse Is. 55: 10 compares His thoughts to the harvest. Incidentally, thoughts written or spoken become 'language') we also understand that He spoke creation into existence. It was/is this same language. If we're not seeing similar results whose fault is that and why aren't we? Friends, herein lay the objective of this work, to provoke you toward putting this Word-Seed-Language in your heart that you might become an ambassador capable of working for The King!

To do so, we must understand it. We must regard it as Sacred and become adept in applying it to every facet of our lives and finally, as it is restored, we must guard against the counterfeits. Frankly, there's an interesting verse in 2Timothy 3:3 that you really should look at. The English won't tell you what I'm about to reveal, mind you, so we'll look here at the Greek words. Grab your seatbelt! The description that follows is specifically directed toward 'The Last Days' and thus, our generation. Here's verse two and three:

> **2 Timothy 3:2-3** *For men shall be lovers of their own selves, covetous, boasters, proud, blasphemers, disobedient to parents, unthankful, unholy, Without natural affection, trucebreakers, false accusers, incontinent, fierce, despisers of those that are good.*

The phrase I want you to focus on is 'False accusers' in verse 3. It sounds rather innocuous in the English. Though some translators have it as 'slanderers', or malicious gossips, it is well understood, though ill-favored, that this group is deeply entrenched in most Congregations and we're quite fond of them, so we tend to overlook this description. However, note the Greek #1228, diabolos; you've seen how it's translated, but, metaphorically it indicates a person said to act the part of the devil or to side with him in opposing the Creator! It is quite often rendered plainly as 'devil'! This isn't saying we'll have lots of devils running amok within our groups (Though it is plausible). However, what is being said is there will be many people *speaking the language of the devil!* The false language isn't often directly opposite of the Truth, which would make it easy to recognize. More often, it's an intentional misquote of Scripture, something taken out of context and manipulated to fit the personal agenda of the flesh! This is far more diabolical (*Note that Greek word) than an abject lie!

This could be frightening to some, for how can we know the false if we haven't been familiar with the genuine? Right now is always the best time to begin any endeavor!

Thus far we've seen the introduction of His Word as "Seed" into the earth. To countermand that, the enemy finds a suitable host

(Adam and Eve) in order to inseminate them with a perverted alternative. Losing access to the Life of that Seed or Word first breathed into the Adam opens the doorway to death. Without the shielding provided by the Light of His Word, both spirit and flesh experience death. The authority of Adam represented by that Word or Light is compromised. A Megalomaniac called Lucifer a.k.a. "That Old Serpent" is now able to exercise dominion over the regent of YHVH. This presents a conundrum of epic proportions! It is as if the declaration of Isaiah became a self-fulfilling prophecy!

> ***Isaiah 14:13*** *For thou hast said in thine heart, I will ascend into heaven, I will exalt my throne above the stars of God: I will sit also upon the mount of the congregation, in the sides of the north.*

YHVH immediately intervenes by demonstrating the power of His Voice who physically walks onto the scene in Genesis 3! This sets into motion the pattern of Redemption as the Word physically offers Himself as the substitute for Adam. A temporary injunction in the offering of the sacrificed Lamb stays the hand of the Enemy until such time Yahshua enters the physical realm in the same flesh as Adam to reassert the role of the Word as the authority in the earth!

Though Adam is expelled from the Garden he is reminded to work the ground. This euphemism implies that his access to the Tree of Life is on a limited basis, guarded by the Sword (word) which turns H#2015, הָפַךְ haphak, to turn, transform oneself, to change oneself, he must work to excavate truth from this Word who has become flesh! YHVH in His infinite wisdom is able to provide access to the Tree by this disguised – transformed Sword/Word. The precedent is set. You can now have access once again to the authority and power of YHVH – His DNA changing Seed through this living Sword. The only drawback being the disguising of the Word to those who are entertaining the Serpents' seed. We must learn how to recognize Him! He is revealing Himself now! A return to Eden is imminent! He is inviting you to examine Him, handle Him, to probe the depths of the disguise and unmask the Sovereign King long camouflaged from those who refuse to know Him. The Seal upon the Book – the cloak is removed; the Pure Language is being restored! What are the clues to identify Him!

Chapter 2

The Investigation Begins

Previously, we've documented several adjectives used to describe this purposed Word or language. Let's refresh our memory, they are: **Light, Sound (Voice), Seed, Sword, and Fire**. If each of these describe a particular attribute of the language and thus, of YHVH Himself, and if His word is who He is, can we assume this word functions as His DNA (From which everything is created) and could each of the above attributes serve as a coded marker within the DNA strand of the Great King? Look at this quote from Wikipedia:

A genetic marker is a gene or DNA sequence with a known location on a chromosome that can be used to identify individuals or species. It can be described as a variation (which may arise due to mutation or alteration in the genomic loci) that can be observed.

If we display the above attributes are we being identified as Sons of YHVH?

> **Romans 8:17** *And if children, then heirs; heirs of YHVH and joint-heirs with Messiah.*

An heir is one who receives his allotted possession by right of sonship. The latter part of the verse qualifies how this is achieved: ...*if we suffer with Him*...the Greek word used for suffer, hints at partaking of the same type of hardships, but, also hints at undergoing, to have a sensible experience! In other words, to see or experience the same results with this word/language in the midst of trial, as He did! It would seem that exhibiting or demonstrating His word is mandatory for Sonship!

If we display a false, mixed, or mingled word (Perhaps a touch of our traditions rather than Truth) are we revealing a mutation or alteration in the genomic code, which can be traced back to Gen. 11 and further? You make the call. Can this mutated genome be repaired? Resoundingly – YES! We'll see how later!

If we expect you the reader to concur with this mind-bending '*assumption*' (sarcasm mine), then perhaps we need to examine, carefully dissecting each individual attribute mentioned above and see if our line of reasoning is sound. Let's look at those attributes used to describe Him and His Word. We'll begin with...

Light

To properly treat any Biblical subject we always consider the 'Law of First Reference'. That is, the place where it is first mentioned. This sets the precedent for how a specific word or subject should be considered thereafter. At times, it may deviate, but nonetheless, it will always be linked to the first mention. In the case of 'Light' it is first mentioned in Gen. 1: 3 where YHVH said, "let there be light: and there was light." This is a releasing or dissemination from the Creator which follows the event of Gen. 1:2 where the Spirit of Elohiym moved upon the face of the waters. The word here for moved, H#7363, רָחַף rachaph, is translated by most as meaning to hover over, to brood, or to tremble. However, it comes from a root-stem Resh-Pey, which describes a shaking or vibration, a trembling in anticipation of intimacy.

It shouldn't strain one's imagination to see sexual overtones within the Hebrew text. Light was/is the Seed/Word released by YHVH into the earth. [The virility of English is questionable; though it is in fact, seed as well, the potency level has never been there. Its' senescent nature allows for a hit and miss 'spiritual' fertilization at best] The Hebrew is different, though pre-dating all languages (In my opinion) It is the Voice/Word and Light of Creation still at its Masculine Best! The entrance of this word still brings *LIGHT-Energy*!

Look at the Hebrew word used here for light - H#216, אוֹר 'owr, indicating light, illumination. This light must not be confused with the illumination provided by the Sun or stellar luminaries in Gen. 1: 14 – 16. The word intentionally inserted there is H#3974, מָאוֹר ma'owr, which reveals 'that which affords light, a lumi-nary'. As such, grammatically, it can take the plural form. How-ever, the word 'owr is always in the singular with the exception of one example: Psalm 136:7 which says, *"To him that made great lights –* אוֹרִים*...owrim"* Most scholars feel this is in refer-ence to the verse following with details regarding the sun, moon and stars. But, is it really? Could this be a pointed reference to Gen. 1: 1-5 and indicate the creation of both Messiah and Luci-fer, themselves great lights, one who would pervert his role, yet, still 'seed the earth with the darkness of his kind', while Messiah, The Light, would literally be separated from him? I believe it is! The Hebrew refers to this Tov (good) light as the אֶת־הָאוֹר, the Et-ha'owr, Alef-Tav- The Light! Yahshua reveals who this light is/was when He declares Himself as the Alef-Tav (Rendered Al-pha and Omega in the Greek: Rev. 1:8, 11, 21: 6, 22: 13). He is described as The Light of the world. This pattern was understood by those during both the Tabernacle and Temple periods, who recognized the role of the Great Lamp – The Menorah – which illuminated the house, as a prefiguring of the Messiah!

Why was it necessary for Light and Darkness to be separated?

Our first clue is found in Gen. 1:4, 5 where we see a distinction made between Light & Darkness: Let's examine some evidence. Here we see them being referred to as Day & Night.

> **Genesis 1:4-5** *And God saw the light, that [it was] good: and God divided the light from the darkness. And God called the light Day, and the darkness he called Night. And the evening and the morning were the first day.*

♦ Light, H#216, אור *'owr*

A masculine noun meaning light, fire. This light exists before the stellar luminaries. It is created, and given a form called 'day'. *Note the gematria: 207, the same as H#718, 'aru, meaning lo, behold. The same Hebrew consonants can also spell H#7299, Resh-Vav, and Rew, indicating a form or appearance. Thus, this original LIGHT represented the Presence of YHVH being introduced in a form [Body] and attention being called to 'Him'. He is referred to as 'Day'.

♦ Day, H#3117, יום *yowm*

Translated, day, time, year, a division of time. It becomes evident this 'form' is temporary!

♦ Darkness, H#2822, חשך *choshek*

Darkness, obscurity, secret place. It also carries the idea of withholding, to refrain, restrain, to spare, to hinder. It has the same gematria as H#6162, 'erabon, a pledge, something given as evidence or proof that something else will be done.

◆ Night, H#3915,   ליל   *layil*

Night, gloom, a protective shadow. It is from H#3883, La-med-Vav-Lamed, lul, a masc. noun indicating a spiral or winding staircase. A DNA helix? Hmmm? Its value – 70, is the same as H#3651, ken, kaf-nun, to stand upright, to estab-lish. A foundation.

It would seem that Light had to be introduced into a *body-form* for a season in order to become the pledge or guarantee of re-demption, which would change the DNA of darkness and birth those who would stand upright – Y'shar el, Israel!

Afterward, this same Light is then transposed onto the stellar lu-minaries to establish a witness in both the heavens and earth. *Note verse 14:

Genesis 1:14 *And God said, Let there be lights in the fir-mament of the heaven to divide the day from the night; and let them be for signs, and for seasons, and for days, and years.*

Now, we must examine the Hebrew again:

◆ Lights, H#3974,   מאור   *ma'owr*

Translated light or luminary. Note the Mem prefix indicating from or out of, place of origin, followed by Alef-Vav-Resh, 'owr. These lights are from or out of the ORIGINAL LIGHT source! Ironically, the gematria of ma'owr equals 247, the same as the Hebrew word H#2167, Zamar, a verb meaning to play an instrument, to sing with musical accompaniment. This is seen in Job:

>*Job 38:7 When the morning stars sang together, and all the sons of God shouted for joy?*

If we understand the concept of light in the original creation and its sustainable affect upon all life we can surmise that post-Fall, the resultant curses upon the earth would have restricted the access to the light, denying Plants (photosynthesis) and Animals (food, healing, etc.) while Man himself is denied (physical life and spiritual access) the sustenance that Light once provided. Light, literally is life! Scholars admit light functions as the messenger and color the message! Like plants, humans are photosynthetic, absorbing light directly through the "solar panels" of our skin and eyes. Take a look at Psalm 27:

>*Psalm 27:1 The LORD is my light and my salvation; whom shall I fear? The LORD is the strength of my life; of whom shall I be afraid?*

If He is light and salvation, then He must be light and the light our salvation, how hard is this? Now, for Scriptural confirmation:

>*John 1:4 In him was life; and the life was the light of men.*

Matthew 6:22 sums this up quite succinctly:

>*Matthew 6:22 The light of the body is the eye: if therefore thine eye be single, thy whole body shall be full of light.*

Healing with light, or phototherapy, is gaining acceptance among medical practitioners, skin care providers and home enthusiasts as research and personal anecdotes verify the benefits of color light therapy for everything from treating cancer to skin care.

With the discovery that our cells continuously produce light, or photons, and that these photons carry information throughout the body's energy field, healing beings of light with light just makes sense. Ancient Egyptians understood that certain colors affect the mind and body. They used panes of colored glass in ceilings so people could benefit from the incoming colored light. Your Eyes function in much the same way. Why not the 'Spiritual Eye' – the mind? In fact, in every spiritual conflict, the battle is won or lost here, in the mind. Is it possible that we've been told lies regarding the powerful effects of Sound, Light and Color which are intangible attributes of His Word? From our former perspectives these were only associated with what we considered the impalpable aura emanating from the Creator alone. Yet, in the New Testament book of Hebrews, chapter 4 verse 12 we're told that same word has the ability to pierce to the dividing asunder of soul and spirit and of the joints and marrow (DNA?) and is a discerner of the thoughts and intents of the heart! Therefore, its' power is just as applicable to and on behalf of – YOU!

The metamorphosis that occurred as the Light is diminished is apparent in Gen. 3:22 when Adam and Eve (Chavah) are driven from the source of Life/Light – the Tree of Life! Our lives have continued to degenerate since. But, what must it have been like before? Wouldn't Adam and Chavah (Eve) literally have exuded, reflected, been permeated, perhaps clothed with, the Light in the Garden? If YHVH's words were light and He breathed that life into Adam birthing him, then wouldn't Adam and Eve (Chavah) also have exhaled the breath or light – word of YHVH? The word for breathed in Hebrew is H#5397, נְשָׁמָה, neshamah, a breath, a blast. *He had breathed into him the POWER OF SPEECH*, in other words, speaking breath! At this point man became a living soul, 'lanefesh chayah', literally a speaking soul! It can also be translated as meaning 'the mind'!

This adds a new dimension to Philippians 2:5:

Let this mind/word/light be in you which was also in Messiah.

Its (Neshamah's) root is interesting as well; it comes from nasham, which is used of a woman panting in child birth. Isn't it curious to note the two-letter root in both words? The Shin-Mem that spells Shem; this word can be translated name, but it also indicates CHARACTER! One's nature or attributes! If this is true, and it is – then we can expect a reverse metamorphosis to take place as the Word – Light – Seed becomes more prevalent. Romans 12:2 engages our imagination with this very thought!

> **Romans 12:2** *And be not conformed to this world: but be ye transformed by the renewing of your mind, that ye may prove what is that good, and acceptable, and perfect, will of God.*

Please make note of the Greek word used for 'transformed'. G#3339, metamorphoō from which we get our English metamorphosis!

If Adam and Eve underwent a degenerative metamorphosis after the Fall and the Plan of YHVH to redeem Man from the lien of Sin, whose payment can only be satisfied by death, yet remained in force, by what method or device do you suppose He plans on using to restore or extricate Adam from his mortgaged soul? I contend, the very device used when Creation was in a waste and desolate – Tohu v'bohu – condition. He will restore the Light – Word! The inevitable result of the account of Genesis 1 saw the DNA of that 'waste and desolate' creation change! His methods and He have not changed! Change is coming to those who will embrace it. However, for us to properly diagnose our own present condition and seek a remedy, we need to return to the scene of the 'Crime' and find out what happened in Genesis 3 and simply retrace the steps of Adam.

Chapter 3

A DNA Change Occurs

Now let's peek into the Garden and see Adam before the fall to determine if we can understand these changes and the resultant necessity of our implementing the DNA reparation His Word-Light-Seed and what it affords us! Frankly, as we begin our detective work, if we just look at the KJV, we find them both without clothing of any sort; in fact, Gen. 2: 25 describes their physical condition after the creation of Eve (Chavah) as 'naked'. But, what really does the original text say?

♦ Naked, H#6174   עָרוֹם   *'arowm*

Rendered naked or bare. Yet, the same Hebrew letters can also indicate to be subtle, shrewd, crafty, or prudent.

Though some scholars may argue, the fact remains, etymologically, the Alef & Ayin are silent letters depending on vowel pointing to give them their sound. Thus, they are interchangeable. The Ayin-Resh root-stem could just as easily have been the Alef-Resh root of the Hebrew word for LIGHT! In addition, Ayin-Vav-Resh is a masc. noun that can mean skin! We see it used later after the fall, in Gen. 3: 21 to describe the garment of blooded skin, H#5785, עוֹר 'owr that YHVH clothes them with. *Remember this.

Is it possible that Adam and Chavah (Eve) were clothed with a Light Skin or garment? Is it possible they were prudent, shrewd or crafty in the use of this Light Garment – this aura created by the Word/Light/Seed that had just overshadowed them while their bodies – the DNA – resonating in both of them are changed?

Today, scientific research pioneered by Semyon Kirlian (Kirlian photography) has proven that living objects have an electromagnetic field or light around them. [Biofield Global Research Inc. www.biofieldglobal.org/what-is-human-aura.html] (As though His word needed scientific affirmation)

Another peculiar and misunderstood, though interesting, event takes place upon Adam and Eve (Chavah) discovering their naked condition. What follows becomes the hallmark of human nature down through the ages. When one loses the "Fellowship with YHVH" that is His Light – Word – and the Covenant garment it provides (As did Adam and Eve) the natural, carnal tendency is bent toward an attempt at replicating it, with a manmade 'lookalike'. In the Garden encounter theirs was a fig-leaf garment. To gain the proper insight concerning what is taking place I suggest you refer back to Genesis 3: 7, where the KJV reads *'they made themselves aprons of fig leaves'* The word apron, in Hebrew is H#2290, חֲגוֹר chagowr, and is translated as a belt, specifically designed to cover the loins. Well now, what's this? Do their actions infer that the seat of procreation is uncovered? (See Ephesian 6 and the instructions regarding having ones' loins girt with Truth) If you examine this Hebrew word for 'apron' there are two different, two-letter root stems to look at: The first is that formed of the Chet-Gimmel, which indicates to twirl, dance or encircle. Next, the Vav-Resh hints at the root of Light – 'Owr! What you're witnessing is a fleshly, carnal attempt to replace the original Garment of Light with a man-made replica! It is said that the ancient mystical Freemasons themselves wear a green apron after the fashion of Adam's fig leaf. The Mormons are said to also wear them within the walls of their Mormon temples. [Decker's

Complete Handbook on Mormonism, Ed Decker, 1995, Harvest House Publishers, Eugene, Oregon, pg. 53]
[http://www.theforbiddenknowledge.com/hardtruth/washingtons masonicapron.htm]

We must not leave here yet. The Hebrew word for Fig will jump out at you! This word is not the same as the word we'll be addressing in the following paragraphs, but, you can see the intentional use by YHVH of this word here to paint a specific graphic picture. The Strong's number H#8384, for this Hebrew word is, תְּאֵנָה, te'enah, loosely translated as 'fig tree'. However another related word spelled with the same Hebrew consonants is H#8385, ta'anah, and infers the heated encounter of copulation, an occasion or opportunity where carnal intimacy occurs. By further breaking the Hebrew apart, we note the Tav appended to the front which indicates 3rd person future tense, 'you shall'. This leaves us with the Alef-Nun-Hey root which spells 'anna', which is an interjection of entreaty to seek remedy for an urgent or grave situation. It is used to express the desire for forgiveness!

Of a sudden our image of Adam and Eve begins to alter somewhat. It seems highly evident that Adam and Eve knew the deadly consequence of their heated, intimate sexual encounter with the Serpent's Seed. Their shame is evident and they immediately seek to clothe themselves while crying out in desperation for forgiveness! The fig-leaf garment doesn't suffice. Though in the aftermath of this travesty (YHVH does empathetically re-clothe them, in what I believe was the first Yom Kippur – where the lamb is slain for the sins of the world still in the loins of ADAM) their aberrant behavior launches a battle with the fig leaf of our flesh that has no man able to gain victory over the sinful nature. The Apostle Paul fittingly describes the situation in Romans 7 until crying out in desperation he remarks:

> ***Romans 7:24*** *O wretched man that I am! Who shall deliver me from the body of this death?*

He gives the only suitable answer in chapter 8: 1 acknowledging that no condemnation i.e. no law curses, the one who is "IN MESSIAH YAHSHUA". This is a covenant term indicating to have 'put on' or taken on the same Covenant Language, or Legal terminology wherewith one is able to combat sin in the flesh!

It is for that reason that we see the relic that is the fig tree upon the loins of fallen Adam until the Sovereignty of the Last ADAM a.k.a. Yahshua the Messiah, the Word made flesh is able to gain the ascendancy, and thus breaks the power of the fig tree! Oh yes! This literally occurs! We find the metaphorical fig tree displaying its barren loins in the presence of the True Seed or Word (Messiah Himself). (Matthew 21: 19) Once an erstwhile power, this 'soon to be neutered' leaf garment is strategically placed to oppose the True Garment of Light – Yahshua –while He sojourns between two very appropriately named cities: Bethany and Bethphage: Bethany translates as "House of Misery" while Bethphage is defined as "House of Figs". Upon encountering this false garment, Yahshua immediately curses the Fig Tree because it doesn't produce fruit! Neither does the Serpents' Seed produce Light! You can see the same parallel with the fig tree in the story of Jacob in Genesis

> **Genesis 32:1** *And Jacob went on his way, and the angels of God met him.*

In the next verse as Jacob sees the Host – *machaneh*, he called the place, *Machanayim*! The fig tree is here, you just need to look closer though, because a different Hebrew word is used: A fig tree by any other name would cover the same... (Sorry about the poor humor) Let's get back on track.

I want to show you this interesting link. Here we're going to look at another Hebrew word for fig. In fact, it is the etymological source of the English word we ourselves use for fig: So, the Pey-Gimmel root should be familiar to you. Look at the place in the above verse where Jacob meets the angels:

◆ Met, H#6293   פָּגַע   *paga'*

To meet; or to encounter – to establish a boundary to reach a certain point. Here, the division of the Physical House of Jacob takes place and this division – boundary would continue until the Last Days – Ezek. 37: 16 – 22! This word 'Paga' has the two-letter root, Pey-Gimel H#6291, pag meaning an early fig, a green fig. It is this same sign of the FIG TREE mentioned in Matt. 24: 32 which becomes a prevalent omen of the end days signaling – the TWO HOUSES BEING RESTORED INTO ONE! It is in the previous verse here in Matthew 24 that you can see the parallel to Ezekiel 37 where Yahshua mentions gathering His elect from the four Winds, GK. #417, anemos, a violent agitation or stream of air – it is not a coincidence that the word for Torah – Law, is GK. #459, anomos, spelled the same with only a vowel point change in the Greek. The Word or Torah will be a violent, agitated breath that fills the BONES OF EZEKIEL 37:4, 5, 9, and 10!

Here we recall how Yahshua earlier cursed the fig tree (Matt. 21: 19) because it had no figs on it, *Remember he came specifically to restore the Whole House! Thus, the fig tree was cursed because it lied! The fig tree implies the flesh! It will always agree with the Serpents words! In this case it indicates a false, fleshly attempt to join the House together, this will be exposed for the counterfeit that it is! The Ayin as a suffix indicates to, 'see, perceive' to fully understand! *NOTE, look at the gematria of this word 'paga'; Pey-80, Gimel-3, Ayin-70 = 153, the same as the phrase 'B'nei Elohim, Sons of YHVH'. You should also recognize it as the number of fish caught by Yahshua's disciples after His resurrection. Could the actions of the fig tree above be further evidence of a false attempt to join the House together by counterfeit means, which gets foiled by Messiah? You will see this again!!!

This brings us back to the place where Jacob wrestles: The River Jabbok. In Hebrew H#2999, יַבֹּק Yabboq indicates to 'empty or pour out', signifying the emptying of Jacob's flesh and here accordingly, it becomes a paga - a boundary. Jacob will never cross it again as a divided House! These boundaries between flesh and spirit are very real and one crosses at his own peril. This opens the door for further explanation of Genesis 3. Where Adam, Eve and the Serpent cross these boundaries themselves! Opening the doorway for the introduction of the Fallen Ones into the earth! This also helps to illuminate Jude 6:

> **Jude 1:6** *And the angels which kept not their first estate, but left their own habitation, he hath reserved in everlasting chains under darkness unto the judgment of the great day.*

The Greek language indicates a crossing of these same boundaries!

I'll point out a few words here that should pique your interest a bit.

◆   First, G#746, *archē*

Translated here as; beginning or origin. It is used absolutely to denote that. It is from a root implying the establishment of precedence.

◆   Left, G#620, *apoleipō*

To desert or forsake, to leave behind.

- Own, G#2398, *idios*

Pertaining to one's self. It is used in a number of places to indicate to do one's own business (and not intermeddle with the affairs of others).

- Habitation, G#3613, *oikētērion*

A dwelling place or habitation. Used of the Body as the abode of the spirit.

Even in the Greek the text is plain enough that one can easily see how the Fallen Angels followed Lucifer's' lead and crossed over the spiritual and physical boundaries established for them. They were not alone in this endeavor, in each case there had to be a willing (suitable) host who opened the doorway for this seed line: First Adam and Eve, later the 'daughters of men'! Whether you are able to grasp the horrific consequence of opening the womb of your mind to this seed, much less the shivering thoughts of a physical intimacy, the fact remains: It happened before and after the Flood and is predicted to occur again soon by no less a prophet than Messiah Yahshua Himself in Matthew 24: 37. This seems to establish a powerful principal. Word and Seed and light are indeed synonymous. If the Creators' word is seed – Light then there must of necessity, be a counterfeit light or seed. If the entrance of His word brings light, what must the entrance of the counterfeit produce? This may force you to rethink your former paradigm regarding the Word, Seed or Light of YHVH, while at the same time shuddering to think of the alternative! Though we say we believe in the veracity of the Scripture, if an outside source confirms what has been written we're left with no excuse. So, though you've had your spiritual guard up for some time to protect you from the contamination of false teaching and my words have alarmed you. Remember this: His word can stand scrutiny. Why don't we step outside the comfort zone if it's not because we're afraid to find out we've been taught wrong! Ouch! That one hurt didn't it? Come on; let's see if there is any logic to the idea of being clothed with a Garment of Light! What does this Word, Seed, or Light consist of anyway?

The only conclusion a reasonable person can come to forces a juxtaposition of the two garments: One a spiritual shroud or cloak of Light the other a work of the flesh devised by the hand of man i.e. the 'Fig Leaf' of carnality! Quite frankly, we've worn the fig leaf for so long that today's Church wears its specious covering proudly! Simply because our feelings and emotions are woven into the fabric of the flesh. We've become so 'sin conscious' that the notion of living a righteous lifestyle where one can indeed be clothed with the Garment of Light has become an abstraction. The idea that one can walk in power and authority is relegated to antiquity along with the Old Testament accounts of men who did exactly that while exercising the Lashon Qodesh – the Holy Tongue – Hebrew! The stupefying, yet incredibly shameful fact that science has advanced the theory (That man can indeed generate a resonating power able to change DNA) rather than the Believing Community exercising it serves as an indictment against us! The Hebrew Scriptures are veritable treasure troves of proof that it has happened and it is prophesied to occur again by no less than YHVH and Yahshua to be the defining characteristic of the Last Day generation!

Chapter 4

Lights, Science and Scripture

Science is always playing catch-up with Scripture. *Finally*, scholars conclude that light vibrates! *Light is vibration.* Gen. 1:2 told us eons ago! So how do these vibrating, frequency emitting, visible descriptions of light apply to the purposed logic of a luminous garment clothing Adam and Eve (Chavah) in the garden?

The entire electromagnetic wave spectrum of visible light produces different colors. Colors are simply waves vibrating at different frequencies. On one end of the spectrum you have red; on the other end you have violet. Red has the longest wavelength and the lowest frequency, violet has the shortest wavelength and the highest frequency. Blue light and red light are both just light, but the blue light has a higher frequency of vibration (or a shorter wavelength) than the red light. In fact, when you 'see' white light with the naked eye it still contains these 'colors'. "Color is the visual effect that is caused by the spectral composition of the light, emitted, transmitted, or reflected by objects." [Quote courtesy of Prof. Jill Morten of Color Logic]. The varying velocities of light contain all the splendors of the universe. The velocities decrease from white light (186,000 miles a second) through violet, indigo, blue, green, yellow, orange, and red to black (140,000 miles a second). It is by the varying movements of these velocities that the eye is affected by the sensation known as color. Color is, therefore, one of the manifestations of vibration and all vibration manifests in corresponding color, the color being merely an indication of the occult or hidden chemical activity.

To add another twist to this already thickening plot, modern scientists are now convinced that Light has in fact slowed down since Creation [Setterfield and Norman SRI 1987] If Light and Word are 'One', and since both light and sound are measured as frequencies in cycles per second, mathematically, if you speed up a sound's frequency by doubling it forty times, you come up with a frequency that is within the parameters of light. Conversely, if you slow down light's frequency forty times, you have a frequency within the parameters of Sound. Is it possible thus, to consider a simultaneous slowing of the light which coincides with the restoration of this Pure Language – the Lashon Qodesh that we mentioned in Zeph. 3:9? In other words, is it possible, as a result of our degenerative condition (Brought on by the increasing presence of sin – that darkness which was separated from the light/word at creation) that Mankind is slower – farther away from the light source? Yet by virtue of YHVH once again, allowing us access to the restorative, creative power of the very language that enveloped Adam in the garden, we are allowed to push the envelope of those conventionally excepted limits which have kept us from the source of His Light-Word.

> ***Ephesians 5:8*** *For ye were sometimes darkness, but now are ye light in the YHVH: walk as children of light.*

As a side note regarding the idea of this generation being the farthest and slowest generation (Spiritually) from the Light; it is easy to see why rabbinic scholars teach that the generation of the last days will be the lowest generation, i.e. the farthest away from the Torah. Is it coincidental that the portion of the Body of Messiah used to crush the head of the Serpent, the heel, (The Y'aqov – Jacob) the lowest member, the one farthest away, can be considered also as the last generation, the one who has been detached longest from Torah? Now you understand why this Language of Light and Salvation is being restored as we speak. What role do we play in our being restored to the original light source – this Rainbow of Creation?

Moshe reminds us, in Deut. 7:6-13, (Particularly verse 12) it will be simply, because we harken H#8085, shama, to hear intelligently and obey. However, the Hebrew word is the future tense "ti'shma'un." It reminds us that Moshe is talking to a future generation. One who is not here while this is being written and thus cannot be the Joshua led group he is currently addressing, and which later enters Canaan.

> ***Deuteronomy 7:12*** *Wherefore it shall come to pass, if ye hearken to these judgments, and keep, and do them, that the LORD thy God shall keep unto thee the covenant and the mercy which he swore unto thy fathers.*

Again, the Hebrew language has hidden treasures for those who will search. The word "if" in the same verse, is H#6118, eqeb, translated 'because of', from H#6117 & 6119, 'aqab, which may also indicate the heel who eradicates another by force! The true intent of the word Jacob, H#3290, יַעֲקֹב Ya'aqob as "Heel Catcher" becomes evident! If – 'aqab – Jacob hearkens...

Because he Hears and obeys the Commandments of YHVH, the "Heel", The House of Jacob who destroys the enemy, will enter and occupy the Promised Land!

Why is this line of reasoning hard to swallow you asked? Do words actually have vibrational tones connected with light, sound and color? *We don't seem to have issues once the established scientific community confirms it!* [Sarcasm mine] Why not try something radical and just believe there is Power resonating in His Word? In consideration for the skeptics among us, here is another mind-staggering confirmation from, of all sources, what was once held as a predominantly atheistic group – the Russian scientific community: who, while working on the human genome project, found there was language and syntax within our DNA and that it could be changed and re-encoded by frequencies, sounds or even words within a laser light beam. Recent research has confirmed this area of DNA has triggers or switches which can be turned on and off (for example by the environment, words, or trauma), and that what they turn on are genetic abilities and weaknesses. We can be conformed to the image of YHVH, and again become a transfigured being of light, because our DNA has the capacity to be re-sequenced by the same Word/Light said to conform us into His image! Using the very method of Creation, the Spoken Word, The Russians were able to influence cellular metabolism and even remedy genetic defects.

The team achieved incredible results using vibration and language. For instance, they successfully transmitted informational patterns from one set of DNA to another. Eventually, they were even able to reprogram cells to another genome — they transformed frog embryos into salamander embryos without lifting a single scalpel or making one incision! In another experiment, their conclusion determined that human DNA is reprogrammable by our own speech when specific frequencies are sounded.

Did you hear that? They were able to modify amphibian DNA simply by manipulating specific frequencies in the spoken word. Is it a stretch then, to assume Airport scanners, X-rays, EMF & Micro-wave frequencies, Scalar pulse and HAARP waves, (Don't forget your egg frying cell phones) and genetically modified foods, to mention a few, may have the ability to manipulate the human genome? How many of you remember the subliminal snack messages at the Drive Inn theaters of the 60's? How many of you, suddenly hungry, rushed out to purchase popcorn? Admittedly, were I reading this, I would begin to educate myself concerning what we've been taught regarding these potential DNA manipulating, life-altering issues! (Oops, was that a subliminal hint?)

Linguistics, Light & Frequency

Honestly, those who are like doubting Thomas among us reading this will not believe that words have such power. Perhaps you recall the child-hood rhyme: 'sticks and stones may break my bones, but WORDS will never hurt me'? Many believe this was originated to bolster the attitude of a child on the receiving end of bullying taunts, etc. However, nothing could be farther from the truth! Bruises will heal, but the effects of the spoken word into or over us has the potential to shape our destiny in the realm of the spiritual, physical and mental! Words are indeed powerful! Even the innocuous words of inanimate objects like your computer or the cell phone that speaks to you cannot be dismissed as harmless, as such, we must re-examine our former paradigm concerning their influence in our lives! Let me show you clinical evidence!

Linguistics (the science of the structure and construction of speech) can be used to explore not only natural speech that has evolved in individual countries and cultures; it equally can be applied to artificial speech: for example, computer programming languages. By examining speech, one ascertains the basic rules of syntax (the creation of words from letters or characters) and semantics (the study of the meaning or content of words). Together, syntax and semantics make up the foundation for a grammar. By applying this scientific form of linguistic examination to the genetic code, scientists have found that DNA follows grammatical rules similar to those used in human speech. *Fosar and Bludorf* explain that, apparently, the structure of DNA does not correspond to human speech structures, but rather all human languages follow the pattern of the genetic code. After all, DNA and the genetic code existed long before the first human uttered the first word. DNA functions as a superconductor and is able to store both LIGHT and INFORMATION!

These same scientists state bluntly, that humans are crystallized or precipitated light! It shouldn't shock you to consider that Lucifer, according to 2Cor. 11: 14 can transform himself into an angel (messenger) of light. This points us immediately to Gen. 3 and the encounter with the Serpent, H#5175, נחש nachash. Though translated serpent, this word more accurately defines one given to divination or the practice of observing omens, each of which is expressly forbidden by Scripture. Ironically, as with all Hebrew words & letters, nachash has a numeric value which equals 358, the same as the Hebrew word for Messiah, H#4899. Mashiach) It is here in Genesis 3 where we see the genetic code of Adam & Eve and all those who would issue from his loins forever changed. My point being: if there is a counterfeit light producing 'seed' there must of necessity be a genuine light seed.

This same pattern is seen again in the flood account of Gen. 6 and as revealed by Yahshua, it will occur again shortly before His appearing!

> **Matthew 24:37** *As it was in the days of Noah, so shall it be also in the days of the coming of the Son of Man…*

It is this serpent's seed, whose manipulative words of divination and enchantment – allowed the Fallen One to vocalize and then later, physically materialized himself once again, through the Angels, Messengers or Fallen Ones and their Nephilim or Giant offspring. These same are later found attempting to destroy Noah. The Hebrew word for serpent, nachash, is spelled Nun-Chet-Shin: Pay close attention because the word-picture of the Hebrew language is compelling here! The Nun-Chet root spells NOAH, while the Shin attached means to devour! Prophetically, even before his (Noah's) birth the aim of the enemy is exposed. He must Devour Noah! Coincidence? I think not! Noah literally means rest, or comfort. It can also be rendered, 'to lead or guide', the conducting of one along the right path. As in Noah's case, what happened to and with him will also happen in our day. Make no mistake; we will see the introduction of a perverted Seed/Word that will issue forth out of the mouth of a False Messiah, an Enchanter, who will attempt to destroy the People of Yahweh. We must be able to counter this perversion as Messiah Himself did: with "It is written". It can only be effectively spoken through the Rainbow Language of Truth – Hebrew. In comparison, it is significant to note the competing lineage of Cain (as opposed to that of Noah) in Gen. 4. Once again a picture of the counterfeit which mirrors the genuine, yet who ends up in the land of Nod (Restless Wandering). The Law of Genesis determines that everything reproduces after its' kind. Quite naturally, shouldn't we expect these Fallen Angels and their offspring the Giants to have followed in the role of their father – Satan?

Additionally, if we're to expect the same conditions in the days just before the coming of the Son of Man to be like those which existed in Noah's day, then perhaps it would benefit us if we could see how this attempt to devour Noah mentioned above may impact our own future and the methods by which it becomes a fulfillment of the prophetical declaration made to the Serpent – Nachash in Gen. 3: 14, where he's told he would 'go upon his belly and dust (H#6083 עָפָר 'aphar, dust, that which is without color) shalt thou eat' (akal, consume, devour, to destroy). Most reject this out of hand as the fantastic ramblings of a conspiracy theorist. Yet, the evidence abounds to confirm that we've been conditioned to accept their return for decades – at least if you've paid any attention at all to the media.

What clues regarding our future survival against this Perverted Seed Line can we ascertain from those imbedded in this Genesis account? Come on and we'll look at the place just four verses later, where 'The Voice' is found speaking to Adam, he, who the Creator declares will also return to the dust. On the surface we see a bit of what seems a contradiction: Yet, if you recall, Adam was formed from the Adamah – ground, whereupon, he became red, ruddy, which lead to his being named 'Adam' indicating a future tense, "I Will Blood You". Couldn't this also indicate that he is one who has life, light, and seed in him perhaps? In this latter declaration where he is said to return to the dust, it would seem that this could also example a person who walks according to the lusts of his flesh and as such, is being referred to as returning to or existing in a state of death – much like Adam, returning to the dust. Could it be that the Serpent is said to be able to consume, destroy the dust metaphorically pointing to those who are carnal, lustful, those who do not have the life, blood, light, word in them? If this is true, then something must have taken place which made Noah different; at least it seems so, since he's declared as 'perfect'?

The Characteristics of Noah and how he implemented the Light – Seed – Word of YHVH in his daily life while standing against spiritual opposition that will not been seen again until just before the 2nd advent of Messiah beckons our study. Just as in Genesis 3, the distinction between the two seed lines was never more apparent. The same can be said today. Men are able to excuse their tendency toward perversion by calling evil good and light darkness, the paradox of which causes a blind eye and a receptive womb to be turned toward the Powers of Darkness! How will we survive the assault of the Fallen Ones that is prophesied to shortly begin and which is surely to bring extinction the human race unless another Noah arrives? Perhaps we should learn about the Days of Noah and the Man himself in order to ensure our survival?

Chapter 5

The Generations of Noah

This word 'generations' in English comes from two separate Hebrew words used to describe Noah. The first word H#8435, תּוֹלְדוֹת, toldoyt - refers to the future or the offspring or issue of Noah (His sons) and with the Tav prefixed [which grammatically indicates future tense] there seems a hint at an additional, future group related to Noah! The 2nd word, H#1755, דּוֹר dowr, translated generation, hints at the past, up until this time, or period. It is during this segment of 'time' – the dowr - that Noah is described as being just, H#6662, צַדִּיק tsaddiyq, (Just and/or righteous, and used of a judge or king who maintains right and dispenses justice. It indicates to be put something right in relation to a legal cause or standard). What legal cause could have been in jeopardy here? In context, the only abrogation of a legal cause in this chapter has been the introduction of the Seed of the Fallen Ones into the earth through Adam's seed which was/is contrary to Torah (Gen. 6: 1-7). The crossing of those established boundaries were prohibited from creation. Yet, cross them they did!

Noah is – as a result – of his handling of this legal cause, wherein he maintains both the spiritual and physical integrity of the Seed, Word, or Light – referred to next as 'perfect', H#8549, תָּמִים tamiym, complete, whole, without blemish. This word can also carry the idea of something shut up or closed. As a short aside, let me give you an example of another familiar Hebrew word which adds clarity for us. This Hebrew word is mentioned in Ex. 28: 30 in a vivid description of the vestments of the High Priest. With the undeniable connection to the perfection of Noah. Perhaps we should pay close attention to see what else is revealed. The word in question here is the Hebrew word Thummim, describing an article, of which little is known, yet evidence proves it was part of the High Priest's vestment and as such (if Ephesians 6 is true) it should be part of the DAILY GARMENT YOU'RE WEARING! It is always linked with its' conjoined twin – Urim, translated as Lights! All Torah scholars acknowledge these two articles as part of the mechanism by which the High Priest and YHVH communicated. Now, watch this:

The Urim (Lights) and Thummim (Perfections) which enabled communication with YHVH were worn upon the breast and symbolically allowed the Cohen Gadol to bear the judgment of Israel upon his heart. This connection to the shroud of Light that we've referred to as the DNA of YHVH and as such, that which sufficed as a 'visible cloak' shielding the Priest while in the flesh, does indeed point toward the DNA of YHVH – His Torah. In this example of the High Priest, the function of this "lights and perfections" would also seem to give you and I insight as to how Noah may have been protected against the perverted fleshly advances of the Nephilim and to what extent he used this same device - Urim and Thummim - to judge the people who indulged in the same moral decadence. This would seem to fit the spiritual barometer of most today who oppose the Word of YHVH!

It shouldn't be a surprise to find at no time does YHVH engage in verbal minutia. He simply doesn't mince words; Our conclusion regarding this precise, intentional description of Noah is that it came as a result of obedience to YHVH and by apparently, not mingling his seed with that of the Nachash or Serpent! In other words, Noah's bloodline was shut up, closed off, to the Serpents' seed! In an interesting segue into this discussion of Noah's generations we find the Creator in Gen. 6: 7 lamenting because of the extent to which His creation is found to have perverted their way.

Nevertheless, it is said of Noah: *"But Noah found grace in the eyes of the YHVH"*. This is the first mention of GRACE in scripture and should be used to set the standard for its understanding. Noah is graced because of his obedience to the Voice, Light, and Word of YHVH! This is a far cry from the traditional 'free-unmerited favor' embraced as doctrine by today's liberal church which seems often employed as a license to continue in sin! Did you note the connection between Noah and Grace? Oops, you didn't look at the Hebrew did you? If not, you missed it! Grace, in Hebrew is H#2580, חֵן chen, translated as favor or good will, but spelled with the Chet – Nun; exactly backwards from Noah, Nun – Chet! He found chen – grace in the eyes, H#5869, עַיִן 'ayin, translated as an eye, a well or fountain; a womb! Noah found the favor of YHVH in the fountain – Well of Salvation (The Hebrew word is Yahshua).

Isaiah 12:3 *For with Joy shall you draw waters out of the wells of salvation.*

Noah stayed within the boundaries of the Torah – Word – Seed of YHVH not exposing himself to the counterfeit seed!

It would seem by employing sound investigative techniques we can affirm in the Hebrew that Noah was entrusted with and therefore, protected the Seed Line of, the Woman through whom Messiah would come (Gen. 3:15). You can easily see this because the Hebrew word dowr (generations) is connected to the verb 'Hayah', meaning to be, to come about, as a result. In other words, it came about that Noah walked, H#1980, הָלַךְ halak, to walk with, to go toward, and to walk in, אֶת־הָאֱלֹהִים the ET-haElohiym! Noah walked with the Alef-Tav of YHVH! Sound vaguely familiar? Enoch did the same! Interestingly, the Nun-Chet (Noah) word picture is that of One who fences in – protects the Seed!

Now, to look at Noah's offspring – Toldoyt: Perhaps we'll find some clues about future generations through the names of Shem,

Ham, and Japheth.

♦ Shem, H#8035   שֵׁם   *Shem*

It is defined as: name, reputation, character.

♦ Ham, H#2526   חָם   *Cham*

Hot, lustful passion, to be angered or enraged.

♦ Japheth, H#3315   יֶפֶת   *Yepheth*

To be opened, fig. one whose mouth is open to slander or lies. It was Japheth who would dwell in the tents of Shem. Could it imply that many who have dwelt with us will turn to slanderous ways falling away from the truth of Torah and Shabbat in the coming days of seduction? You be the judge...

Again, here the names themselves lend credence to our position: HaShem, the Character of He Who is THE NAME will become enraged against those who lie and slander against Torah! We know Torah is the Word or Seed of YHVH! We see two groups polarized over the issue of obedience to/reception of – this Torah as the Seed of YHVH. We see the resulting judgment separates the True Bride from the False, Adulterous Bride. Are there other patterns in Gen. 6 that yield insight for our day?

Preservation/Restoration
of the DNA-SEED of YHVH

It becomes quite obvious that Noah's lineage is preserved in order to secure a proper bloodline through which Messiah would come. This is a physical demonstration of a spiritual Seed which would also be preserved by our guarding it. That seed line is packaged as The Pure Language! As corroboration, the Rainbow would become the eternal symbol of a Covenant Promise to those who would follow Noah's example! Do you need more confirmation? Consider this: But, ruminate on it first, because it's a big piece to swallow if you're having difficulty connecting the dots thus far!

Noah is told to build an Ark, H#8392, תֵּבָה tebah, which means a basket, Ark or vessel. However it is related to Tav-Vav-Hey, teiva, which means to mark, or write, it can also infer 'word'. Now regarding this ark, aside from the dimensions, only one item is described as being built into the Ark – said item was a window, from H#6672, צֹהַר tsohar, noon, midday, light [as in exposed to the sun] (Gen.6:16). This word has confused scholars for generations because it does not mean an opening in the truest sense and is quite different from the same English word translated as window and used in Gen. 8:6, H#2474, חַלּוֹן challown, a perforation, to pierce, to open. In fact, the meaning of tsohar is exhilarating! We find where it is used (24 times in the Old Testament – 24 is the gematria of the Hebrew word Achiydah, meaning an enigma or riddle), its meaning is given as "a brightness, a brilliance, the light of the noonday sun." Its cognates refer to something that "glistens, glitters or shines."

Many Jewish scholars identify this "tsohar" as a light which had its origin in a shining crystal or jewel suspended (Similar to the Lamp or Menorah in the Tabernacle?) within the Ark and which, when exposed to the Sun would refract in the same RAINBOW colors that would later be used to remind Noah of the Covenant of YHVH! The Rainbow then would not have been a novel idea to Noah. In consideration, once again it is highly plausible that Noah is charged with protecting the LIGHT/SEED/WORD/LIFE [Nun-Chet = a fence or protection for life]. Was he the Caretaker of the Seed or DNA of YHVH in verbal, spoken form just as he protected his own bloodline from corruption? In retrospect, doesn't this sound remarkably like the description of the Ark of the Covenant which would have the Tablets of Stone representing this same Light placed within? The Hebrew phrase for Tables of Stone is quite telling I might add: Tables, H#3871, לוּחַ, luwach, though rendered as table, or slab, its' root stem, the Lamed-Chet indicates the spark or drive, the energy of life. The word for Stone, H#68 אֶבֶן 'eben, is defined as a stone, but, comes from the root of H#1129, banah, which indicates to begin to build, as in building a family name, for which the first born son is purposed. These 'luwach eben' – tables of stone within the Ark, were themselves symbolic of the Seed, Light, Word deposited into Creation whose spark ignited Life! Though Noah gives a clear indication of One who obeyed YHVH, he is sadly, also vividly described as a man who struggled with his flesh as seen in later chapters. Once again, you'll have to look at the Hebrew to see this. It would seem Noah lets his guard down which results in the events as described in the text of Gen. 9:20. The Hebrew verbiage alone reveals the makings of another downward spiral, where the seed is left unprotected, both spiritually, and naturally and sexual perversion (The crossing of those boundaries again) occurs once more.

Genesis 9:20 *And Noah began to be an husbandman, and he planted a vineyard.*

וַיָּחֶל נֹחַ אִישׁ הָאֲדָמָה וַיִּטַּע כָּרֶם:

Vayachel Noach Ish haadamah vayitah karem

The root for 'began' is also the Hebrew word for profane – chalal. While the word vineyard – kerem, and its root, Kaf-Resh spells the Hebrew word for a Male Lamb. The Mem indicates a womb or birthing. It would seems that Noah profaned his role as did his predecessor, the First ADAM – the Ish from the adamah – the ground, who like Noah, functioned as the Earth's husbandman charged with the planting of the seed of the Messiah in the ground!

Let's link Noah's issue here with something rather curious in our

'Word is Seed' theory:

Genesis 9:21 informs us that the abjection of Noah is directly linked to his wine drinking. What do you suppose is hidden here in the Hebrew language?

♦ Wine, H#3196   יַיִן   *yayin*

Though rendered simply as 'wine' it indicates that which intoxicates.

Ironically, this physiological state is also tied to the intoxicating, seduction of the Nachash (Serpent) or his flattering 'words'. It may come as a surprise, but, it is my opinion that the Greek language, from which most translate their "New Testament", is closely related to that lying, truth altering tongue. The Greek mindset has so permeated the Church of today, that relatively few understand the fallacy inherent in the translation. Curiously, the word Greek, from Greece, is translated in Hebrew as: H#3120, יָוָן, Yavan, Ionia or Greece. It comes from – you guessed it - H#3196, yayin, to intoxicate. You make the call...Be sure to remember; we're called to be Kings and Priests and thus admonished to write our own Torah and administer it properly in the Kingdom. I must say I am not against wine drinking in moderation. Anything else dulls the mind and opens a doorway for compromise.

When the person entrusted with the High Priestly duties fails to handle the Word, Seed, or Light properly, that person is isolated from the Source of Life, much like Adam from the Tree of Life. Hidden similarities can once again be seen in the Tower of Babel account, where YHVH confounds the speech of all Nations (excepting the Shemites) denying them access to the Tree of Life, His Living Word or Light. In Gen. 11:7 the word for confound, is H#1101, בָּלַל balal, to mix, mingle, or confuse, it can also mean "to pour over as in water", from the root Yabal, to flow as water!

This is the same root as the Hebrew word for flood, H#3999, מַבּוּל, mabbuwl. The Mem prefix seen in mabbuwl, hints at a womb, to birth, thus the flood seems likened to a birthing process; Yet, it is a vivid picture of Numbers chapter 5 and the Waters of Jealousy test, where the accusations against the adulterous bride are written, the water 'poured over' them into a cup, which she is made to drink. Go back and read this for an account giving instructions to the jealous husband who lodges accusations against his wife accused of adultery. It also gives the details pertaining to her resultant judgment or exoneration should she not be found guilty. This account is another example of where the seed of the Serpent is destroyed whiles the Seed of YHVH lives, bringing the Remnant to a central place, a destination. Though He had promised to never send another literal flood of water to destroy the earth, this spiritual flood of WORDS at Babel and later in Revelation 12, does far more damage and scatters the perverse remnant. When on the other hand, He is found distinguishing the House of Shem who remains Echad – One i.e. in Union with the Pure Seed, or language. Fast-forwarding, as I alluded to, Rev. 12 we're told of a future flood that will come forth out of the mouth of the Dragon! Where would we be able to see a foreshadowing of this event foretold? We'll look at this later…I'm entrusting you to not forget! However, I want to return to our discussion of the events of Genesis that are detailed in chapter two and three. The unique Garden of Eden venue where this occurs begs our indulgence. Nowhere in the KJV will we find anything but a simple picture of the locale known as Eden, much less the sordid details between chapter 2 and 3. That said, before we leave, I want to show you the rather gerund English definition, followed by the Hebraic Word Picture embedded in this word 'Eden'. Have a look for yourself.

♦   Eden, H#5731   עֵדֶן   *eden*

Though commonly defined as 'pleasure' or 'delight', the two-letter root stem of Ayin-Dalet, pronounced 'odd' signifies

YHVH's dwelling place, it can also hint at the continuance of a King on the Throne. It can also function as a preposition or conjunction related to periods of 'time', while also inferring a testimony or witness. By adding the letter Nun, we see an indication of something diminished or made smaller.

It would seem that EDEN was the place where YHVH diminished Himself – replicated, duplicated, took on a smaller form, in this case the Body of Adam, for the purpose of establishing His Kingdom through His Regent who would continue in His place on this earth. He would also manifest Himself in the flesh in the person of Messiah. The pattern is consistent with that of Ancient Near Eastern Treaty language where the Great Suzerain King appoints one as Vassal Servant in His stead to represent the Throne. The Covenant is written in the Legalese or legal jargon of the Great King! Hence, the Vassal must immerse himself, become One with, and be clothed with, the Word, Light or Seed of the Great King! How Awesome is that? It would be required of the Vassal to act as a testimony or witness of the Great King! What would identify the Vassal as the emissary of the King? The servant would often have something belonging to the Suzerain to prove he represented Him. Such as a special garment, signet ring or document emblazoned with the Seal of the King. One should be able to readily identify the Rainbow Garment, the establishment of the Sabbath (The signet or seal, sign of YHVH) and of course, the Creative power of the language of Hebrew. Adam enjoyed the advantage of this power until Genesis 3 where the Serpent usurps much of that authority! How did that affect man afterward? Glance back at Genesis 2 and 3 with me again. Who said 'rubbernecking' wasn't fun? ☺

In contemplation of what lies ahead for those who would stand against the Enemy, a meticulous examination of the successes of Adam, Noah, Shem, Abraham and others is required. History does indeed repeat itself and thus becomes our surest teacher. Though Biblical precedent exists our separation from its fundamental truths has kept us from acceptance of any possibility that there exists a Garment of Light! Though telling evidence proves we can be transformed into His image by emersion into this healing, cleansing, DNA altering stream, skeptics who profess biblical knowledge regularly pooh-pooh the idea. Thankfully, we have those mavericks in the scientific world who openly challenge the boundaries of conventional scientific knowledge and by exhaustive trial and error often come to the same conclusion as the empirical data readily found in Torah! Let's refresh our memory of the events of Genesis 1 – 4 so that our foundation is sure enough that we can expect the application of His Rainbow Language to change our lives.

Chapter 6

The Rainbow Covenant
Back to Eden...

We've talked about the Garment of Light that surely clothed Adam and Eve (Chavah) in Gen. 2 which must have literally enveloped them in a "COAT OF MANY COLORS" as a testament to their role as vassal to the King. (The symbology is not lost on those familiar with the story of Joseph and of course the garment worn by Yahshua, which I contend was also formed of and emblematic of, the same Light Power) But, to answer the question ending last chapter, what happened afterward, what change did the "Fall" bring? Can we follow this premise any further or is this a dead-end? (Pun intended) Again, let's investigate:

Genesis 3:21 tells of YHVH clothing Adam and Chavah (Eve) with 'skins', H#5785, עוֹר 'owr, some say it was the 'physical skin' we now have. Others like me contend it was the skin of an animal, specifically a lamb, fulfilling Rev. 13: 8 *the Lamb slain before the foundation of the world*...this pattern becomes consistent throughout the Tabernacle sacrificial system whose rituals are found requiring the same blood covering as atonement for sin! Whether a lamb or fleshly skin the argument for one or the other doesn't merit fighting over, because it could just as easily be both! It is worth noting the Torah describes the Skin of the sacrificed animal as belonging to the Priest. Adam had been the Cohen Gadol – High Priest of the earth and now because of the fall must take on the skin of the flesh – the lamb in order to 'live'. Following this same pattern, Yahshua, our High Priest, came in the fashion of Adam, i.e. the same flesh! Yet, without the taint of sin, thus, He is not Naked and made ashamed, but clothed with the original Light Garment – Word! This allows you and me access to the Coat of Many Colors – that Edenic Light Garment – by putting on Him – enveloping ourselves in the Light –Word! Does this make sense or am I a rambling idiot? We do have precedent I might add! Remember after descending Mt. Sinai Moshe's face glowed with light after the encounter with The Word/Fire/Voice for 40-days; while in another example, we see Yahshua Himself transfigured before Peter, James and John.

The significance of wearing a 'blooded garment' is not lost on those who're connecting the dots as we go along. Like myself, there are many (Including academicians) who believe Blood to be congealed or 'slowed down' light. Blood, which is inherently water (About 90%), contains liquid called plasma, which has suspended cells within its flow.

Pursuing this concept, American scientist Dr. Irving Langmuir (1881-1957) studied how ionized gases affected electronic devices. He noted how the ionized plasma fluid within the tubes carried electrons and impurities much like the human plasma. He reasoned blood plasma to be similar to congealed light. If so, and again you weigh the evidence, the blood 'skins' (Remember the Hebrew word 'owr, skin, similar to the word for light) covering Adam and Chavah (Eve) could literally have been a congealed light garment!

In an exemplary fashion, this fleshly skin you're sitting in reading this book, is literally filled with myriads of blood carrying vessels called capillaries. These vessels (messengers perhaps?) carry a DNA coded message which provides a higher variation of color in humans than any other mammalian specie, making your own skin a Blood-Word-Light - Coat of many colors! Furthermore, Gaston Naessens, the renowned scientist who discovered the ultramicroscopic bodies within the blood stream called 'Somatids' seems to concur with our position: Blood is electrically charged, containing Light, energy and frequency in the form of these tiny Somatids, themselves also electrically charged and are what many believe to be the tiniest condensers or energy source ever found! According to Naessens, there is no explanation where cell life comes from except in the concept of pleomorphism; that is, the many forms that somatids go through. Bechamp's German student, Gunther Enderlein discovered likewise, that these tiny bodies, he named protits - predate DNA and carry on genetic activity. It is the first thing that condenses from light energy and is the link between light and matter; ergo, somatids are the link between biological and physical sciences. *Somatids are none other than condensed biophotons or light energy. We know that the human body glows and emits light often referred to as an aura.* [http://goarticles.com/article/SOMATIDS-THE-MYSTERIOUS-DNA-PRECURSOR – author Sai Grafio: Writer, poet, author, lecturer, astrologer, psychic]

It would seem all one would need is to plug themselves into the receptacle of the Word and become a 'charged Being', capable of reproducing and releasing that power upon contact with a grounded source! HalleluYah!

If you should delve further into the Hebrew language you'll see the confirming prophetic declaration of this very thing in Gen. 1:26 where the first mention of creating man occurs. The word man, H#120, אָדָם 'adam, is rendered man, from adom, meaning red, or ruddy. The Hebrew letter Alef appended to the front indicates a future tense, "I will". While the Dalet-Mem root spells, dam, the Hebrew word for blood! Thus, prophetically, declaring the intent of YHVH toward Adam as, "I will blood you". Adam was to become a walking Dynamo! The phrase encompasses every facet of Salvation poignantly hinting at the fall, Adam's death, subsequent covering and atonement by blood, etc. All of which, Adam would himself have been very aware of! This power was given to us upon the Ascension of Messiah.

Luke 24:49 And, behold, I send the promise of my Father upon you: but tarry ye in the city of Jerusalem, until ye be endued with power from on high.

*Note: The Greek word for power? Dynamis!

If you're still reading this far, you're probably concerned with what many would consider an asinine effort on my part, to convince you of the existence of the very garment – the Coat of Many Colors found clothing Adam and Chavah (Eve) in the garden. I believe it is also available – though having been intentionally hidden for a season – to those of this Final Generation who will step into the realm of The Word – His Word, and put it [Him] on! Gal. 3: 27, Roms. 13: 14 ...*put on Messiah.*

Bear with me as I attempt to convince you further, by showing you some powerful patterns that YHVH uses as teaching tools regarding this very issue. Let me provoke you with a question first. Aren't we created in the image of YHVH and thus, expected to emulate Him? Of course, you'll agree! Take a look then, at Psalm 104

Psalm 104:1-2 Bless the YHVH, O my soul. O YHVH my Elohiym, thou art very great; thou art clothed with honour and majesty. Who coverest thyself with light as with a garment: who stretchest out the heavens like a curtain.

The Creator Himself is clothed with a garment of Light! Is it stretching things to believe that we were and will be again, clothed with that same glory? I don't think so! This is all well and good. But, how can I tie the events of Eden and that of Noah's covenantal Rainbow together? It just doesn't seem to fit. Or, does it? Let me present you a bit of a teaser, to get the juices flowing!

If in fact we can agree that YHVH doesn't change then Adam should have been aware of the Covenantal sign of the Rainbow given to Noah. Is this possible? First, it is my contention that the Torah (Teachings and Instructions) of YHVH would have been known before the creation of Adam as is revealed in Genesis 1:14 where the message is written in the Stellar Luminaries. These original visible planets – 7 in number – represented the Heavenly Tabernacle Menorah. Those 7 branches, each light arching to meet its fellow on the opposite side would have formed a natural circle much like the 7 colors of the rainbow seen from a bird's eye view. The Covenant is eternal, thus, its sign would be as well. We should expect the restoration of the Tabernacle Menorah and the Rainbow Language as conjoined twins, to become the prevalent sign in the coming days as well.

Essentially, the foregoing story of Noah and the promise made to him by YHVH to never destroy the earth again by a flood is a mainstay in most religious circles. Surely, there's more to this innocuous event than merely the great deluge and the resultant destruction of the earth. Something of this magnitude would without a doubt, require a promise as a guarantee for future generations and as such, merit a Sign or seal far more meaningful than just a colorful display after a rain shower. I needn't remind you the token or sign for that covenant was the rainbow. In consideration, I submit there's more than meets the eye and by this time our evidence should be piquant enough to provoke you to dig further. Perhaps you need a bit more convincing? If so, let's look at a few words from Genesis:

> **Genesis 9:13** *I do set my bow in the cloud, and it shall be for a token of a covenant between me and the earth.*

In order to avoid any ambiguity, we'll look at this verse from an unconventional perspective; – rather than the KJV – we will see what the Hebrew yields for our understanding:

♦ Set, H#5414   נתן   *Nathan*

To place, put, spread out. *Remember the language of Hebrew uses letters for numerals, thus each letter has a numeric value which, once examined will confirm the message of the letters themselves. Following that premise we find the numeric value of Nathan, Nun-50, Tav-400, Nun-50 = 500, the same as the Hebrew words, H#8269 & 8270, pronounced 'Sar'. It means prince, ruler, chief one, and priest. It can also mean 'Navel' - umbilical cord, or body, flesh. It is the root stem of the Hebrew word Basar – which means flesh! If we break those letters apart - look at the word picture given basar; i.e. our flesh, should be [Bet – house of, SAR – the Chief One] the residence of the Prince or Chief One. This is important, simply because there are Hebrew word pictures inherent in each individual letter. Once the cipher of the letters is revealed it seems evident (Though it is hidden to the casual observer) YHVH in this one word – natan - is alluding to the Rainbow functioning as the UMBILICAL CORD OF THE PRINCE. Need we say more? Perhaps a clinical approach will suffice?

Science has proven DNA travels through the navel cord from mother to child and 'pieces' are transferred to both! [Mary-Yahshua?] Because He had no earthly father [We know because the very pattern of Gen. 1: 2 where the Ruach ha Qodesh -Spirit of Elohiym, moved, I.E. literally vibrated over creation is repeated at the description of His conception, foretold to occur by the Malak (Angel) Gabriel in Luke 1: 35] *The Holy Spirit would come upon her and overshadow her...)* which would result in a 'sacrifice without blemish' therefore, the 'pieces' of corruption mentioned above, whether through an earthly father or mother, could not be transmitted to Him. Thus, He must be born of the WORD and as a result of His atoning work; the same opportunity is given to you which provoked the startling conversation with

Nicodemus who came to Yahshua by night! You must be born again! In fact, this is also echoed in 1 Peter:

> ***1 Peter 1:23*** *Being born again, not of corruptible seed, but of incorruptible, by the word of God, which liveth and abideth forever.*

Following this same formula for creation in the natural realm, couldn't the event of Jacob's ladder also have metaphorically depicted an umbilical cord carrying the DNA of the Son of YHVH into the earth? Gen. 28:12...*behold a ladder set upon the earth*...I personally believe this was a DNA helix, revealing the messengers/angels of YHVH ascending and descending via this 'gateway' or umbilical cord. Later, we find in John 1:51 the Messiah making reference to this very event; by declaring to His talmidim (disciples) how they would see the same *messengers ascending and descending upon the Son of Man*!

To the Rainbow again Gen. 9:13

Let's get back to our verse and look at the Hebrew word used for 'BOW'.

♦ Bow, H#7198 קֶשֶׁת *qesheth*

*Note the Hebrew phrase: אֶת־קַשְׁתִּי ET qashti, Alef-Tav - My Bow! Qesheth is translated: 'Bow', rainbow. The gematria of qesheth, Qof-100, Shin-300, Tav-400 = 800, the value of the final form of the letter Pey – mouth. 80x10. 10 is a picture of order and is also the gematria of Alef-Tet which means secrecy, to conceal. This is an example following the order of what issues out of His, the Creators' Mouth; concerning things kept secret & concealed from the enemy – yet revealed to those in Covenant! Does YHVH conceal things from some?

> **Proverbs 25:2** *It is the glory of God to conceal a thing: but the honour of kings is to search out a matter.*

Of course He does! You'll understand more after you remember that Daniel is told to seal up the books in Daniel 12: 4: To seal and keep them for a season. By the way, this subject will be addressed in another chapter which will stretch the limits of your traditional views even farther. So, keep your finger here, while we move on.

The Hebrew word qesheth – bow, has a numeric value of 800. This is the same as the Greek word Omega - the last letter of the Greek Alpha-Bet and used to reference Yahshua 4 times in the book of Revelation. This letter corresponds to the Tav in Hebrew, the sign of the Covenant!

Where exactly would that Rainbow sit, in other words, is the placement of the Bow a clue regarding its' use?

◆ Cloud, H#6051   עָנָן   'anan

Translated cloud, but if we break the word apart, we see the letter Ayin – a well, or a womb, It is literally a pictograph of a human eye indicating to see, perceive. The last letter is the symbol of life - Nun. Is this a challenge to view the Rainbow as life-light-word in the womb? You decide.

◆ Token, H#226   אוֹת   'owth

A sign, or marker, something that conveys information! Remember the first usage of the word establishes a precedent: Gen. 1:14 where the stellar luminaries are set for SIGNS! It is a fact; the stars themselves were given Hebrew names

(Though perverted to Greek and Arabic at times) which convey the entire salvific message.

What possible way could the lights in the firmament transmit a message and by what medium or 'language' would it travel? Would it be a specific type sound or light? Perhaps a radio wave frequency? What are the possibilities? Remember the movie from 1977 "Close Encounters of the Third Kind"? In it, scientists attempt to communicate with an Alien Mother ship using light and musical tones! Science fiction you say? It is also well known that Stars have varied colors thus producing variable musical sounds and tonal frequencies! Look at the following well documented information.

NASA has discovered a group of massive red stars that are actually humming to themselves. The planet-hunting Kepler space telescope recently spotted sound waves emanating from the stars, the Wall Street Journal reports. NASA recorded the tune, and played it recently at a press conference in Denmark. "It is a giant red concert," says the astronomer who made the recording. "They have many different frequencies and overtones." Is this Biblical?

Job 38:7 *When the morning stars sang together and all the sons of God shouted for joy?*

Creation is a symphony! [www.newser.com/story/104101/nasa-finds-singing-stars]

Put yourself in the place of Noah. For all intents and purposes, you're alone in the world, with the exception of 7 family members. You've just witnessed the greatest devastation of man or creation imaginable. Your nerves are a bit frazzled. You've walked with Yahweh for generations. He hasn't failed you yet. The Signs of His Presence have confirmed your steps. This time, you alone are tasked with the very assignment your ancient Forefather Adam failed at. You need direction! Now, fast forward to our day…It was promised by no less than our Messiah that conditions would be the same at His 2nd coming much as it was in Noah's day. If there was ever a generation who needed a discernable gesture of the Creators' Promise wouldn't it be this one? The malevolent intensity of Anti-Torah bias and the mocking nature of those opposed to anything remotely Biblical has increased: Their purpose? To flush out and then violently crush the faint-hearted!

How probable is it that you will get discouraged without an understanding of these signs of His Covenant? Note what Messiah says in Luke:

> *Luke 21:26 Men's hearts failing them for fear, and for looking after those things which are coming on the earth: for the powers of heaven shall be shaken.*

Without a fundamental, working knowledge of the Creation Language the odds are infinitesimal in favor of your survival. Isn't it time we began to recognize more of those signs and to read the message underscored in each? Read on as we continue to look at the prophetic declaration of Genesis 9:13.

♦ Covenant, H#1285   בּרית   *bĕriyth*

Covenant, treaty. We know the normal two-letter root, Bet-Resh can mean son, bar. However, the Resh-Yod-Tav connection is intriguing as well, it infers to be indulgent, lenient, to pity. This reveals the nature of the heart of the Father!

Our Extrapolated Definition

After having reduced the definition in Hebrew to its most concise, we're left with what in my judgment, should provoke a powerful, visceral reaction from you, dear Reader.

"I do place, in the House of the Chief One, My bow, the Alef-Tav (releasing out of My mouth – secrets concealed in the Well [womb-Mem] of Life) engraved there as a Sign between Me and the earth!"

This Bow became His banner. How does this affect your understanding of the Lovers' declaration in Song of Solomon?

> **Solomon 2:4** *He brought me to the banqueting house, and his banner over me was love.*

Do you recall our earlier discussion of Noah and the episode with the "fruit of the Vine"? If you look at the verse above you'll see the same word used for wine, H#3196, יַיִן yayin, which is translated as the word for 'banqueting' in the book, Song of Songs. How ironic, to find the very place designated for enjoying the intoxicating fruit of intimacy – the bridal chamber - (which should also be found emblazoned with the banner of His Spoken Word, illuminating us with His Presence) could in turn become a place of debauchery much like occurred in the illustration of Noah? Do you see how the Language or Seed which is being contemplated by the Bride determines what or whom is birthed out of that intimate encounter? Now you understand why the Greek language – (which incidentally comes from the same root – Yayin) and any other tongue or seed which seduces one away from the Truth leaves you in a naked condition much like Noah and Adam. As a result, we've lost our garment of Light. The Rainbow language. Perhaps if we re-gain understanding and therefore, begin to 'hear the Voice of the Shepherd' we will once again, as children of the light, walk in it! What then has happened to remove us from the Source of Light and His Covenant sign – the Rainbow? Walk with me a few more paces and we will endeavor to find out.

The Rainbow only occurs when moisture refracts or bends the light, revealing colors. Throughout Torah, Light and Word are synonymous. Thus, when YHVH says, "let there be light", He speaks or vocalizes the light! He slows the light down so that it can be heard or seen in the physical realm! Remember from earlier on we found that most Physicists agree that light is sound that is sped up, and sound is light which has slowed down. If you slow lights' frequency 40 times you have a frequency within the parameters of sound. If you speed sound by doubling it 40 times you have a frequency within lights' parameters!

The number 40 above is interesting; it is associated with trials, testing, proving. It is written in Hebrew with the letter Mem, meaning WOMB and it is the number symbolizing Chaotic Waters – just like Gen. 1:2 where the waters/Mem of Creation were in Chaos! Thus, when light-word, is spoken - sounded into the Waters of the Womb - conception takes place! During the birthing process as the labor pains increase, the embryonic fluid becomes troubled ultimately breaking forth in a deluge or flood as the womb is breached.

Humans are 60-65% water! Therefore, light when it is released into these water vessels, becomes sound!

Dr. Bruce Lipton, PH.D professor of Anatomy at St. George's University School of Medicine teaches that cells are liquid crystals! Exposing them to an energy source such as Light, radio waves, musical notes and colors, causes them to resonate sympathetically and even change physical shape – NO WONDER THE ROCKS CRY OUT!! This is akin to the vibrational frequencies of Creation in Genesis 1: 2 where the Energy Source – the Ruach haQodesh (Holy Spirit) moved (H#736 רָחַף rachaph, trembled, to shake, or release vibrational energy) upon the waters! The Light moved – was refracted – upon the amniotic fluid of creation, the rainbow is born! For those who refuse to acknowledge the chaotic events between Genesis 1: 1 and Genesis 1:2, the introduction of Light into a world that is without form and void is easily skimmed over. However, the Hebrew phrase is rendered 'וָבֹהוּ תֹהוּ' Tohu v'bohu and indicates that which is laid waste, made void and empty. It hints at a present condition that exists as the result of a previous chaotic event. It would seem natural to see the healing power of His Word, in the form of Light, being introduced to 'heal or rejuvenate' the DNA of Creation. One could easily view these events as a 'redemption process' being initiated.

It is no accident the number value or gematria of Hebrew letters in the Hebrew word for redemption, H#1353, גְּאֻלָּה gĕullah equals 39, the number of stripes (40-1) (Deut. 25: 3) received when one was to be scourged. Let's examine Is. 53:5 where we're told, *"With His stripes we are healed"*. We understand this as a Messianic reference, and we freely acknowledge the importance of the Stripes received upon the back of Yahshua to purchase that redemption. But, what did those stripes really indicate?

Examine this Hebrew word for Healed H#7495, רפא rapha', it implies far more than physical healing - actually inferring to MEND, REPAIR, TO SEW TOGETHER. (Perhaps like the skin parchments of a Torah scroll?) The word for 'stripes' from the Hebrew is H#2250, חבורה, chabbuwrah, and can also infer to make strokes on parchment and as such, reveals a rather amazing scene. Viewed from this context we're told these stripes were STROKES ON THE SKIN, LIKE WORDS WRITTEN ON A SCROLL! Imagine if you can, Yahshua being tied to an upright beam with his back to the scourge. Each stroke of the whip would have made stripes in blood, which would have resembled the strokes of a scarlet pen upon a Torah scroll. It is my opinion when Moshe was shown the 'hinder or back parts' of YHVH in Exodus 33 he was literally being shown the Back of Messiah striped by the scourge to purchase the redemption of His Bride! If blood and light and words are interconnected, those stripes of Light, Sound, and Color, which are all connected to the HEBREW LANGUAGE, would each nourish and restore the natural, fleshly, carnal Body! Thus, the Stripes would sew, mend, and knit together, restoring harmony to the broken, disease affected, DNA corrupted areas of our bodies, Spirit, Soul, & Flesh.

In fact, Music- Sound & Color-Light are harmonics of each other. For example: The Musical note C on the piano is 256 cycles, while one octave higher (high C) is 512, go up 39 octaves – STRIPES – and double the number and you get the vibratory rate of the color RED, making the two exact harmonics of each other! It is this color of blood that marked each stroke on the LIVING TORAH MADE FLESH – YAHSHUA!

The Gematria of Chabbuwrah, (Stripes) (Chet-8, Bet-2, Vav-6, Resh-200, Hey-5 = 221) is the same as: Yori, Yod-Alef-Resh-Yod, which means, He (YHVH) gives light and H#3138, yoreh, a word defining the Early Rain that fell during the Fall Festivals. Another word 'Yeor' is the Hebrew word for NILE (The River of Egypt). This ancient river was connected to the Constellation Canis Major and in particular the Dog Star – Sirius, the brightest star in the heavens! Karl Guthe Jansky a physicist at Bell Laboratories in 1932 proved that stars emit both light and sound (radio waves)! Once more this word 'stripes' connects us again to both sound and light.

Why should a rainbow be able to convey a message, if any, and what could the message possibly be? Remember, Noah's flood was a foreshadowing of Numbers 5:23, where the Adulterous bride had her curses written in a book, H#5612, cepher. The root stem of cepher is spelled in Hebrew: Samech – Pey – Resh. The two-letter root, Samech – Peh spells Saph, H#5592, which means a cup or bowl and it also pictures a threshold, the boundary crossed over as one enters the Marriage Covenant. The word – picture of the letters tells the story of the Adulterous bride. She brings 'another lover' across the sacred boundary of the intimate place and the curse of the book is invoked against her. These words were written and had living water poured over them, washing them, along with the dust of the Tabernacle floor (Genesis 3: 19 H#6083, aphar, written Ayin-Pey-Resh: Pey-Resh, par = the fruit of our lips) into the Cup of bitterness from which she drank. If guilty as accused her belly and thigh would rot out. If not, she would conceive and bear children.

The Rainbow is a Sign of this same Covenant – and as such, this sign conveys message/words AND APPEARS ONLY WHEN WATER IS POURED OVER IT washing it into the earth! Thus, a promise to not destroy the earth with the Bitter Waters of Jealousy – a flood - is written in the Rainbow to remind us Messiah paid the penalty for the guilty bride. The Outcasts of Israel have played the harlot and the bitter waters are being offered. Yahshua drank the cup on her behalf and at this critical time in history, when Babylon the harlot is forced to drink from the cup again the prophetic words of Revelation 18: 4 admonishes "My People" to come out of her. This seems to follow in the same fashion as the command to Adam, Noah, Abraham and others.

With that solemn admonition at this most opportune time in history there should be no surprise The Rainbow (language) appears once again, after the season of our exile, the period when the House of Israel, after the manner of Genesis 1:2 was 'Tohu v'bohu' – waste and desolate. We can see each successive era of the Patriarchs following much the same pattern: Noah, Abraham, Moshe and finally, Israel's 430 years in bondage are all foreshadows of where we are now after 2730 years of our own exile. Our release comes, when, along with the advent of the Covenant Promise - the RAINBOW APPEARS AGAIN! In Matthew 24: 37 Yahshua declares His second appearing would parallel the days of Noah. It would seem logical for an expectation of the restored Rainbow Language to occur as well. For who then is this Pure Language prepared and for what purposes its use? The description of Noah's birth may lend a hand at deciphering this clue.

The language structure of the Hebrew text indicates how the birth of Noah – Gen. 5:29 (whose name means rest, and typified the Sabbath) would eradicate the enemies of YHVH and restore Adam as a race. He would "...*comfort us concerning our work and toil of our hands, because of the ground which the LORD hath cursed."*

- Comfort, H#5162, *nacham*, to console, comfort us.

- Work, H#4639 *ma'aseh*, to relate, tell, declare, by setting something right!

- Toil, H#6093, *itstabown*, hardship, labor.

- Hands, H#3027, *yad*, hand, authority, power, strength.

- Because, H#4480, from, with, H#4482, mane, stringed instrument.

Our Extrapolated Definition

Noah, the last generation before the flood, would console his people regarding the restoration of the power and authority of the Living Man that "Stringed Instrument – called Adam" and the place he held in Creation before the ground was cursed.

No wonder Creation now awaits the manifestation of the Sons of YHVH – Romans 8: 19. You have vocal cords; as you exhale, air pushed across the cords produces sound. You are a living stringed instrument who loudly proclaims the Glory and Power of YHVH via His Word! It is at once, the Light, Sound, Music and Color vividly displayed in the Rainbow Covenant of Re-Creation! You must be fruitful, multiply and replenish, subdue and exercise dominion through this Word! We are indeed, Children of the Light. Yet, how can we walk in the Aura that was once the Cloak of Adam and Yahshua? How did Adam function in Eden? Prima facie evidence is conclusive: Adam was the earth's regent representing the Great King and as the office would warrant, he used the language of the King to speak prophetically to the subjects of his realm. Every form of life was subject to Adam, including the Nachash. Yet, the serpent cunningly used the legalese of the same Covenant to seduce Adam and Eve. How could this be? First, we need to see how Adam functioned in Eden.

We've discussed the principal of Adam being clothed with a Light garment, which essentially represents the over-arching banner of YHVH's word. Like its primitive 'fiber-optic' cousins of today light would have offered the fastest means of communication. Adam thought it and was there. If light vibrates at a certain frequency which determines its speed, then to slow the light down would seem to have made it capable of being heard. In fact science confirms that the Earth's electromagnetic field is the source that enables every known biological specie to communicate. This same principal is seen on a reduced scale when one considers how the Hebrew language and its individual letters are themselves musical notes; each letter lending its peculiar sound. This enables the Hebrew language to have an effect on both what we see and what we hear. Coupled with the vibrations associated with each, it could also be 'felt'. How else can one explain a blind person 'seeing the word', a deaf man 'hearing the word' and finally a dead man or girl neither of whom had the physical capability, being obedient to what they heard Yahshua declaring? Have we truly explored the dimensions of His word? Can the healing 'sounds' themselves alter our DNA? Our understanding of Genesis 1: 2 where the Spirit of YHVH moved – vibrated – producing Sound, while interacting with the crystals of water would have converted the energy in the sound to light energy! Today this is known as 'sonoluminescence'. In Genesis 1:3 the Creator simply says: "Let there be Light."

What then must Eden have been like? With its garden permeated by a perpetual mist the Sounds of His voice must surely have amplified the Light of His Presence. What melodies would have been possible! Surely Adam was the conductor of creations' greatest orchestra! Shall we see?

Chapter 7

The Sound of Music

Many Scholars believe the conditions in Eden were such that; light, color and sound would have been amplified exponentially. It is also highly likely that Adam's sensory perception would have been heightened to a degree far above ours, allowing him to differentiate between frequency patterns of light, color and sound; the limitation of which, preclude us from experiencing, much less, appreciating them. It is highly probable, that Adam enjoyed hyper-dimensional abilities that enabled him to transcend the physical constraints of time as a result. To a lesser degree, these boundaries are being approached and may be crossed entirely, in our near future. If so, it will be by those whose walk with YHVH becomes similar to that of Enoch, Elijah and Phillip the Evangelist, and of course Yahshua, each of whom was translated from one dimension to another. Indeed, there are people today that experience something similar in my estimation, to Adam, at least, in the realm of sight and sound. In doing so, demonstrating a rare phenomenon called 'Synesthesia'. This peculiar ability allows some to see colors simultaneous with the hearing of sound or music and often, when seeing visible numbers. Ridiculous you say - as if, once more, scripture needed clinical confirmation. (Sarcasm again, sorry) Yet, Modern Science has proven an association between certain sounds, colors, light and musical notes and their ability to affect the human body. It is a palpable and irrefutable fact: the Original Hebrew language was designed to be sung (each letter represents a musical note). Words set to music are easier to commit to memory, go figure this one! Now we no longer wonder at Mark 4: 24 and the 'parable of the Sower' where the Messiah stresses the inestimable power of hearing:

> ***Mark 4:24*** *And he said unto them, Take heed what ye hear: with what measure ye mete, it shall be measured to you: and unto you that hear shall more be given.*

Incidentally, the word measure here can also indicate a melody, tune or rhythmic structure or movement in a musical score.

There is a Hebrew word pronounced Mozenim, and translated as meaning a set of balances or a scale. The root is ozen, the Hebrew word for ear. How like YHVH to place on either side of your head a set of balances to measure what you hear? Again, the Calvary of Science rides to the rescue of Scripture. The ear is proven to contain the sensory organs for hearing and balance! It is also filled with a 'water-like' fluid. Water crystals receive and transmit light as wells as, sound and electrical current! Sound is formed from vibration whose length is measured as 'frequency'. The sensation of a frequency is commonly referred to as the pitch of a sound. There are seven colors in a rainbow and seven notes in a musical scale. The first, third and fifth colors of the rainbow are Primary colors... red, yellow and blue. The first, third and fifth notes of a major scale is a Major chord... root, third and fifth. Something quite amazing happens when we tie all of this information together (that's Physics, Optics, Light, Sight, Sound, Hearing, Art, Music, and Neuroscience) and line up the two groups of seven up together... Primary Colors literally become Major Chords!

If you could actually "hear" the extremely high frequencies in which the red, yellow and blue (primary color) light waves are vibrating at... you would hear a Major chord.

If you could "see" the sound of notes in a major chord relative to the same "rainbow scale" used by light... you would see notes and chords in primary color. This would seem to be supported by the phrase repeated more often than any other in the New Testament by Yahshua: "Let he that hath an ear; hear". In truly hearing we become doers as well. The Messiah has restored our ability to hear, we just need to deal with our flesh which is the filter through which everything heard passes! Let me show you an incident involving Messiah that may add a little 'oomph' to your understanding.

Our setting is in the garden of Gethsemane, (Since we will also mention the Tabernacle Menorah, remember this word Gethsemane is translated; Oil Press) where you surely remember Yahshua shortly before His arrest? Look closely:

> **John 18:10** *Then Simon Peter having a sword drew it, and smote the high priest's servant, and cut off his right ear. The servant's name was Malchus.*

Simon comes from Shema meaning "to hear" while Peter is translated as a rock or stone. This reminds us of the Rock who heard in the wilderness and judged the People. This smaller rock – Peter takes a sword, the word, and cuts off the ear – the hearing of Malchus, which is translated as meaning Kingdom. This is a prophetical enactment pertaining to the House of Israel who became dull of hearing and were cut off from the Living Word, and Light, accordingly. However, Yahshua reattaches the man's ear! This indicates a future restoration of the Hearing of the Torah for the House of Israel and Judah! Hallelujah!

There is another function of this word normally rendered 'ear', H#241, ozen; in this case it's H#240, אָזֵן 'azen, translated in Deut. 23: 13 as an instrument to remove excrement from the Camp lest YHVH refuse to walk among you. Hmmm? Few of us relish the removal of spoken excrement in the form of; gossip, backbiting, slander, lying and such, but without the surgical use of this tool/weapon, you will not find the King in the Camp! Now, think about that for a spell!

Allowing for that slight detour – perhaps you'll excuse me for stinking things up a bit! As we continue our journey, we'll look at the Sciences where, once again in its' plodding gait, it has given the nod to Scripture by recognizing the role of the human ear: (You thought you knew its role until the above) In several studies it has been shown that sound (light that is slowed down) has a profound effect on the human body. Sound enters the ears, H#241, אֹזֶן 'ozen, which act as a balance to adjust, accept or reject what is heard/seen. Thanks to the ground breaking findings of Dr. Alfred Tomatis, we have come to understand the extraordinary power of the ear. In addition to its critical functions of communication and balance, the ear's primary purpose is to recycle sound and so recharge our inner batteries. According to Tomatis, the ears' first function, in utero, is to govern the growth of the rest of the physical organism. After birth, sound is to the nervous system what food is to our physical bodies: Food provides nourishment at the cellular level of the organism, and sound feeds us the electrical impulses that charge the neocortex. Just as the Ruling Elite have compromised our food system, genetically altering the DNA of most plants, & foods, in order to compromise the Human Body, so also has the Sound been altered to produce an inferior spiritual being incapable of proper thinking! All this since the Tower of Babel encounter! Pray tell, how has sound been manipulated you ask. Well, let's look at some musical connections.

Within the last twenty years, the most common relationship found between musical notes – sound, is that their colors match the notes of one octave with the colors of the electromagnetic spectrum, starting with the note C. Red = C, orange = D, yellow = E, green = F, blue = G, indigo = A, and violet = B. Is it possible that Josephs' Coat was a physical manifestation of a spiritual/physiological change that would begin once Joseph and later the Bones of Joseph seen by the Prophet Ezekiel often referred to as "The Outcasts of Israel" began to put on the garment or Coat/Sound/Light/Language? Without this 'Coat' our hearing is distorted. How can we know the Voice of the Shepherd and truly follow him?

The ear that doesn't "hear" correctly, cannot process the auditory tones necessary to properly understand language. The ear that does hear is able to sequence and process information. ASP (auditory sequential processing) is the building block of thinking and enables one to receive, hold, process and implement what is heard. Now SHEMA (The ability to hear and then obey) becomes more apparent! If YHVH is restoring the Pure Language of Creation – Hebrew, shouldn't we prepare ourselves to hear it properly? How can we do that? Our bodies must be tuned 'in'; the flesh acts as a filter through which everything we hear is processed! So when you are learning this new language, you should "tune your ear" to the sounds by getting as much listening practice as you can, even if you don't understand the words very well. As your ear becomes accustomed to the sounds of the language, you will gradually start to recognize more words. Once you are able to recognize the words, you will more easily be able to attach their meaning to them. It's the same way our children learn the language of their parents! Without this tuning we are 'hearing impaired' i.e. what we hear is affected, quite possibly by our own flesh and by the machinations of the Prince of the Air, who is able to distort sounds, thoughts, etc. We should be careful to note the power resonating in the form of sound, light, and music. The latter being the most familiar and probably most powerful medium of communication in today's culture. We should also be careful what music we 'hear'! How so? Isn't it a relatively harmless, form of relaxation? Read the following and answer later.

Music is heard because of the frequency or number of vibrations per second that the ear is able to hear. The ancient Musical or Solfeggio scale was quite different from that of today and knowledge of it suppressed. Why? Because each note vibrated at a specific frequency that had a profound effect on the body & mind.

It is the note C that is closest to MI (Transformation and Miracles) on the ancient Solfeggio scale vibrating at somewhere near 528 cycles per second, when sped up by doubling it 40 times you are in the color spectrum closest to green! The first mention of the color green is found in Gen. 1: 30, H#3418, ירק yereq, this word has the same two-letter root, the Yod-Resh, as H#3384, Yarah, which means to shoot, throw, to teach. It is the root of Torah! But the Yod-Resh root is also connected to the word 'iyr', meaning city, gate, or Watcher (Another word for Fallen Angel). Now add the letter Qof – the back of the head, the hinder part, that which comes at the last.

We see that the restoration of the language of Genesis that brought life to every GREEN thing will also be restored at the end, our day! The gematria of yereq, Yod-10, Resh-200, Qof-100 = 310, the same as Ayin-Resh-Mem root, H#6174, arowm, which means naked! If we refresh our memories, we recall Adam and Eve were first clothed with this garment of light and naked (without) fleshly garments, with no apparent shame. *See Gen. 2:25. This same root is seen in Gen. 3:1, 7 where the serpent is described as subtle (arowm – naked, without this covering) inferring that he perhaps had the garment at one time (Ezek. 28:13). In the former, Adam and Eve are naked and not ashamed, H#954, בוש buwsh, ashamed, *note the two-letter stem Bet-Vav of Buzi, (my shame, contempt) the name of the Father of Ezekiel, whose vision of the restoration of the Dry Bones living again follows this same blueprint. It is interesting to note that YHVH says in Gen. 1:30 that He has given the green herb for food, H#402, אכלה 'oklah, meaning food, to consume. However, the Kaf-Lamed-Hey root spells Kallah, the word for BRIDE! This is the same word translated in Gen. 3 where we're told the serpent would consume, eat, 'akal, the dust. By adding the Hebrew letter Hey to the end making it a feminine word 'oklah, the hint is: Is this green herb (green being the color closet to the note MI for transformation and healing) food for the Bride? What you take in you will either consume you or make you fertile! Truly, you are what you eat! Can you see why almost every food source is now contaminated with GMO's: genetically modified organisms? We're told both in Deut. 8:3 and two places in the New Testament (Matt. 4:4, Luke 4:4) *man shall not live by bread alone, but by every word that proceedeth out of the mouth of YHVH!* The first reference is connected to the feeding of Israel by the Manna in the Wilderness. By the same token, Yahshua became the Living Bread or Manna. The Word of YHVH which sustains us! Is it possible the Torah (implied by the Green color) is made to come alive as the language is returned to His People? The Sages teach Chlorophyll does not capture green, it reflects it. That's why plants are green. The Mashiach is called a plant. He is human photosynthesis. Even the High Priestly garments lend credence to the importance of hearing and seed bearing as shown by the bells (sound) followed by pomegranates (representing seed or fertility) upon the edge of the garment! As we examine the Hebrew word for green, H#3418, יָרָק, yereq, it's interesting to find that it comes from H#3417, yaraq, which means to spit. Since we're inferring this color has having a connection with the life that is protected or renewed by the word in the last days, then perhaps it helps us to remember that Yahshua took clay and SPIT and placed it upon the eyes of a blind man, restoring the light – sight to his eyes. This man sees men as 'Trees'. Ironically, in Rev. 9:4 Yah's protection is afforded to the green things and 'trees'. Coincidental? I don't think so!

It is also interesting to note Rev. 9:4, where the locusts released out of the pit are told to not touch any green thing, but only those men who had not the seal of YHVH in their foreheads! Will this protected group speak a language that encompasses the vibrational frequencies of Light and Music? The previous chapter tells us a third part of the trees and all green grass had already been burned up. What's really being said here? Remember the Locusts, H#697, ארבה 'arbeh. It was this specific plague which began the birthing pangs that would eventually deliver Israel out of

Egypt. These Birth pangs are assigned to Jacob, both past and present (Jacobs Troubles) yet were first prophesied to in relation to Eve: Let's look:

> **Genesis 3:16** *Unto the woman he said, I will greatly mul-tiply thy sorrow and thy conception; in sorrow thou shalt bring forth children; and thy desire [shall be] to thy hus-band, and he shall rule over thee.*

YHVH tells Eve, He would greatly multiply (her sorrow) *Note the redundancy of the phrase in Hebrew! הַרְבָּה אַרְבֶּה HaRabah Arbeh! Do you remember the word for Locusts? It's this same root H#697, ארבה 'arbeh. The above phrase [HaRabah arbeh] connects Eve's birth pangs with 'The Many Locusts' of Revela-tion 9:4! What brought about Eves sorrow at conception: Since she had been commanded to be fruitful and multiply, conception and birth were natural results right? It seems very plausible her reception of the Serpent's Seed was, of course, the missing con-nection! The sexual tryst which cost her Coat or Covering of Light/Language/Color began the introduction of the metaphorical 'locusts', the sorrows. Thus, is it possible that YHVH will at some point, again multiply the source of her sorrow, [fig. of the locusts who represent the Serpent's Seed] to test her? Are those locusts a.k.a. the HaRabah arbeh - the greatly multiplied sorrows of Eve, indicative of a mass attack against humanity in order to compromise the bride again? Makes for interesting reading doesn't it? How then will she survive? Hmmm? Let's see. As we mentioned earlier, Gen. 1:30 speaks of everything that has life (חַיָּה נֶפֶשׁ) the Chayah nephesh - as having access to the previous-ly mentioned green color. Don't get hung up on the English word green, rather look at the Hebrew word, yereq. From this root we get the Hebrew word TORAH - The teachings and instructions of YHVH. Is it possible these same teachings and instructions, the Breath of lives breathed into Adam at creation, will once again be introduced at this final restoration, affording you and I the protec-tion and security of the Great Coat, the covering - the Language of Creation, Color, and Light? Will it become the mechanism which separates the Light from the Darkness found within man during this plague? The Hebrew word for 'sorrow' in Genesis 3: 16 continues to provide insight.

- Sorrow, H#6093, עצבון *'itstsabown*

Translated as 'hardship, labor'. It is spelled with the Hebrew letters: Ayin-70, Tzade-90, Bet-2, Vav-6, and Nun-50, for a total numeric value of 218: This value is the same as H#3391 Yerach, the Hebrew word for moon.

What is the connection between the moon, this word sorrow and the Bride? The moon regulates the months, the (Hebrew) Mo'edim, and in its' course, also regulates the gestational cycle of the woman. The root of itstsabown is: Ayin-Tzade-Bet, etsev, a noun depicting an idol – false god. The word for moon, yerach, is from the same root as (H#3384 Yarah) from which we get the word TORAH – SEED/WORD and also connects us back to the color GREEN, H#3418. Thus another confirmation that a future attempt to compromise the Bride will occur at the Mo'edim – Holy Convocation, the time set aside for intimacy with the Creator and the optimum time for ovulation in order to produce offspring! Matt. 24: 37 reminds us: "*As it was in the days of Noah...*" this gives a hint at the timing of this event when the Bride is almost overwhelmed by the plague of these same beings/locusts who will issue out of the pit! If you rearrange the Hebrew letters to form H#84, 'ebrah, meaning wings, you get the Hebrew word for the wings of an eagle (Upon which YHVY led Israel out of Egypt and whereupon she will again be delivered) you see also the root of ABRAH-am. (Abraham) His seed are the people who will be delivered by those wings! (Deut.32:11, Rev. 12: 14). Another cognate Hebrew word for wings is H#3671, כנף kanaph, wing, covering, skirt or corner of a garment! It is within the Wings or folds of this Garment that Israel is cradled like an Eagles' young! These colors, musical notes and sounds aren't as easily brushed aside now are they?

After that our interest should be piqued! So, let's briefly examine those ancient Solfeggio notes:
[*See www.redicecreations.com/specialreports/2006/01jan/sol]

UT – 396 Hz – Liberating Guilt and Fear

RE – 417 Hz – Undoing Situations and Facilitating Change

MI – 528 Hz – Transformation and Miracles (DNA Repair)

FA – 639 Hz – Connecting/Relationships

SOL – 741 Hz – Awakening Intuition

LA – 852 Hz – Returning to Spiritual Order

As we've shown you before, the third note of the original 6 Sacred Solfeggio frequencies is "MI" for "Miracles" and vibrates at 528 Hz. It is the exact frequency used by genetic engineers throughout the world to repair the blueprint of life, DNA, the healthy core of which is a six-sided crystal of structured water. This Note, 'Middle C' – which we've seen connected above to the color green, yereq, (Torah) could be part of the healing codes embedded in the Rainbow language necessary to restore the compromised DNA of the House of Jacob/Israel!

The number 528 is the gematria of H#4669, מפתח miphtach, used in Prov. 8:6 to infer the opening of the lips that enable one to speak of *excellent* (nagiyd, princely – to expound about the prince) *and right* (meyshar, upright, straight – the root yashar is the same as that of Yishar'el – Israel) *things.* Hmmm? If I can't sing this note properly (Don't know the Hebrew) does this infer that I may not speak properly or have an intimate relationship to the Prince or King? *Remember the word picture of Set – Nathan? From which we saw how The Rainbow functions as the umbilical cord of the Prince! The cord sends information – nourishment - to those who remain connected. If you're hungry and thirsty for Righteousness, you shall be filled. Maybe this unravels the mystery of Yahshua's statements in Matthew:

> **Matthew 7:21-23** *Not everyone that saith unto me, Lord, Lord, shall enter into the kingdom of heaven; but he that doeth the will of my Father which is in heaven. Many will say to me in that day, Lord, Lord, have we not prophesied in thy name? And in thy name have cast out devils? And in thy name done many wonderful works? And then will I profess unto them, I never knew you: depart from me, ye that work iniquity.*

(Oh, the Greek word here for iniquity is G#458, anomia and means 'a' WITHOUT – 'NOMOS' meaning without law, Torah, Word, Light. Ouch, hurts good doesn't it?)

The only possible conclusion regarding the restoration of this tongue is to allow us to speak properly of the King of Israel! Whether before Him or in representation of Him - while in confrontation with His enemies!

This also reminds us of Yahshua's remarks in Luke 19: 40 *"if these should hold their peace, the stones would immediately cry out"*. The stones of that area were marble/granite in origin and proven to have the ability to receive and transmit sounds much like a C/D disk! They are crystalline in nature. You are described as LIVING STONES with a body comprised of at least 60% water (brain 70%, lungs 90%) which is, as mentioned above, also crystalline in composition. The study of wave phenomena, the ability of sound to organize and re-pattern matter, is called Cymatics; Form is the more elusive component of sound. Sound-forms can be seen by subjecting mediums such as sand, water, or clay to a continuous sound vibration. When sounded properly, the Hebrew letters will form in the different mediums of sand, iron filings, and water crystals! This may sound alien to many but two dear friends of mine, who should be credited with much of the last 20 years' worth of information about the real Mt. Sinai in Saudi Arabia, Jim and Penny Caldwell, have actual photos of snowflakes in the form of the Star of David! If you know the Paleo-Hebrew Alef-Bet, this star is formed by the overlay of two Paleo letters, both Hebrew Dalets – one atop of the other! [http://splitrockresearch.org/content/109/Video_Clips/Snowflakes]

The Ancient Paleo letter Dalet would have resembled an equilateral triangle. By transposing one atop the other and looking down upon it from a 3-dimensional view, it could resemble a DNA helix. Here's a picture of the Star of David – Double Dalet!

Armed with such phenomenal information, long withheld from us, it would seem the aim of the spoken WORD – specifically HEBREW – is to engage you, the individual and we, the corporate body in exercising this ability, that we may begin to effect the repair of our own DNA. The residual effects should impact ones' surroundings in powerful ways! Now I understand better the command of Mark 11: 23 *...speak to the mountain!* If the former Exodus saw a migratory community who were without sick or feeble individuals among them, then I propose, this latter, Greater Exodus should have exponentially more! We are on the cusp of the greatest Ingathering and subsequent wilderness excursion, the world has ever seen!

Chapter 8

DNA Manipulation

Why wouldn't it become important at this juncture in time, for one to be able to speak to his/her body or that of someone else, or any adverse circumstance for that matter and witness the transformation of DNA? This is a NO-BRAINER! It has been the method of Satan since Gen. 3 to attempt to manipulate or corrupt the gene pool by the insertion of the serpents' seed. Today we see genetically modified food (GMO), beverages, seed, animals and HUMANS! In addition to the genetic mutants depicted in the media and hailed as 'superheroes'. Could it be that this is in preparation for an encounter with that same serpent's seed – those monsters Noah stood against? Out of our ignorance have we allowed the science of Genetics to cross boundaries that have opened the fountains of the deep in preparation for the flood that will issue out of the Serpents' mouth (Rev. 12:15)? Is this current mingling of the Seed of the Fallen One with that of Man another attempt to corrupt the seed-line again? *See Dan. 2:43 & Matt. 24:37 ...*as it was in the days of Noah...*

This has been the pattern since creation. Satan attempts to manipulate human DNA for the purpose of creating a suitable host for his Seed. This is his effort to counterfeit the methods of YHVH. *Note Gen. 6:2 where the Fallen Ones, a.k.a. the Sons of Elohiym - בְּנֵי־הָאֱלֹהִים, took wives of all they chose, H#977, בחר bachar, to choose. It literally means to try by example, to examine. It is a fact: trial which precedes proof produces choice. It is quite plain they chose these women because they were suitable hosts! Have you; are you a suitable host for the words/seed of the Fallen Ones? Or, have you remained chaste before the King of Creation, your blood-line pure, your generations perfect? Be careful…There is hope.

Just as Jacob stopped the genetic flaws of his flock at the water trough of YHVH's word, you shall draw water with Joy out of the wells of salvation translated as Yahshua. (Isaiah 12:3) Oh, stop a second and look at the Hebrew word for draw in that verse; H#7579, שָׁאַב sha'ab, to drink, to slake one's thirst. The main idea is 'taking off the surface'. It is cognate with H#2834, חָשַׂף chasaph, which indicates to make bare or strip off. It is used figuratively of Babylon stripping off her garments. Do you suppose, coming out of Babylon (As commanded in Revelation 18:4) involves the removal of the harlots' garment in order that one be able to draw from the well of Yahshua? The term well is a euphemism for the seminal waters of the husband! This sheds more light on the first commandment: Thou shalt have no other gods before me. The literal Hebrew rendering indicates you can't bring them before my face! I.E. don't bring your Pagan gods/lovers in the intimate chamber to spoil the Father's bed thus making one naked before Him!

> ***Malachi 2:15*** *And did not he make one? Yet had he the residue of the spirit. And wherefore one? That he might seek a godly seed…*

Unlike Abraham Yahweh is not beyond childbearing! He is still bringing forth sons! B'nei Elohiym – Sons of God!

As a side note, the gematria of b'nei Elohiym happens to be 153, the number of the fish caught by Yahshua's disciples and thus, a reflection of the gathering of the Sons of YHVH! Again, Gen. 6:1 reveals a counterfeit group claiming son ship, but whose sons were these! Remember how these fish of Yahshua's disciples are caught in a net? The Hebrew word for net, H#7568, רשת resheth, comes from the root yarash, meaning to take possession of, to occupy, to expel an occupant, to drive him out. YHVH is a gentleman and does not force Himself upon man; however, as seen in Gen. 6, Satan and the Fallen Ones have no qualms in doing so. Are there other examples of a future DNA manipulation? Perhaps a clue can be found in Daniel:

> **Daniel 2:41-43** *And whereas thou sawest the feet and toes, part of potters' clay, and part of iron, the kingdom shall be divided; but there shall be in it of the strength of the iron, forasmuch as thou sawest the iron mixed with miry clay. And as the toes of the feet were part of iron, and part of clay, so the kingdom shall be partly strong, and partly broken. And whereas thou sawest iron mixed with miry clay, they shall mingle themselves with the seed of men: but they shall not cleave one to another, even as iron is not mixed with clay.*

This prophetical explanation is in regard to the vision had by King Nebuchadnezzar. Yet, it bodes ill for future generations. The phrase 'iron mixed with miry clay' is acknowledged by most as a metaphorical term speaking of a co-mingling of the Seed of the Fallen Ones with that of Man once again. Their offspring are acknowledged as the giants of antiquity, men of renown. Evidence of their existence has been intentionally covered up and so far removed from modern history that most have a difficult time accepting the potential of this having ever occurred. I contend that not only has it occurred, but has continued to happen, and every effort of the *Powers That Be* has been garnered to hide this fact from the People. For our book's sake, Nimrod is the earliest, if not the most well-known of this Specie! His lineage suggests he was from the line of Cush who himself was a son of Ham and as such, this association is an indicator of his carnal, debased nature. Gen. 10: 9 describes Nimrod as 'a mighty hunter before YHVH'. Again, the English isn't worth the ink it took to write. However, the Hebrew for 'hunter', H#6718, צַיִד tsayid, has a root which can indicate to hunt men! Many Scholars believe he was in fact, a cannibal feeding on the flesh of men. Furthermore the origin of his lineage can be traced in antiquity, back to that of the line of Cain, the first 'anti-messiah' figure.

Curiously, the origin of the word Cohen – Hebrew for 'priest' is thought to have been attributed to his (Cain's) name. An etymological search reveals that 'Canni-bal' is most likely a rendering of 'Priest of Baal' [Cohen of Baal]. Sadly, there are fringe elements whose perverse interpretation of Scripture assiduously pictures Nimrod's connection with Cush; thereby, asseverating his loins as the origin of the Black Race which, quite frankly, is a heinous lie. Etymologically, it doesn't mean 'black skin', as most translate, though it does infer rather, a dark, blackened, countenance – I.E. a sinful, evil nature. This seems to put a rather enigmatic verse in Jeremiah in much better perspective, especially when the KJV's English leaves no real substance. Let's look:

> *Jeremiah 13:23 Can the Ethiopian change his skin, or the leopard his spots? Then may ye also do good, that are accustomed to do evil.*

The root of Nimrod is the same as the Hebrew word used here for leopard H#5246, Namer, something spotted, a leopard. Nimrod was the founder of the first Cult of Sun Worship, Nimrod, Semiramis, and Tammuz. History records this cult as also being referred to as the 'Leopard Priesthood'. This symbol is seen throughout ancient history! However as revealed in Eph. 5 Yahshua, the Living Water, the Light of the World, the Language of Creation washes away the spots!

Curiously, the Leopard is seen in both Daniel and Revelation and is historically associated with the ancient Grecian empire, which included: Greece, Iran, Iraq, Ethiopia, Libya – North Africa, Syria, Lebanon, etc.

It is highly probable, following the Torah patterns, the future Anti-Messiah will emerge from here! If so, since Ancient Tradition teaches that Nimrod stole the Light Garments of Adam and Eve, in doing so, he is said to have exploited the garment's power. In this vein, it is quite possible that the future Anti-Messiah will attempt to twist public sentiment regarding the restoration of the Rainbow Language – Hebrew - into a tool he himself can use to garner power and influence over the Nations, much like Nimrod. It is believed that Nimrod was the originator of the Babylonian Mystical Religion, which flourishes today. Deeply hidden within the Cult of the Harlot and among her harlot daughters is a hidden, mystical, influence, wielding intoxicating power over the masses. Faultily, this group exhibits a tendency toward the perversion of the worship of the True Creator with Music and Song and whose inculcations often are seen imbued with – yep, you guessed it – the Hebrew Language! This has never been more apparent than the compromise revealed in the Musical Scale whose tones have been adulterated.

Let me show you a few more facts in this area before we move on. Oh, digress though I may, once again, Science comes to aid my work. In what could be packaged as a modern "Pied Piper" cult, much investigation has proven certain binaural beats (frequencies) are purportedly being used to digitally create the same physiological effects with musical tones as demonstrated by known hallucinogenic drugs such as: LSD, crack, and heroin. In plying their knowledge to benefit the Craft, they have also produced tones that produce 'doses' of a sexual nature and other less sinister applications. If this is foreign to you, have you ever heard the term "Verbal Intercourse"? Sound is indeed – Seed! [http://www.huffingtonpost.com/2010/07/15/digital-drugs-get-teens-h_n_647397.html]

Thus comprised of Words, Light, Sound, and Frequency, is it really possible for music to exhibit a power capable of resonating within the molecular and cellular level of the human mind and body, producing the desired effect it is 'programmed' for, perhaps even altering DNA? Perchance we should remember the Being who had musical instruments created in his body.

Ezekiel 28:13b *...the workmanship of thy tabrets and of thy pipes was prepared in thee in the day that thou wast created.*

Couldn't he have had pipes built for singing? You have! You're a stringed instrument, one where wind from the lungs passes through the 'pipe' across the 'cords'. Stop trying to overthink things and let's try and be a bit more pragmatic as we examine evidence. Shall we look a bit deeper in the well?

2 Timothy 2:15 *Study to show yourself approved a workman that needs not to be ashamed; rightly dividing the word of Truth.*

Forgotten in Time: The Solfeggio Scale

Some surprising facts about the above Solfeggio frequencies are now being confirmed quite often from the scientific community. According to Dr. Leonard Horowitz, 528 Hertz is a frequency that is central to the "musical mathematical matrix of creation." More than any sound previously discovered, the "LOVE frequency" resonates at the heart of everything. It connects your heart, your spiritual essence, to the spiraling reality of heaven and earth.

The Love frequency is the "Miracle" note of the original Solfeggio musical scale. Independently confirmed by researchers, these core creative frequencies were used by ancient priests and healers in advanced civilizations to manifest miracles and produce blessings.

Mathematician/Scientist Victor Showell describes 528 as fundamental to the ancient Pi, Phi, and the Golden Mean evident throughout natural design. Vic Showell and John Stuart Reid (a pioneer in acoustic research and Cymatics measurements) have proven that 528 is essential to the sacred geometry of circles and spirals consistent with DNA structuring and hydro sonic restructuring.

528 reduces to a 6, the icon for physical manifestation. That is, 5+2+8=15; and 1+5=6 (using Pythagorean math). The symbol "6" reflects the "spiraling down from heaven into the wholeness of earth." In fact, the Love frequency can be fundamental to broadcasting all matter and energy into reality according to the laws of physics. The number 6 is represented in Hebrew by the letter 'Vav'. Its picture is that of a nail, or connector, and it is said to represent the bent-one or humbled man, Messiah Himself. Should you observe a Torah scroll closely, you'll see each page beginning with a letter Vav! This healing frequency is connected to the master healer who identifies Himself in Exodus 15:26b, *for I am YHVH that healeth thee.* The phrase in Hebrew: יְהוָה רֹפְאֶךָ: כִּי אֲנִי, Ki ani Yahweh Rophecha!

There is also a preponderance of clinical evidence of its use. One instance saw these frequencies used in cleaning the polluted water of the Gulf of Mexico. In 2010, John Hutchinson, an electromagnetic energy expert from Vancouver, B.C. Canada and his research partner Nancy Hutchinson used the 528 Hz frequency and other Solfeggio tones were used to reduce the oil and grease in polluted waters. The area was treated with the frequencies for four hours the first day, and by the next morning, the waters were cleared. Four more hours of treatment completed the test, with the results certified by Dr. Robert Naman, President of Analytical Chemical Testing Laboratory, Inc. of Mobile, AL. who confirmed the removal of oil and grease from the after treatment of the sample source tested.
[http://528records.com/pages528hz-sound-miraculously-cleaned-oil-polluted-waters-gulf-mexico-according-new-study-canadian-r]

Why would something that happens in the Gulf be pertinent to this study aside from the obvious 528 solfeggio frequency connection? Quite a lot in fact: This incident of April 20th, 2010 mysteriously parallels the Bitter Waters of Jealousy Test recorded in Numbers chapter 5.

The Gulf of Mexico is the Womb of the Nation! (It looks like it). If you've not read Jonathan Cahn's book 'The Harbinger', you won't notice the connection with the Mississippi delta and the line the flows from the Gulf Oil spills' location northward, bisecting the birthplace of this Nation – New York City. What makes this significant? In close proximity are multitudes professing themselves "Believers" and loudly proclaiming the area as the Bible belt.

This is a mockery of Ephesians 6 where we're told to have our loins gird – belted with the word of truth. How is it a mockery? Because many indulge in anti-Torah traditions, and explicit sexual perversions that openly embrace every debauchery including homosexuality, all in the name of RELIGION – including the flaunting of their pagan 'holy days' in the Face of the Great Suzerain King. In fairness, this is happening across the Nation, yet the Southern Gulf states comprise mainly the location referred to as the Bible-Belt. To continue, when the Gulf's bottom was ruptured and crude oil began to flow I began to hear YHVH speak to me about Numbers chapter 5 and the bitter waters of jealousy test for the harlot. If guilty her belly and thigh would rot out. Most industry professionals who are familiar with the oil industry will know that crude oil is called the "blood of the earth". Flowing blood makes one unclean, like the harlot above. But, that's not the only connection to this book. We started early talking about the Tower of Babel incident and frankly, we also made a comparison to the harlots' judgment as well.

If you look in Gen. 11: 3, you'll note the compound used for the mortar to secure their bricks in the 'Tower' - H#2564, חֵמָר chemar, the ancient Hebrew word for Crude Oil! This is the same substance used to water-proof the Basket that Moshe was placed in when left to float upon the Nile – by the way, the Nile was the symbol of life for Egypt and the first source to be judged in the 10 plagues. It was turned into blood! The womb of Egypt was declared dead – just like the Gulf! It is not an accident that the Pharaoh of Egypt was said to not know Joseph. It was he who introduced the Language of Creation – Hebrew, bringing life to a 'dead' nation. Forgetting Joseph, like forgetting Yahshua, subjugated the People of Israel to a cruel taskmaster. YHVH sends a deliver name Moshe which is literally translated 'One out of Whom Water is Drawn', to restore a Pure Language to the People! They carry the bones or DNA of Joseph with them! As this final restoration begins and the People of YHVH begin the Greater Exodus, the Rainbow language – the Etsem – Bones – DNA will be evident among the House of Israel once more, enveloping us in a variegated garment of Light!

Let's remember Joseph's coat of colors once more.

Chapter 9

The Joseph Connection

Zephaniah 3:8 which precedes the verse regarding returning a pure language, tells us YHVH is determined to *gather* H#622, אסף 'acaph. (...*My determination is to gather the nations...*) This word means to gather, to collect, but it is also the root of Joseph). This could say, just as easily, "I am going to JOSEPH the Nations! Curiously, this verse contains ALL 22 LETTERS OF THE HEBREW ALEF-BET, INCLUDING THE 5 FINAL FORMS. Is Joseph somehow connected with this cup of jealousy and the language being offered to the world? Ps. 81:5 tells us Yah *ordained a testimony*, (H#7760, שׂום suwm, to appoint, to change, and to charge. It also conveys the idea of the placement or the laying of beams in a wall, or THE IMPRINTING OF A SEAL ON SOMETHING) *in Joseph*, H#3084, יְהוֹסֵף Yĕhowceph, to make doubly fruitful. *NOTE THE ADDITION OF THE HEBREW LETTER HEY IN THIS WORD, IT IS AN ANOMALY ASSOICATED WTTH YHVH ADDING A LETTER OF HIS NAME INTO THAT OF JOSEPH – Adding the letter 'Hey' indicating to become fruitful, would seem most important to the generation who arises AT THE END! This same thing happened with Abram and Sarai (AbraHam & SaraH.) Let's look at some additional evidence. If the letter Hey indeed indicates to become fruitful, then what makes it so? Apparently, it is by the seed of the word, light. A clue can be seen in the example below of Joseph and Benjamin.

Allow me to take a short look at Genesis 44:2 and Joseph's silver cup placed in the mouth of the sack of Benjamin.

◆ Silver, H#3701   כֶּסֶף   *keceph*

Note the Samech-Pey root again! Keceph – Joseph. This root indicates a Cup or bowl. Interestingly, the Samech and Shin are interchangeable, thus it could read Shin-Pey, sap, the word for LIP – MOUTH. The Kaf, represents authority, ownership, it was the Kaf engraved upon the land that proved Israel's title deed. Thus, Joseph had the Authority of the MOUTH, WORDS, and LANGUAGE! He, like YAHSHUA WENT DOWN TO EGYPT! Even more interestingly, he, like Yahshua was thrown into a pit (A euphemism for hell or the grave).

◆ Cup, H#1375   גְּבִיעַ   *gĕbiya'*

Cup, bowl, specifically, the golden cups and calyx on the flowers of the Menorah. The calyx is the hard cover protecting the SEED!

Out of deference to our older brother Judah, who has guarded the Torah with his life, what I am about to say will be painful: There is also an excuse; Judah simply doesn't recognize Joseph – yet! As a result, the Torah isn't taught of the Jews to anyone who is non-Jewish. This limits the outreach of Judah to the Nations. On the other hand the current awakening and return to Torah en masse can only be attributed to the efforts of one group. That group is referred to as the House of Israel or Joseph and as a result a sobering event is taking place worldwide. All the while, inconspicuously, in the ancient pattern of ignomiry that was Josephs' at his brothers' hand, it is he who is teaching the Torah to the Nations – NOT JUDAH! (I know my Jewish Brothers will surely OY VEY here, but, self-examination is painful) At pre-

sent, there is a great rift between Judah & Joseph, with both mis-
understanding the others place in the Kingdom! This was apparent during Messiah's 1st coming also, as He declares, "I come in
my Father's Name" (Jn.5:43) and then that He only came for the
Lost Sheep of the House of Israel! (Matt. 10:6, 15:24) What was
Yahshua's name in Hebrew? The same as Joshua, H#3091,
יהושוע Yehowshuwa: (Yahweh is Salvation). Curiously, Joshua
son of Nun was originally called, H#1954, הושע Howshea', son
of Nun (Life) until changed by Moshe. This is the same name as
Hosea who married the harlot and whose children epitomize the
scattering of the House of Israel! The Pharisees, like many of our
Jewish brothers today, WANTED NO PART IN THE
GATHERING OF THE GENTILE NATIONS who had prostitut-
ed themselves by selling the birthright. The same is reiterated in
the parable of the Prodigal Son in Luke. 15. Oh, by the way, following this same pattern of Hosea: Tradition says that Joshua
married the Harlot Rahab! Go figure!

Joseph's Connection to the Coat of Many Colors!

I know we've been a bit long winded in our ranting. But, I am
convinced Adam and Eve were clothed with this same light, with
its' rainbow of Color, Light and sound, known as the Word! It is
highly probable the latter Coat, the Coat of Blood – represented
the position of Adam as regent in the earth. Tradition hints at
Nimrod stealing this coat and later getting slain by Esau who then
takes it, and as he flees for his life, he falls prey to such exhaus-
tion that he becomes willing to sell his birthright. Was it possible
this 'Ancient Robe' represented a power so alluring to Esau, he
becomes willing to denigrate his birthright and thus, his present
and future worth, knowing he would be able to exercise this
power and realize what he had loss? How apropos that the conflict is foretold before Jacob contends for this same birthright
with Esau, as he exits the womb catching the heel of his brother.
This ancient conflict was first prophesied in Gen. 3:15 where the

serpent is told of mortal combat between his seed and the seed of the woman. I believe taking back this 'coat' - if it did exist - was part of the arrangement when Esau sold the birthright to Jacob. However, before we go there, I can assure you Jacob understood the latent power of this DNA of Creation. Now, I know the chronology is wrong here, but, let's linger a bit on Jacobs' son Joseph, before we come back to Jacob, the dad. You know the story; Joseph would (and in fact, did) receive this coat from his father, in all probability, committing him to the charge of the language, seed, and word as Jacob's Firstborn! If you want further proof, go with me to Genesis:

> **Genesis 37:3** *Now Israel loved Joseph more than all his children, because he [was] the son of his old age: and he made him a coat of [many] colors.*

As is our custom, we'll break the KJV apart and let the Hebrew expose its' truths!

* Coat, H#3801   **כתנת**   *kĕthoneth*

A feminine noun indicating a coat, or a garment, it is cognate with the root formed of the Kaf-Tav, to write. The Nun-Tav is the root of H#5410, to pave the way, a pathway. This is the same word used in Gen. 3:21, where YHVH makes the same type "COAT" for Adam and Eve. By definition then, the coat represents a 'paving of the way for what is to be written'. This puts the words of Yahshua in John 14:6 into better perspective:

> **John 14:6** *Yahshua saith unto him, I am the way, the truth, and the life: no man cometh unto the Father, but by me.*

In actuality, the events of Genesis 3 and Genesis 37 were examples of the plan of YHVH to introduce His Son – the One who would be written – in the earth. This puts another well-known event into better perspective: John 8:4-11 tells of a woman caught in adultery. Her accusers bring her before Yahshua (The High Priest). He follows the protocol of Numbers 5 regarding the bitter waters of jealousy by writing the accusations against her in the earth. He stoops down again to write the 2nd time. Many have speculated regarding what He may have written. If you learn to follow the patterns of the Hebrew language, you can see how the woman avails herself of the forgiveness of the Living Waters – Yahshua. Yet, the others walk away. What happened? I believe Jeremiah 17:13 gives the answer:

> ***Jeremiah 17:13*** *O YHVH, the hope of Israel, all that forsake thee shall be ashamed, and they that depart from me shall be written in the earth, because they have forsaken the YHVH, the fountain of living waters.*

If we look further at this Hebrew word for coat – Kethoneth – the dots become easier to connect to form a viable picture. By dissecting or breaking the word down, it contains the 3 -letter root (H#3674) kenath כְּנָת which indicates an associate, a colleague or companion, one who performs the same function, from the root kanah כָּנָה meaning to call one by name, it indicates an intimate knowledge of the individual that's being called, while also to give a title of honor to; We see inserted in the middle of kenath the Hebrew letter Tav - ת whose word picture is: A sign of the Covenant; in other words as long as Adam and Eve (as well as you and I) chose to be in the Covenant/Torah, then we can be seen as companions/colleagues, one who performs the same function!

Could it be that when Yahweh clothes Adam and Eve with this blooded-light, coat, it was symbolic of them being restored to a place of honor, clothed again with the Light in a limited measure? Once more confirming the promise of the resurrection of these fleshly bodies whose power would enable us to have our own Edenic Light Garment restored. The first Adam and Eve failed but, the second Adam (Yahshua) and second Eve (His Bride) are once again put into the position of Co-Regents in the Earth, functioning on the behalf of the Great Suzerain King Himself, Yahweh. This garment replicates Him in other words, transforms us into His image? On to the Coat of *Colors…*

♦ Colors, H#6446   פַס   *pas*

A long coat or tunic, richly ornamented and multi-colored. This garment was worn by the first-born as a sign of inheritance. Thus, Joseph who would have had the right of firstborn, wore the same tunic as Adam, the firstborn, and later, Yahshua, whose tunic was gambled over because of its' value. The Pey-Samech is the two-letter root of Pesach or Passover! It is not an accident that Joseph is 17 years old when given this coat (the numerical order of the letter PEY – mouth, voice) and is later thrown into a dry well at Dothan, translated 'Two Wells'. It is a fact this pit exists today and has a source of living water that is supposed to supply both wells, yet, Joseph's – the House who is scattered – has been a dry source!

This word Dothan, H#1886, דֹּתָן Dothan, has a root stem, Dalet-Tav which is translated as knowledge, specifically of the Torah. The Nun suffix when added implies to diminish what it follows I.E. to make light of or to diminish the knowledge of Torah. This is the place where Joseph finds his brothers instead of where they were supposed to be: at Shechem, a Hebrew word which indicates shoulders, the place of bearing burdens or responsibility. The Brothers sound like many today who flee from the personal responsibility of The Word to a place where its' effect is diminished in our lives. Much like the answer of Yahshua to the Scribes and Pharisees of his day, who He described as: *making the word of God of none effect through your tradition, which ye have delivered: and many such like things do ye. (*Mark 7:13*)* The Scribes were charged with 'writing the Torah', making it plain that others might read it, while the Pharisees [taken from the Hebrew word H#6567, parash, to separate, or scatter] were the preeminent theological group of the day. These two definitions remind me strongly of the Tower of Babel encounter where the language is mishandled by Nimrod and the nations are scattered as a result! How ironic, to find this word Dothan from above, spelled with the same consonants as H#1885, Dathan, the rebellious Levite (one entitled to wear the Coat) who challenged Moshe's position "over them" refusing to submit to Torah! The moment the House of Joseph challenges the authority of Moshe/Torah like Dathan, they are stripped of the Coat and thrown alive into the pit! This puts the vitriolic accusation, so often leveled at many of us who espouse the Torah, of 'going back under the law' i.e. shouldering the responsibility – in quite a different light doesn't it? Perhaps a reminder of the dry conditions of the well is in order!

The Wells of Dothan

If you do the research the physical wells of Dothan exist today. However, what about their spiritual implication? It is far more significant to the House of Joseph than most can fathom! An oft quoted verse may lend insight. Spend a bit of time here with me as we catechize Isaiah 12:3.

> *Isaiah 12:3 Therefore with joy shall ye draw water out of the wells of salvation.*

You won't regret the spiritual repast this verse affords. Even the gematria or numeric values found in the text point to the King of Creation! If this doesn't fire you up your wood's wet!

In this verse there are 26 letters. The significance is lost if one isn't willing to approach these boundaries that were once thought taboo, but, were by clear design of the Creator! 26 is the gematria of the Hebrew word Kavod, glory, and also that of the Tetra-grammatons' -YHVH! It is the glory of YHVH to hide His Presence in the Wells (the Hebrew word for wells, is H#4599, מעין ma'yan, an underground source of water! The root is the word Ayin – the word picture of an Eye, that which sees light, color! The Mem prefix means the womb or source) of Salvation, H#3444, ישועה yĕshuw'ah.

Psalm 36:9 *For with thee [is] the fountain of life: in thy light shall we see light.*

Truly, the entrance of the word into the womb brings light! The above word 'fountain', in Hebrew is; H#4726, מקור maqowr, it indicates a spring, as a source of life, or, conversely, the menstrual flow or flow of blood after childbirth. Remember life is in the Blood. A Niddah condition is one which involves an unclean flow or 'dead' blood. The choice is ours, life or death. The waters of this Well are for some life, for others who rebel, the choice is death. Blood, like the Word, separated from the source, dies.

Science today concurs that Blood and light are connected. Many, like me believe, Blood is light that is slowed down – thus, it is connected to SOUND-Color. Blood's color is Red, yet Dr. Gaston Naessens found microscopic, Light-emitting, living organisms that he named somatids in every cell. Is it possible that the more we're IN THE LIGHT – Torah, the more we'll see these Somatid begin to illuminate or clothe us with Light? Don't forget – Light contains Color! Who was charged with bearing the Torah on his shoulders/Shechem, like a garment? JOSEPH! Red, the color of blood, is unique; it has the longest wave-length of the primary colors and is thus, the farthest away from the original source – RED –ADAM in Hebrew - needs to be restored to/by that Great Light!

Another curious but often overlooked example of how the enemy attempts to circumvent the Plan of YHVH is by attempting to stop the source of flow – whether it's light, sound, color, the

Voice, or the waters of the well. This example can be seen throughout Torah where the enemies of Abraham, Isaac and Jacob are found stopping up the wells dug by the Patriarchs. Each successive generation had to work to ensure these wells were reopened. It is by the sheer Mercy of YHVH that He is now, by His ruach – spirit unstopping the wells, bringing back the LIGHT to the Ayin-Well, the Eye! He is literally restoring sight (Light) to the blind. Thus, as the eyes/wells of Joseph are unstopped, the Light returns! The gematria of Joseph, H#3130, יוסף Yowceph, is 156. The gematria of Well – Ayin, עַיִן, is 130. If we subtract one from the other? The difference? 26, the value (Not coincidentally) of the Tetragrammatons' YHVH! Once again, Yahshua – The Living Word is healing the Blind Man! This time it's you and I who have been blind! We need our wells – eyes, opened to the underground spring that will clothe us in Light again. We find evidence of this in the Gospel accounts of the blind man from Bethsaida, #G966, translated house of fish. Could this be a hint of the Constellational sign of the House of Pisces – pictured as two fish connected, and thus, representing the restoration of both houses of Israel? Mk. 8:23 tells us Yahshua led the man out of the town/Bethsaida, to heal him. Since it is translated "House of fish", and we find that Yahshua summarily fishes him out of that location, is it possible His action points directly to another alarming connection regarding future prophecy of our day: Watch this…

Bethsaida has another meaning as well. Beth indicates house, of course, but the second root word comes from H#6718, Tzaid, to hunt, track down. Jer. 16:16 tells of a day when the hunters will finish the work of expelling the House of Joseph. The Fishers arrive first, then the Hunters! This implies persecution baying at our heels as we make the Greater Exodus!

On another occasion, Yahshua heals a blind man from Jericho who willingly throws off the garment of blindness in exchange for the garment of light. The ancient city of Jericho belongs to Manasseh, the son of Joseph! What really restored this man's sight? His eyes, like wells, being empty, were dry, dark pits or wells. It was Yahshua the Living Word, the Light of the World! As in all Covenant making, the parties exchange garments. He exchanged the garments of blindness for Yahshua's Coat of Many Colors! We see the same pattern in the account of Luke 15:22 the Prodigal Son, who as he returns to the Fathers' House, like – Joseph gets the best robe, #G4413, prōtos, first, in place, time, as in succession. #G4749, a robe or stole, the outer garment of a priest or king! Yes, it was the Rainbow Coat of Colors!

Genesis 37:31 shows us another parallel between Joseph and Yahshua. *And they took Joseph's coat, and killed a kid of the goats, and dipped the coat in the blood*; the same thing happened to Adam whose Coat of Many Colors is hidden within the fleshly veil, and covered by the blood. Yahshua breaks down this fleshly barrier to reveal the *Light TO The World*, the DNA of Creation, those living organisms within the blood, restoring the language of the Rainbow!

Now as we continue to contemplate this Coat of Many Colors it is intriguing to see how the plural form of the word for colors - Pas, passim, פַּסִּים spelled backwards gives you the Hebrew letter Mem- which means 'from, out of, a womb or place of birthing the origin from whence something comes'; this is followed by the -YOD-Samech-Pey, which spells – you guessed it - JOSEPH! Indicating a future birthing that connects us to Joseph in the last Days, as the source of this Coat of Colors – light – word! The responsibility of this garment, Kethoneth, rests upon the shoulders of the wearer. Veritably, it would for our benefit to find out if the restoration of this garment is to be considered a genuine expectation. If so, is it possible for us attempt to place its future occurrence within a specific time-frame? Or, is that stretching things a bit too far? Perhaps we can shed more light via this next verse.

> ***Zephaniah 3:9*** *For I will turn to the people a pure language…*

(H#8193, שפה saphah, to become visible. It also means the lip, language, edge, and border, as in the lip of a cup of divination. The two-letter root stem, Shin-Pey is etymologically the same as Samech-Pey and also infers a cup or bowl) [The Shin-Pey is also the root of Joseph]

...that they may call upon the name of YHVH to serve Him with one consent

(H#7926, שכם Shechem, shoulder, consent)

Shechem, as we've discussed, is the name of the valley located between the famous Mountains of Ebal and Gerizim – the Mountains representing the blessings and cursing of the Torah! Joseph has the title deed to this place where the Language is restored! This helps to explain the rancorous attitude of the 10 brothers toward Joseph who feel their father has treated them unfairly. They did not want the burden of the Torah, and resented the fact Joseph did. It is apparent, in all honesty, the deference came as a result of Joseph spending time in the tents of Shem and Eber, the two Patriarchs who brought the Rainbow Language across the flood.

The Sages teach that before Jacob went to the home of Laban, he studied the "Torah of Exile" in the tents of Shem and Eber.

History makes it painfully evident that another, even greater Exodus, exiling us from the nations, will occur where the outcasts of Israel – the House of Joseph – will once again experience the frightening threat to our existence, because of our refusal to compromise before the last Pharaoh, a.k.a. 'The Anti-Messiah' who will not know Joseph! We are now being given the same opportunity to reside in the tents of Shem! The Double Portion of manna is being poured out. Get it while you may, it is found in the Tent of Shem. Incidentally, this Hebrew word for 'tent' is fascinating in view of our study thus far:

♦ Tent, H#168 אֹהֶל *'ohel*

Rendered simply here, as tent. It comes from the root of H#166, 'ahal, translated as: to be clear, to shine, to be bright, luminescent. Its' two-letter root stem is Hey-Lamed, which according to Klein's Etymological Dictionary of the Hebrew Language means, brilliance, radiance. I find it interesting to trace this to Isaiah 14: 12 where we see this Hey-Lamed root in H#1966 הֵילֵל heylel -בֶּן ben-שַׁחַר shachar, the phrase describing Lucifer! Heylel is rendered LIGHT-BEARER! Because of his own rebellion this place or position, is wrested from him and given to ADAM! Though the latter word, Shachar is defined as meaning dawn, or morning, it is better rendered 'to seek early or earnestly, to break or pry into something! How Lucifer must have detested Adam for being given access to the very Rainbow Language of creation that had embossed him as a breastplate yet was wrenched away as he rebelled. Do you long for; have you pried into the depths of His Word?

If we remember, Lucifer wore the breastplate while in Eden walking amidst the 'stones of fire'. Ezekiel 28: 13 – 15. What do these 9 stones (3 less than the Breastplate of the High Priest who wore 12) represent?

Scripture makes it plain that Lucifer was indeed fitted with 9 of the 12 Breastplate Stones (Ezek.28:13) listed in Exodus 28:17-20. For time's sake we'll reserve our study to the 3 stones *not worn by him*: They are as follows:

♦ Ligure, H#3958 לֶשֶׁם *leshem*

Opal, a precious stone. As a preposition it can mean, for, for the sake of.

♦ Agate, H#7618   שבו   *shĕbuw*

Agate, a precious stone. However, it is from the same root as, H#7617, Sabah, to take captive, prisoner.

♦ Amethyst, H#306   אחלמה   *'achlamah*

A precious gem. Also translated 'Dream Stone', from the root H#2492, Chalam, to dream!

Remember, the word Chalam-dream, is etymologically similar to the word for ladder - H#5551, סלם cullam, I.E. Jacob's ladder, representing the DNA helix, the language of Creation. It seems rather obvious the Redemption plan of YHVH existed long before Adam, Joseph, etc. I firmly believe the conspicuous addition of these specific stones to the High Priests' Breastplate could literally be telling us they were added for: *The sake of the One who would be taken Captive, The Dreamer, and (Jacob/Joseph)! These stones would play a part in the restoration of the DNA of Creation – The language of Torah!*

Thus far, we've considered the Rainbow as our symbol of the Covering of Light. Seldom do we see but half of the bow, when it is in fact a full circle. If we transpose this circle of light that is usually seen on the horizon and place it above our heads it becomes a condensed picture of the 12 Houses of the Zodiac. Each house, like the stones, representing one tribe of Israel! These luminaries convey the message of the Redemption Plan. Inherent in them is a promise to restore, just like the Rainbow given to Noah! What will this restoration look like? The prophecy of Ezekiel's dry bones serves as an interesting hint.

After speaking to the bones to stand, the prophet watches as they come together with flesh and skin. Following our eternal pattern set forth in Genesis where the body is formed, the breath, H#7307, רוח ruwach, translated 'Spirit' of YHVH then comes.

However, an intriguing thing is taking place, the same word ruwach can also indicate to touch, to gain quick understanding and to accept. Again, this follows the template of Gen. 1 and Gen. 2: 7 where YHVH breathes into Adam! It is this breath that lives, brings life, light, and sound, while enveloping these newly formed bodies with the Rainbow Coat of Colors! This begins the Union of YHVH's house. We will need the collective touch of that breath to give us quick understanding. This should help those of you who think you may have a problem learning the Language!

The vision of Ezekiel focuses on 'dead bones'; bones that have no life in them - as readily ascertained from the Scripture. Even though the Prophet speaks to the bones, following the pattern of Genesis 2 and the creation of Adam it is the Breath – or DNA of YHVH that enables them to live and as we read later, to join collectively with their brother Judah in UNITY to form the Body or House of YHVH in the earth. It is my opinion that the Hebrew language alone is the most important 'missing piece' that inhibits our union. Its restoration will cause the Whole House to function in the capacity of the Priest of the Earth as Yahweh intended. Look at Psalm 133 for confirmation!

When Joseph meets his brothers in Egypt they are not able to identify him. Today, Judah doesn't trust Joseph, and frankly will not formerly recognize who we are. Something must occur to change that. The Sages teach Joseph showed them his circumcision and spoke the Hebrew tongue. Perhaps if we spent time looking at those ancient bones of Ezekiel and begin to 'speak to them' and call for the Wind or Breath of YHVH to come, The Sticks of Joseph and Judah would unite.

Chapter 10

Ezekiel's Two Sticks

It is made very plain in Torah - the intent of YHVH is to reconcile the two estranged houses of Israel: Judah and Joseph. It very well may be the restoration of this Rainbow Language which ignites the spark that sets afire the stubble of ignorance and bias dividing the two brothers. If so, the blueprint followed will be that of Joseph, who was not identifiable to his brothers until he spoke Hebrew and showed his circumcision to his brothers. Ezekiel tells us the TWO will be melded into ONE stick. Ezek. 37:16. This word begs further examination.

 ◆ Stick, H#6086   עץ   *'ets*

Tree, wood, timber. It also in its' plural form, Etsem, means, bones. The numerical value of Etz = 160, the same as the name, 'Ben Chanan' a son of Judah, known as the "The Son of Pity". The bones are where DNA residue is found long after the flesh dies. Joseph's bones were carried out of Egypt and buried at Shechem, thus the connection is irrefutable! The sticks of Judah and Joseph will become One – Echad - in Messiah, the ETZ CHAIM, and THE TREE OF LIFE! At present, our UNCIRCUMCISED LIPS – have caused us to be disconnected from Torah. Without being circumcised (This involves more than physical circumcision) in the lip or tongue, i.e. the carnal flesh cut off, Judah will not recognize us. This will not possibly happen, until the Hebrew language, without which you absolutely cannot begin to plumb the depths or ascend the heights of who He Is – is first acknowledged, dealt with, and then applied to our lives. Else we will perish; it's as simple as that. Moshe declared he himself had uncircumcised lips after being in exile 40 years (Ex. 6:12). We've been in exile 2,730-years from the time the Northern tribes went in to captivity as a result, I would certainly agree, our lips are uncircumcised.

The Zohar [The foundational work in mystical Judaism] infers that without Torah (HEBREW) and community – the fellowship of others – Moshe's lips were obstructed. His impediment was not physical but spiritual. We need the Unity of the whole house and the restoration of the language of Creation and Torah – Hebrew to be able to demonstrate to both the world/Egypt and Judah our own circumcised lips. Just as Joseph did before his brothers in Egypt!

Now, I saved Jacob for the last example, simply because the true definition of his name means 'One who catches the heel'. The heel is the last part to be seen as a man walks away. It hints at the one who comes last! It is another of those patterns that YHVH hides from the casual search. It is during the coming time of Jacob's Troubles that Jacob will once again be an exile; yet, his time in the Tents of Shem will enable him to prepare the way of Messiah.

Let's see what we can find here. Jacob happens to be the 22nd in the line of Patriarchs from Adam. There are 22 Hebrew letters that he saw while having the dream. These same letters will later impact his life exponentially. From the accounts of his life, the pattern of Jacob is eerily similar to Messiah! He has ransomed a remnant bride and is bringing the SEED – WORD (The Hebrew) back to be united (Yachad, H#3161, to join, be united) with the other HOUSE. It is both Houses that are collectively promised the Inheritance. Incidentally, 22 is the gematria of H#3162, ya-chad, Yod-Chet-Dalet, and means to be united, to gather together, to be in Harmony-Union.

When one hears musical sounds that are off key, out of place, they are comprised of words or letters that don't fit, (Improper words spoken, out of anger, hate, resentment, and etc. fall in this group) and though similar to sounding a wrong note, leave lasting impressions or seed, of their kind. The 22 letters of the Alef-Bet are a symphony, that when sounded properly – will gather things together – Yachad – much like the OUTCASTS OF ISRAEL, those people who are separated, from the Commonwealth of Isra-el! They are part of the DNA, the Symphony of Creation, the Language of YHVH, which are giving an UNCERTAIN SOUND until brought back to the group! The Yod (Yachad) acts as a pre-fix and indicates 3rd person, action, 'he does, he is doing'. The Chet-Dalet, H#2298 indicates ONE. Thus, the 22 letters with their individual and collective values tell us of the intent of YHVH to make us ONE with HIM! The number 22 is written Kaf-Bet, which supplies the root of several words, not the least of which is H#3513, kaved, which infers, weight, heaviness, glory, or splendor. These letters are vividly descriptive in relating how the Creator conceals the Dabar or word, (Alef-Bet) spoken of in Proverbs:

Proverbs 25:2 *[It is] the glory of YHVH to conceal a thing: but the honour of kings [is] to search out a matter.*

The phrase, 'to conceal a thing' is written in Hebrew: דָּבָר הַסְתֵּר it is the KAF-BET, KAV(ED) GLORY OF YHVH TO CONCEAL THE DABAR – WORD! The word Samech-Tav-Resh, H#5641, סתר Cathar, is the same 3-letter root as ESTHER – which means 'hidden'! The Megillah or Scroll of Esther is the very book that seems to be lacking an overt picture of YHVH or Messiah. Both are there, but as a result of the intentional efforts of YHVH both would therefore, remain concealed, within its' pages, from the casual observer! It was this same "Hidden One" whose Manifest Presence is revealed to Jacob in his well-known dream. I believe there was a powerful revelation of the Person of YHVH – Messiah and a demonstration of that power inherent in His word. From a Hebraic perspective far more than just a dream occurred! It would take this exchange in the dream to set Jacob on a path of Redemption. When he leaves Padan Aram some 20 years later he is not the same man! What happened?

Jacob's DNA Changed?

We're all too familiar with many of the next incidents of Jacob's travels; however, the one I want to focus on here is where Jacob wrestles with "the Angel", which results in his name being changed. Look here:

+ Wrestled, H#79   אבק   'abaq

Translated, 'wrestles', it is from the word H#80, 'abaq, meaning dust, to be ground into dust. This doesn't give much of a clue until we examine the results of this struggle and the numeric value of the word 'abaq'. It has a value of 103, which is the same as H#4264, מחנה machaneh, meaning hosts or camp, which incidentally, is the name of the place where Jacob earlier divides his house! It is also the numerical equivalent of H#3934, la'eg, Lamed-Ayin-Gimel, which means a mocking, or stammering. This word is used to describe a tongue spoken by a foreign lip as in Is. 28:11. Ironically, it is also the gematria of H#2673, chasah, Chet-Tzade-Hey, meaning to divide: a word also seen in this same chapter! Another ominous numerical connection is that of H#4023, megidon, (Megiddo) the place most often associated with the Apocalypse of the end [Armageddon] – and seen framed in places such as; Zech. 12 where those who pierced Him, will look upon Him and mourn as for an only son! Ironically, Jacob is pierced in his thigh – loins while struggling! What is really happening in this wrestling match? Our extrapolation follows…

It would seem this struggle is one to eliminate, to grind into powder, the seed of the dust, the carnal flesh of Jacob and his house and the foreign tongue/language associated with it. The changing of his name infers the changing of his DNA and thus, that of his house. The language of a spiritual house/family must be consistent with Torah or it becomes a stammering tongue! This struggle takes place in Gen. 32:25 (24 in the KJV) where Jacob wrestles with a man until the breaking of the day. *Note the words 'man & breaking' used here in Hebrew:

♦ Man, H#376   אִישׁ   'iysh

Tthis is the same root from which we get the Hebrew word 'fire.' He wrestles until the days breaking, H#5927, עלה 'alah, rendered 'offering', to lift up; though translated as above, it could also be rendered "AN OLAH (offering) made by FIRE! You have a picture of this Man – Yahshua being lifted up, as he wrestles with the flesh of Jacob. It's a picture of His sacrifice as an olah or fire offering on Jacob's behalf! This fire purges the flesh of Jacob allowing the change of his DNA. If you subtract their numeric value 311 – 105, it leaves 206, the same as DABAR – WORD. It is the fiery language of the Alef-Tav that changes the DNA once it is offered or lifted up – spoken in the Earth. This is exactly what Yahshua meant in John 12:32:

> **John 12:32** *And I, if I be lifted up from the earth, will draw all [men] unto me.*

♦ Lifted in the Gk. #5312, *hypsoo*

Means to be exalted, to rise to the summit of opulence and prosperity, to rise to dignity. While the word translated 'from', G#1537, 'ek as a preposition can mean from, it also infers AN EMMISSION OUT OF! Thus, part of the re-gathering involves a future wrestling with the Man of Fire (Cloven tongues?) who being lifted up, and exalted will draw the OUTCASTS to Him! How long will you wrestle with Him?

Facing YHVH!

Jacob describes this place of wrestling with a word that is used two different ways. In Gen. 32:31 (30 KJV) he calls it Peniel, *be-cause I have seen the face of Yah and lived*. It is written in the first person, פְּנִיאֵל MY FACE [IS TOWARD] YHVH. However, the next verse has it written: אֶת־פְּנוּאֵל Alef-Tav Peniel. The tense of the word changes to the future imperative, YOUR FACE [WILL TURN TOWARD] THE ALEF-TAV (word) YHVH, *Note the Alef-Tav, Messiah that confirms again to whom our face turns! Jacob was later able to 'face' or confront Esau as 'Is-rael' because of the paniym al paniym, face to face encounter with the Word – Light – Messiah!

Now Esau!

Facing Esau is no task if one has their face turned toward YHVH.

> **Genesis 33:4** *Esau ran to meet them. He hugged [Jacob], and throwing himself on his shoulders, kissed him. They [both] wept.*

Vayarats Esav likrato vayechabekehu vayipol al-tsavarav vayishakehu vayivku.

In the original language there is an anomaly seen in the text just above the phrase 'vayishakehu'. Placed atop of every letter is a dot. The word 'kissed', H#5401, נשק nashaq, means to kiss, but it is closely related to H#5402, weapons, battle, and the above H#5404, eagle. It is evident that Esau is attempting to destroy Jacob and fails. The Battle for the House of Jacob is set into motion and Jacob is delivered on Eagles' Wings! The Sages teach this was the origin of the "kiss of death" where Esau attempts to bite or devour his brother only to fail because Jacob is no longer a carnal-led man. He now walks in the Spirit and Power of the Word – Light. Illuminated by the Rainbow Garment!

Jacob's story is one of transformation. He pictures Messiah, who came in the flesh to "Y'aqov", catch the heel of the Serpent who would attempt to bruise (Gen. 3: 15) his head, the sign of authority, power, the kingdom. *Note the word bruise: H#7779, שׁוּף shuwph, to seize, or to 'gape upon' in order to devour. In this instance, Esau's' rankling frustration maddens him to the point seen above. This should help you understand those who 'gnashed upon Steven with their teeth' as he recites the Torah to them. *I'm sure Jacob would never have been guilty of quoting Torah to Esau!* (Sarcasm mine). The restoration of the Holy Language will surely coincide with the restoration of the Whole House of Jacob, particularly Joseph. Which I believe to be the inherent shadow picture of Ezekiel 37 where the dead bones are made alive!

Jacob and the Bone Connection

The evidence of resonating DNA in the bones of the *deceased* Patriarchs is not that far-fetched. We do have another Scriptural example of the Power of the Holy Spirit residing in the bones of a deceased one – Elisha – whose bones caused another's' dead body to live.

> **2 Kings 13:21** *And it came to pass, as they were burying a man, that, behold, they spied a band of men; and they cast the man into the sepulchre of Elisha: and when the man was let down, and touched the bones of Elisha, he revived, and stood up on his feet.*

The latter part of the verse – he revived and stood up on his feet – is rather innocuous in the KJV English. However, the word 'revived' in Hebrew is H#2421, חָיָה, chayah, meaning to live, to be restored. The phrase 'stood up on' is from one Hebrew word, H#6965, קוּם, quwm, and does infer to rise, to stand, but, can also indicate to ratify, to establish. Now, here's where it gets interesting! The word translated 'feet' is H#7272, רֶגֶל regel, rendered as feet here. Yet, it metaphorically becomes an indicator of the loins of the man! This hints at a promise to restore the Seed – DNA – of the one resurrected. How? Because of that Double Portion Anointing – this by the way has nothing to do with the 'catch phrase' of the 1990's coined by the Pentecostals and Charismatics. This has to do with the Double – Portion of the Manna – Word – Seed – Light promised to be available on the 6th-day, 6,000 year of Creation - the very day we are living in! However, this anointing of Elisha originated from THE MANTLE OF ELIJAH WHICH FELL UPON ELISHA! Many Scholars believe this was the same Mantle of Adam, Shem, Abraham, Elijah and here. It is thought to have been passed to John the Baptist, who passes it to the Messiah! Could it have been the Rainbow Coat of Many Colors, representing the Language of Creation? You decide. However the intrigue doesn't end here. The Dead Man in the story above (According to tradition) is quite interesting as well.

The touch of his (Elisha's) corpse served to resuscitate a dead man. A year after Elisha's death and burial a body was placed in his grave. As soon as the body touched Elisha's remains the man "revived, and stood up on his feet". [23] It has been said, that this dead man was Shallum (son of Tikvah), keeper of the temple-wardrobe in the reign of Josiah [24] and husband of Huldah the prophetess. Source: [*http://en.wikipedia.org/wiki/Elisha*]

*Note the part about being a "keeper of the temple-wardrobe". Could this have been the Rainbow Garment? Mere coincidence?

Perhaps the Prophetic nature of the Names of the individuals above contains a clue to add to our position. Let's look:

> **2 Kings 22:14** *So Hilkiah the priest, and Ahikam, and Achbor, and Shaphan, and Asahiah, went unto Huldah the prophetess, the wife of Shallum the son of Tikvah, the son of Harhas, keeper of the wardrobe; (now she dwelt in Jerusalem in the college;) and they communed with her.*

♦ Huldah, H#2468   חֻלְדָּה   *Chuldah*

The common translation of her name is in my opinion a lazy effort at extracting truth. It's defined as 'Weasel'. However, there are two separate roots of the form חלד (Hld) in the Bible, and they obviously have nothing to do with each other: From one of these her name is translated to mean to dig or hollow out. In Aramaic this verb means to creep or crawl. The derived masculine noun חלד (holed), meaning mole or denoting some kind of rat or burrowing animal, is used only once in the Bible and you wind up with 'Weasel'? Naw! (no pun intended) On the other hand, this same obscure root is defined as meaning: The entire tenure or length of one's life as in Job 11:17, Isaiah 38:11, and Psalm 89:47. As such, it is sometimes translated as 'world', hinting at all of life's action on the earth. It is apparent that Hulldah is the wife of Shallum.

◆ Shallum, H#7967   שַׁלּוּם   *Shalluwm*

From the same root as Shalom – Peace. Shallum ben – son of – Tikvah.

◆ Tikvah, H#8616   תִּקְוָה   *Tiqvah*

Translated as 'hope', expectation. It is also rendered as 'a rope or cord'. Like the scarlet cord of Rahab.

Is it just me, or can you sense the connection with this 'dead man' being made alive, resurrected, simply because he was a 'keeper of the Garment', that brought an expected Peace? Wasn't 'Peace on Earth, goodwill toward men' the initial salutation of the Melakim – Angels regarding the first coming of the Prince of Peace! There's seems a definite connection to the DNA of this language resonating in the bones of Adam!

So, as you can see it's not happenstance that Ezekiel also has the vision of the Dry Bones. Dry implying without marrow, the place where blood and DNA are formed! The Breath of YHVH breathed into these bones infuses them with His DNA, thus, enabling them to be resurrected! Could these bones seen by Ezekiel be a picture of the bones – DNA of Joseph that were carried out at the Exodus as a reminder of the future gathering of the Bones or House of Joseph who would be scattered/buried among the nations? Can these bones live?

We've already established that YHVH breathed life, His word into these bones. Words are sounds with distinct vibrational frequencies much like the different ranges of the Light or Color spectrum. It is also quite an established fact the Human Body itself is a natural resonator. We exhibit electrical current through the synapses of the nerves, which transmit 'coded messages' throughout the body. This resonance is greatly enhanced by the crystalline nature of this water-filled chamber! It can transmit and receive Sound, Light, and Color and seems to have a specific tonal (musical) frequency when in optimum health; while demonstrating a propensity toward disease when the specific frequency is disturbed. Modern Massage Therapy has concluded that our spinal column, filled with the life giving spinal fluid which conducts and transmits through this vast nerve trunk is wonderfully capable of absorbing different kinds of vibratory energy and responding with harmonic vibrations. When the spine sings well, it moves effortlessly and harmoniously, with all parts of the body working as an integral unit. When the spine is out of tune, movement becomes stiff, uncomfortable, and, too often, painful. The noted therapist, June Leslie Weider has concluded that bone is an excellent transmitter of vibration and is thus capable of releasing that sound contained within its core. Each individual bone lends its own distinct note when 'tuned' properly. As a result of a properly tuned spine, the body demonstrates better health. Further, *Joshua Leeds, author of The Power of Sound,* stresses the importance of using care with sound: "Be aware of the power of sound; use it consciously. As with any substance, there can be positive and negative applications. Consider music and sound as 'thinking people's drugs.' They can enhance, arouse, or depress. Like food, water, wine, sex, and pharmaceuticals, it all comes down to frequency and dosage. The question becomes: how often and how much? Applied to the effectiveness of auditory stimulation, as well as nervous system balance, the answer is always individual. This is the nature of sound: subtle, powerful, personal." (*The Power of Sound* by Joshua Leeds published by Inner Traditions International and Bear & Company, ©2010. All rights reserved. http://www.Innertraditions.com Reprinted with permission of publisher.)

It is a fact! The Word has a proven therapeutic benefit! Science has also validated that Color and Light have resonating frequencies that can and in fact have, healing powers! Red, blue and white or 'full spectrum light' are the most commonly used colors for healing with light.

Again, science has demonstrated the legitimacy of light therapy. For instance, Red light therapy, or infrared light, was made popular thanks to NASA. They developed this technology as a way to protect the bones and muscles of astronauts at zero gravity.

Red Light Therapy

The National Cancer Institute has research showing a laser beam focused at a tumor site. The light activates a photo sensitive drug which kills cancer cells. Red is the longest wave length. It penetrates skin and soft tissue up to one inch deep without producing heat. This helps to improve blood circulation and relaxes stiff, painful muscles. Red light therapy improves skin conditions including acne, eczema, scarring, burns, skin cancer, cold sores and rosacea. It stimulates collagen producing cells for plumper, healthier, younger looking skin. Exposure to red light stimulates ATP production which provides energy for your body. This ATP increases white blood cells to repair damaged tissues and decreases swelling and inflammation. To help you feel better while you heal, it also stimulates the release of feel good endorphins.

Blue light therapy beds are used by hospitals for jaundiced babies. Babies are also placed in front of a sunny window to help them recover faster.

Ultra-violet light therapy has been proven effective as a treatment for psoriasis. Violet is also used to treat acne because it mobilizes forces within your body that kill acne causing bacteria.

More recently, blue light is becoming popular for seasonal affective disorder and people suffering from the winter blues. Full-spectrum sunlight is light and color therapy at its finest. Sunlight looks golden yellow, but is really all the colors of the rainbow combined together. The Medical community also acknowledges an acute vitamin-D deficiency throughout the U.S. The greatest source of Vitamin-D is pure sun-light!

Each color frequency affects your body and mind in different ways. Such evidence is conclusive. The 'luminaries' (Sun, Moon and Stars) have powerful roles in regulating the health of the human species. Most Scholars acknowledge that prior to the advent of artificial light sources most females of child-bearing age in a given local would have menstrual cycles in common with each other. The arrival of artificial light sources served to 'de-regulate' this internal clock. It is my opinion, that the *Powers That Be,* who serve the Wicked One, knew the end result – and prepared themselves to insert the Serpent's seed at every given opportunity.

From an informational standpoint this is all well and good. But, can we draw the same conclusion from Scripture, regarding the Sight, Sound and Color of this language as it is absorbed within the human mind and body? We fight against an enemy who knows the latent power being discussed and has attempted to harness it for their own purpose. We had better begin to take back what has been stolen from us; lest the days ahead have foreboding consequences.

> **Mark 4:26** *And he said, So is the kingdom of God, as if a man should cast seed into the ground.*

Everything in creation is based on this principal, the power of sowing and reaping. If we expect to see eternal changes in these mortal bodies, then the seed of resurrection power should be evident in every phase of our lives first! Yahshua became the first Kernel of Seed planted. He lives as the proof! Our words should demonstrate the same. He is foreshadowed in the picture of the Ark of the Covenant as the Eternal Light source. The Ark represents Yahshua; the Living Word/Light which served as a catalyst within the Tabernacle whose form resembled that of a Man. The Tabernacle construction ensured that electricity in the form of Static electricity would be created by the friction from its massive veils and curtains and 'caught' within the storage unit known as the Ark! This caused the Tabernacle to be a continuously illuminated structure! Light is the source of Life! Light is Word, the entrance of which brings this light back into the 'body-temple'. If an unclean – Carnal man touches it, he completes the circuit, is grounded and death ensues! *Just ask Uzzah what happens when the Ark is touched inappropriately*! If a spiritual man touches it, his DNA is changed! By touching the Ark – Yahshua, we are resurrected unto eternal life! This electrical (vibrating frequency) power storehouse, the human body - can also be a transmitter of power! The renewal of which begins in the 'Mind'!

The Rabbis teach that there is a bone at the base of the skull called the "Luz" bone. The first mention of Luz is Gen. 28: 19. Luz, H#3870, translated as Almond. The Rod of Aaron (The Priestly Rod becomes fruitful) was hewn from an almond tree. Tradition teaches it is from this "seed" that YHVH will resurrect the body. Jn. 12: 24, 1 Cor. 15: 38, Ps. 34: 20. This bone is situated just where the mind & body connect, at the base of the brain in the skull! The battle is won or lost here. The mind must be renewed by the washing of this word, the illumination by this light!

Is it coincidental that Jacob rested his head upon a Stone at Luz/Bethel, which became a witness of the promise of YHVH to Jacob? This bone bridges spirit and flesh. Within the bones lies the DNA of Creation!

Adam's Bones

Adam says of Eve, "She is bone of my bones". Gen. 2:23 bone, H#6106, etsem, bone – also, essence, substance. Eph. 5:30 Yahshua became the ETSEM of YHVH, the Bones. The em suffix is a Masculine plural form of the word. The root is ETZ, the word for "Tree". How ironic that the word bone and tree have the same root. The bones of the Torah Scroll are called "Etz haChayim". Mans' skeletal system becomes his "tree of life". The spinal fluid, the living water, becomes a conductor for the electrical current of His word, are transmitted through the synapse of every nerve to the extremities of the Body! Individually and corporately! Like Ezekiel you're being asked: "Son of Man, can these Bones live?" Look at this Hebrew word for tree:

Tree, H#6086, etz, is comprised of two Hebrew letters:

- Ayin, to see, understand, to obey, it can also indicate the womb or gate.

- Tzade, the upright or righteous one. The reflection of YHVH. It is the mate to the Aleph (the Creator) representing the Bride! The word picture painted here?

The womb is the gate to understanding the Righteous One & His Bride!

Bone, H#6106, etzem, is comprised of three Hebrew letters:

- Ayin, Tzade, Mem. You've seen the extrapolated definition of Ayin-Tzade above

- Mem, water (the spring / womb of origin of Torah). The mem is an 'open' mem indicating the revealed Word of Yah.

Our Extrapolated Definition: The womb is the gate to understanding the Righteous One & His Bride born from the Living Waters!

Just as the Tree of Life is planted by a River of Living Water, (Ps. 1), man also must seek his existence at this same source. Your spine – your bones, become like this "THE TREE OF LIFE out of which should flow a constant LIVING WATER SOURCE"I.E. the spinal fluid.

John 7:38 *He that believeth on me out of his belly shall flow rivers of living water.*

The man planted by; indicating in covenant with, this water source will see his leaf fail to wither and shall bring forth his fruit in his season! This speaks of both his spouse (leaf) and their offspring (fruit).

Tradition teaches the city Luz, renamed by Jacob to 'Bethel', and was known as the city of Truth A.k.a. the House of YHVH. It is the Word of Truth, the Torah which resurrects the Body. It is at Luz/Bethel, that Jacob had a vision of a ladder connecting heaven and earth, spiritually and physically - the picture of an eternal Luz bone. It is said that this same Almond tree was used by Jacob to enhance the birthing of his flock.

Note how this "Tree" or Rod is planted by the water troughs of Jacobs flocks! Gen. 30: 37, 38. Rods, H#4731, maqqel, a rod, (from an unused root meaning to germinate, sprout, bud). Throughout Torah, this Tree, Rod, etc. demonstrates the capacity to produce seed – I.E. a purely MALE reproductive figure! The Tabernacle Menorah presents the same picture. It is a living Tree – when the Priest (Bride) Aaron – the One who carries the Light – Seed, approaches, the illumination – conception, occurs!

Jacob had two witnesses consisting of both water (at Beersheba The well, the womb of the 7-fold, 7-branch oath, light) and the word, at the place of the dream. Together they produced results! The Apostle John said there are three who bear witness in the earth, The Spirit, the Water and the word/blood!

Tradition teaches that YHVH created the Rod of Aaron at the end of the sixth day as a symbol of Divine authority on the earth. It is passed down from Adam to David and will be restored when Elijah hands it to Messiah at the end of the age. Genesis 17:13 declares that YHVH's covenant will be a sign forever in the flesh of the male (Circumcision) reproductive organ. Out of concern for the delicacy of the ears of my readers, this Rod is a metaphorical linguistic term indicating the male organ of procreation! Aaron's rod was cut off in the natural, yet produced spiritual seed. So was Abraham! This sign is more than just a "physical" circumcision but becomes likewise, a heart matter. Literally affecting one's DNA! Affecting his bones!!

Exodus 6:3-5 are further proof of the Resurrection/Reseeding of the Earth. Yah promises to give the land of Canaan as an inheritance to "them" (Abraham, Isaac, Jacob) who have already died, yet, without possessing it. The sentence structure by nature would have to be speaking to future generations!

Could the DNA that is residual in the bones be used to recreate a new body? Evidently, else HaSatan would not have introduced a perverted, seed-producing Chimera with a different DNA strain. The marrow of the bones produces the Life of the flesh! In fact, genetic modification has been around far longer than modern science, whose feeble attempts at gene manipulation, pale in comparison to what we can see in the Torah. Frankly, few there are who freely acknowledge the evidence. If I show you some, *what will you* do? ☺

Jacob's DNA Clinic

Though shrouded in the compromised English translations, the Hebrew Scriptures reveal what I believe to be a rather unique form of DNA or genetic modification seen used by Jacob in Gen. 30:37-38. Can we examine this a bit? First of all we must remember, once again, Jacob's dream on the way to Padan Aram where he stops at Luz also known as, Bethel. (Remember, we discussed this earlier. Luz hints at a seed being planted) Here at Luz, (translated Almond as in almond tree, the species most believe to have represented the Tree of Life as it did Aaron's rod) Jacob dreams of a ladder, the DNA helix of creation shown us in

Gen. 28:19. There he sees the angels – messengers, word bearers, moving up and down this ladder. Jacob had spent years in the tents of Shem at Beersheba, along with Isaac and Abraham and thus, would have been familiar with the latent power of the Creative Language entrusted to his lineage! This knowledge is why he later is able put the word in action in order to establish the first genome sequencing clinic, which would eradicate the seed line of Laban! Gen. 30:37-38. Let's look at several key words in the two verses:

> **Genesis 30:37-38** *And Jacob took him rods of green poplar and of the hazel and chestnut tree; and pilled white strakes in them, and made the white appear which was in the rods. And he set the rods which he had pilled before the flocks in the gutters in the watering troughs when the flocks came to drink, that they should conceive when they came to drink.*

♦ Rods, H#4731   מַקֵּל   *maqqel*

A rod or stave, it is from a root meaning 'to germinate'. Interestingly, if you break the word apart, the Mem represents a womb, specifically the chaotic waters of the womb. While the Qof-Lamed root stem forms the word Qol – Voice. Did these 'rods' represent the voice/seed released into the womb. Hasn't the advent of the electron microscope shown us the rod-shapes of the human chromosomes? You can see the evidence of the Creators' Chromosomes in our main Scriptural passage regarding the introduction of Light into Creation. It is seen in Genesis

> **Genesis 1:3** *And God said, Let there be light: and there was light.*

There are 23 Hebrew letters in this verse. It is a well-established fact that each human has two sets of 23 chromosomes from their parents for a total of 46 - 23 each from their mother and 23 from their father. There are 22 pairs of autosomes which determine things such as our height, hair and eye color, etc. The 23rd pair is the sex determinant pair. They consist of either X or Y chromosomes. The mother only has X chromosomes. The father has both X and Y chromosomes. If we add 22 + 23, we get 45, the gematria of ADAM as well as, the Hebrew name of Abraham's nephew, LOT, which means to hide, conceal, a covering or veil – the flesh! The first Adam fails and covers himself with a fig-leaf veil of flesh, while the 2nd Adam, Yahshua is born in this same flesh, yet without sin! Yahshua had to be separated from this sin – darkness. In the same fashion, Abraham had to be separated from Lot, the flesh before the blessings began to flow. Ironically, Gen. 1:4 has – you guessed it – 45 letters! Here we see the light, the Menorah, the 22 letters of creation, separated from darkness and deposited into the earth in a BODY – called Messiah! If we add 45 + 23, we get 68, the value of H#1903, hagiyn, a word indicating to appropriate, to cover, enclose. Note the root: Hey = a doorway or as a preposition 'the', while Gimmel – Nun spells the word gan, garden!

Following the above line of thought: "If the sex-determinant pair is matched XX, the child is a female. If XY is found, then the child is a male. Thus we see that the single chromosome provided by the father in this chromosome pair determines the gender of the child". In 1999, Ron Wyatt has a sample of blood tested in Israel purported to have come from a hidden cave containing the Ark of the Covenant with the blood of Yahshua on it. This sample only contained 24 chromosomes, 23 from the mother and 1 X chromosome from the Father to determine a male son, yet there are 22 missing chromosomes, indicating a virgin birth – no physical father! Where are the 22 chromosomes? Here in the 22 letters of The ALEF-BET! The Spoken Word made flesh in the earth, which when received into the womb of the mind by faith, has the power to produce a son in the image of YHVH! Ironically, 23 is the gematria of H#2401, חטאה chata'ah, a feminine noun which can mean both sin and a sacrifice for sin! The 23 chromosomes of

Mary the mother of Yahshua were tainted with sin and thus the Light of YHVH – His Word is interjected into her in order to become the sacrifice to redeem her. (Ps. 51:5). As if to identify Himself, each chromosome is in the shape of an X – the ancient symbol represented by the 22nd Hebrew letter, the Tav! Since the male carries both X & Y chromosomes and the letter Y is written as a Vav (a hook or connector) the significance is overwhelming! Yahshua the Vav-Man connects us to the Covenant – Tav! The Chromosomes contain the DNA particles! The Rod of Jacob lives on!

If we look at the etymology of the word chromosome, we can see another facet of the Hebrew language. Chromo from Chroma infers color, hue (variations of the light spectrum) while, 'some' is from soma, which means body! Is it possible that each of the missing 22 chromosomes and their respective Hebrew letters represent a different color of the spectrum and thus able to affect the physiological side of the Man? It is interesting that the primary colors of the Tabernacle, Blue, Purple, and Scarlet are consistent with the combinations of the color spectrum producing appealing and healing colors. It is these colors which incidentally, are mentioned 26 times in Torah. 26 being the gematria of YHVH! We've made mention in our study of the breastplate which had the same colors of the Tabernacle, blue, purple, scarlet and one more, gold, H#2091, זהב zahab, gold, to shimmer in brilliance and splendor! Its root, the Zayin-Hey, forms the Hebrew word for Lamb, Zeh. The Bet means house. The Lamb of/for the House who will shimmer in glory and splendor! It is this One that we put on and within us: The Word – Alef-Tav. The Rainbow Language!

Back to the key words of Genesis 30:37-38

♦ Green, H#3892   לח   *lach*

New, as in cords or sinews. It can also indicate vigor, strength, the spark or energy of life. If you add the vowel – Vav- you have Luach, the word for Tablet as in Tablets of stone. Jer. 31:33, 2Cor. 3:3. The word will be written – planted in the heart (the womb of the mind). This is a different word than was used in Genesis 3 for green, yereq.

♦ Poplar, H#3839   לבנה   *libneh*

A 'white' tree. From laban, this means white. Funny though, the same letters also spell H#3842, lebanah, a noun meaning a full moon. In keeping with gestational cycles that closely parallel that of the moons cycles this would be the optimum time for Jacob to initiate the repair of his flock's DNA. In keeping with the gestational cycle of the Holy Convocations [Passover/Unleavened Bread and Sukkot] which occur on the 15th of the month, this would also have been the 15th of the lunar cycle, the optimum time for female conception!

♦ Hazel, H#3869   לוז   *luwz*

Translated almond (tree). This was the former name of Bethel (House of El-YHVH) and the place where Jacob first sees the ladder (the DNA helix of the Word) bridging the spirit & physical realms. Gen. 28:12 Jn. 1:51.

♦ Chestnut, H#6196   עַרְמוֹן   *'armown*

A plane tree because of its height. However, note the root, Ayin-Resh-Mem, the word which means naked, subtle, crafty. This describes the condition of both the serpent and the fallen condition of Adam and Eve. Gen. 3.

♦ Pilled, H#6478 פצל *patsal*

To peel, to strip off. The letter Pey indicates the mouth, what is spoken. While the Tzade-Lamed root means shadow, image, to protect.

♦ Appear, H#4286 מחשף *machsoph*

To lay bare. It is from chasoph, to uncover, make bare or naked, to clean.

In keeping with our habit of extrapolating definitions from the Hebrew words or names we find the following:

YHVH's Word released into the womb the spark of life, much like the words/seed released into the heart of His Bride. At the optimum time for conception (Is it that time now?) His DNA spoken into His Bride would change her into His image and protect her from the Serpent, the One who had/would make her naked.

Again, this sounds remarkably like the Garment of Light, the Rainbow Language proven once again, capable of changing the DNA of Jacobs' flocks as a sign that his WHOLE HOUSE would one day be enveloped with this same Covering, forever transforming them into the image of YHVH!

In this brief summary of Jacob's life it is readily apparent he is set on a course that began in the tents of Shem studying the Torah at Beersheba. If we break this word apart: The word Beer, H#875, באר meaning well, womb, etc. also has a unique two-letter root, the Aleph-Resh which means LIGHT, the Bet =

house/bride. The next word, 'sheba', H#7650, שבע is translated, to adjure, covenant, to swear, cut an oath, but it also is from the root meaning seven. This connects us back to the Rainbow and the Tabernacle Menorah, because Beersheba could be rendered, The Womb/Well Which Housed the Seven Lights! THE MENORAH! The Menorah was also a shadow picture of the TREE OF LIFE seen in Gen. 2! This re-enactment of Adam's creation is revealed in the restoration of the DNA of YHVH. This cannot be mere coincidence. Surely, by now you've begun to see the infinite Mind of the Creator at work, weaving this tapestry from the Beginning!

Chapter 11

The Menorah or Lamp of YHVH

Throughout Torah, whenever a spiritual principal is introduced it is always followed by a physical pattern. Something in the natural realm that people can relate to the spiritual. These are simple, teaching tools. (In our case, the simpler, begets the better☺) If our position regarding the Light, Voice and Fire of YHVH literally being a literal representation of a specific Being – YHVH and/or Yahshua, then of course, we should be able to see examples of the physical patterns to demonstrate what we've been sharing about the Rainbow – Light – Language. I'm convinced this pattern is first seen in the Written Form of the language – Hebrew, beginning in Gen. 1:1.

Genesis 1:1 *In the beginning God created the heaven and the earth.*

Well, did you see it? Of course not silly, the English limits us to a basic, rudimentary, statement. However – the Hebrew reveals (Dare I say?) illuminates, much, much more!

בְּרֵאשִׁית בָּרָא אֱלֹהִים אֵת הַשָּׁמַיִם וְאֵת הָאָרֶץ:

There you have it! Seven Words, 28 letters:

B're'shiyth Bara Elohiym ET hashamayim v'ET haaretz.

בְּרֵאשִׁית בָּרָא אֱלֹהִים אֵת הַשָּׁמַיִם וְאֵת הָאָרֶץ:

The number seven is a powerful number seen throughout Scripture and here is apparently representing the Menorah which literally represents the "Lamp or Light of YHVH" I.E. the Messiah. It was one of two pieces of furniture within the Holy Place: the 2nd being the Table of Showbread, which the Menorah illuminated. This 7-Branched Lamp is first seen in Gen. 1:1. Another hint at this same Fiery Lamp is seen in Gen. 2: 20 to describe the need of Adam for a 'Help Meet'. In Hebrew, the phrase is Ezer K'negdo. The root of K'negdo as we discussed early on in this book, comes from the root H#5047 - H#5050, neged or nagad. It indicates to shine forth, to illuminate. Adam, like Yahshua and the Menorah, needed a help meet, in order to reflect or 'carry' his illuminated Seed! This same word nagad is also used in Daniel 7:10 to describe the fiery stream that issues forth out of the Ancient of Days! It is also used to indicate a position or place, as in before, in front of, or corresponding to. Eve (Chavah) was to be a light from the Light Source, Adam. Just as the stellar luminaries were 'lights from the light source'. In fact, the Hebrew word for man in general is H#376, אִישׁ 'iysh, while woman or wife is Ishah, with the feminine Hey added. Etymologically, it is the same as the word for fire! H#784, אֵשׁ 'esh. Curiously, the Man is called ADAM in every instance prior to Genesis 2:23 where his wife is taken out of him! Is this a prophetic hint concerning the name Adam (Alef – "I Will") (Dam – Blood) I will blood you in order to provide a Bride for you who will birth the Light within her! This Menorah begs further examination. Wouldn't you think so? Let's begin with the fuel first. The Oil.

The word for Oil is significant and has a distinctive role throughout Torah: the Hebrew word is H#8081, שֶׁמֶן shemen, oil, to glisten, to anoint. It is etymologically similar to the Latin word for the male seed – semen. If you read Exodus 25: 33-34 the Golden Lampstand had a total of 22 Almond shaped cups. 1 cup for each of the letters of the Hebrew Alef-Bet? The source of illumination is this Oil or Word! Incidentally, its' light giving pattern is somewhat unique: Ex. 25 :37 describes the six individual lamps as giving light toward the center, enfolding upon itself, thus, casting its' light as a single source upon the only other piece of furniture in that location – The Holy Place – That piece was the Table of Showbread! Representing the Whole House of Israel, the Bride. If the Tabernacle design took the form of a man, which I believe it did, then this Eternal Flame – Light, would have illuminated the Head – Mind of the Bride!

According to tradition, it was the Center Shaft alone that was kept burning, the other 6 lamps lit from its' source. This Center Shaft was called the Yarek, and is translated as 'thigh', loins, etc. It is this same area that a Covenanting partner would address, placing his hand under the thigh – loins, Seed – Light, as a symbol of an eternal commitment to the Great Suzerain King! The word yarek, H#3409, יָרֵךְ yarek, is a cognate relative of the word we spent quite a bit of time looking at earlier: The word green, H#3418, יָרָק yereq. This color seems to be somehow connected to the life within the Seed or word of YHVH.

It is not an accident this pure, clean oil - Shemen represents the Seed – Light – Word of YHVH, who is pure, guiltless and declared innocent. He will be placed in an undefiled vessel – Lamp.

His DNA will be written in the pages of Torah. He will be beaten, pounded fine; the enemy will attempt to destroy His seed, cutting off the Name. Yet the Light will plow the earth planting a Seed which will arise for all eternity! It would behoove us to teach who this Tabernacle Menorah, this Niyr Elohiym, Lamp of YHVH really is. His role has been taken for granted, compromised in every way and repackaged in a shiny counterfeit called Tradition. Mark 7:13 shares a scathing discourse Yahshua is having with the Religious group of His day who nullified the power of YHVH in their own lives through these same traditions. I call it the "boomerang" effect, they just keep coming back!

Few understand the dual role of this Light: to bless or curse. The choice of either rests upon the shoulders of the individual. Be obedient or rebellious. Pay attention a bit longer to some vivid descriptions of this Menorah – Light Man!

Zechariah 4:6 identifies this Future Tabernacle Menorah as "The Word of YHVH" – דְּבַר־יְהוָה. quite literally; the Menorah was to be the Light Bearer or Word Bearer! It is this VESSEL – PERSON who is responsible for introducing YHVH's light - seed into the earth. *Note Ex. 37:17 the Menorah is made of one solid piece of beaten work; not from a combination of pieces or materials. Why?

- Beaten, H#4749   מִקְשָׁה   *miqshah*

The idea of a finely decorated work that is related to the twisting or braiding of the hair. The prefixed 'Mem' represents the womb. Now, if we add the connection to hair, Shin-Ayin-Resh, H#8181, se'ar and its related words which convey; to calculate, to become aware, a gate or entrance. Then the puzzle becomes visible: The Menorah was, like Adam & Yahshua, formed by the hand of YHVH in the womb of Torah and would become the gateway for His seed into the earth. The idea of a solid piece seems to hint that Satan – The

Serpent understood this gateway and attempted to co-mingle the "pieces", in order to usurp this gateway!

It should come as no surprise then that the gematria of miqshah – 445 – is the same as H#2120, זֹחֶלֶת Zocheleth, this is the name of a boundary stone where Adonijah, (YHVH is my Master) the 4th son of David attempted to usurp the throne from Solomon. (1Kings 1: 9) Ironically, the word Zocheleth means 'SNAKE STONE' or the birthing stool of the serpent! Further clarity comes via the subtle introduction of the serpents' seed: this is revealed in the word used for branch in Ex. 37:17, H#7070, קָנֶה qaneh, a reed, balance, branch or rod. From Qanah, to buy, acquire, create, possess. This is why EVE names her 1st son – Cain, who becomes the first of the Seed of the Serpent! Another example is found in Gen. 6: 1. CHOSE, H#977, BACHAR, to make a choice based on a thorough examination of the situation and not an arbitrary whim! The two-letter root of Bachar, Chet-Resh, chor, indicates to exercise power over a "lower" class of people. The Bet of course, indicates the bride, wife.

Remember: No stranger, foreigner, or unclean person was allowed access to the Tabernacle. This is a physical pattern following a spiritual one. *See Numbers 1: 51. The word 'stranger' here is zuwr, one who has turned aside, done what is unlawful or profane. Like the actions of an adulteress. It also may indicate one of another family!

Is it possible the construction of the Menorah serves as a reminder to Israel of the pattern of Creation, the intent to create man in His image, intricately weaving His DNA in a fleshly form which would then be 'fruitful and multiply and replenish, subdue and have dominion', becoming the vessel of choice for the Seed of YHVH in the earth? From this pattern seen of the Menorah, though it stands alone as the Light Source within the "Tabernacle Man", it becomes equally apparent there must be a caretaker, one charged with the protection and security of this Lampstand. The physical example isn't lost on the patient observer. Just as sacredly, we should envision our role as caretakers of the Spiritual Light Source – The Rainbow Language of the Covenant! Ours should model the role of the High Priest from its inception. Aaron, brother of Moshe, is the prototypical paragon pointing us in the perfect prophetical direction (Sorry, just a bit of poetic license) of Yahshua! We'll examine Aaron's contribution in this next chapter.

Chapter 12

Aaron's Connection

One of Aaron's many job assignments as we've noted, included the care of this perpetual flame. As I've posited throughout, I believe this Lamp to be a facsimile of the Eternal's Light or Word, first seen in Genesis 1: 3, where "Let there be Light" is first seen. Isn't it entirely possible (Though we have no record) that the High Priest would make this same declaration upon lighting the Menorah? Interesting thought isn't it?

Before looking much further at Aaron, let me call your attention to Genesis 1:3 for a moment. Again, Light is seen released into creation. We can agree that Light is Seed, specifically, the Seed/Word of YHVH. For your information, there's an enigma found within those numbers waiting for you to solve. There are 23 letters in that verse associated with the initial 'dissemination' of the Light. What purpose do you suppose this may have with our understanding of Light, Seed and Word being connected to the earlier paragraphs regarding the Tabernacle Menorah, the Light Source within the intimate Place who illuminates – releases Seed – into the Showbread, which represents the Bride? It's in fulfillment of the first command of Creation to Adam: Be Fruitful...! It's about producing Godly Seed. Now, note this: As we've shared before, there are 23 pairs of chromosomes in the human body: 22 pairs of autosomes (corresponding to the 22 letters of the Aleph-Bet) and 1 pair from the Father that determines the sex. In Gen. 1: 26 the phrase, "Let us make man in our image", נַעֲשֶׂה אָדָם בְּצַלְמֵנוּ (na'aseh Adam betsalmenu) has a total numeric value of 688 - 6+8+8= 22! Both Man and Woman are One - Echad here and it is not until a body is formed for Adam, that YHVH breathes the 23rd, chromosome, the Y-DNA – the breath(s) of Lives that determined the sex – I.E. breathing the ability to reproduce into ADAM! This is why we're told [Gal. 3:28] *there is neither Jew nor Greek, there is neither bond nor free, there is neither male nor female: for ye are all one in Messiah Yahshua.* In Him, that is, in Adam/Yahshua we are ONE again! His Word is the Y-Chromosome – the one who determines whether our words reproduce or not! This same pattern was seen in the example of Jacob when he left Beersheba. There we find Jacob going out from the well – this indicates the place as the source of his origin – his creation! The Hebrew reads, "VaYetze" – and he went out, however, yatsa, H#3318, can also mean to be descended from – birthed out of!

He went out; from Beersheba, מִבְּאֵר שָׁבַע mibeer shava, The Mem, means water(s) of chaos, well, womb – the place of origin. The word Beer, H#875, בְּאֵר meaning well, womb, etc. also has a unique two-letter root, the Aleph-Resh which means LIGHT, the Bet = house/bride. The next word, 'sheva', H#7650, שבע is translated as, to adjure, to covenant, to swear or cut an oath, but it also is from the root meaning seven. This connects us back to the Rainbow and the Menorah, because Beersheba could be rendered, The Womb/Well Which Housed the Seven Lights! THE MENORAH! The Menorah was also a shadow picture of the TREE OF LIFE seen in Gen. 2! Thus, we see a powerful re-enactment of Adam's creation revealed in the example of the Ladder in the dream, literally a restoration of the DNA helix of YHVH – His Word.

Just as we see Jacob being sent out to be "fruitful, multiply, replenish, subdue and have dominion," it would seem symbolically, each time the Seven Branches of the Menorah are illuminated by the High Priest, the same principal as that of the "Sower sowing the Word" can be seen! This should make us view the model of Aaron a bit differently! Let's examine a bit closer the instructions regarding the lighting of this eternal Lamp!

Exodus 27:21b Aaron and his sons shall order it from evening to morning before the LORD.

It would seem the task is more than just physically keeping a fire going. What is the spiritual implication? Let's see if we can find out. Look at the word 'order'.

♦ Order, H#6186   עָרַךְ   *'arak*

To arrange, ordain, to set forth (as in a legal case). To furnish. It refers to the orderly construction of a body or its frame. It can also imply something like or equal to someone else. Hmmm? Its gematria equals 290, the same as H#4813, מִרְיָם Miryam, the name of Yahshua's mother the one charged with caring for the forming of His body and the vehicle through whom the legal precedent of – YHVH's seed deposited in a fleshly body, the Word who tabernacles with us – is established! She declares she knows no man. Indicating there is no other construction material to build this Menorah! She conceives and carries the light!

Is it possible that Aaron, H#175, אַהֲרוֹן, functions in much the same way, as caretaker of the Flame? His name is translated "light bringer", but the Hey-Resh-Vav-Nun forms H#2032, הֵרָיוֹן herown, which represents physical conception, pregnancy. The Alef prefix can imply 'I will'. Is Aaron fulfilling the role of Bride/Mother who upon approaching the Lamp engages in the act of conception? This word herown is visible only 3 times in the Tanach: They are; Gen. 3:16, Ruth 4:13 and Hosea 9:11. The most familiar of the three being the example of Ruth, H#7468, רְעוּת, ra'uwth, a compound word literally meaning "mate of the shepherd". She is the wife of Boaz, the 'Strong One who comes'.

The Hebrew word picture of Boaz is intriguing; it is spelled Bet-Ayin-Zayin. The House/Bride who sees/wombs the seed! Ironically, the gematria of Miryam we've determined to be 290, while the value of Aaron is 262. The difference is 28. Remember the first verse of Torah - Gen. 1:1 which has 28 letters, 7- words depicting the MENORAH? In the beginning…? Wasn't the role of Ruth and Boaz also a rehearsal of that beginning? Her seed line had been cut off, he had no heir and though Messiah was to come through their lineage, the picture looked bleak! These numbers don't lie!

As we look back at Aaron's role with the Menorah it is riveting to note the verse division here in Ex. 27 between verse 20 & 21; the sentence structure indicates no such break.

> ***Exodus 27:20*** *And thou shalt command the children of Israel, that they bring thee pure oil olive beaten for the light, to cause the lamp to burn always. #21: In the tabernacle of the congregation without the vail, which is before the testimony, Aaron and his sons shall order it from evening to morning before the YHVH: it shall be a statute forever unto their generations on the behalf of the children of Israel.*

It is the LAMP, H#5216, ניר niyr, which is to be caused to burn always in the Tabernacle of the Congregation without the Vail…the wording here describing ascending or going up to the Menorah, calls our attention to another who was a counterfeit "Light Bearer" – Lucifer - הֵילֵל heylel - who usurped the Priestly authority.

> ***Isaiah 14:13*** *For thou hast said in thine heart, I will ascend into heaven, I will exalt my throne above the stars of God: I will sit also upon the mount of the congregation, in the sides of the north.*

Ironically, the original pattern of the Menorah was first depicted in the heavens among the luminaries, the very place he brazenly opines that he will ascend or go up to. He is described as fallen, H#5307, נָפַל naphal, fallen (It can also indicate an untimely birth or miscarriage) – from heaven, H#8064, שָׁמַיִם shamayim, which indicates the heavens as a covering. Shamayim also it has the same root as Shemen and the same gematria – 390.

The Hebrew word used above for "ordering" the fire has an ominous use as well. As I mentioned it's the word 'Arak, which also has the two-letter root, Ayin-Resh, the same as the root of H#5894, עִיר 'iyr, meaning a Watcher – Fallen One. The letter Kaf, hints at authority, title deed. Thus, by arranging or keeping the Perpetual Light burning, Aaron is setting in motion a legal cause against the usurped authority and title deed of the Fallen One himself – The Serpent or Satan! If you fail to order the Light Properly, fail to set a legal cause into motion, by either ignorance or disobedience – no matter, the enemy gains the upper hand.

The Priestly Generations

We next see in Ex. 28: 1 the names of Aaron and his sons. What does this order tell us?

♦ Aaron, H#175   אַהֲרוֹן   *'Aharown*

Light Bearer. *Remember our definition above? I will cause you to conceive and bear children

♦ Nadab, H#5070   נָדָב   *Nadab*

To incite willingly, however, the root stem, Nun – Dalet, is the same as Nod, the land of Cain. The Aleph – Bet means house. This infers he incited the house into wandering. It also is the root of Niddah, unclean.

♦ Abihu, H#30   אביהוא   *Avihuw*

He is my father.

♦ Eleazar, H#499   אלעזר   *'El'azar*

YHVH has helped.

♦ Ithamar, H#385   איתמר   *'Ithamar*

Though translated as 'coast or isle of palms', an enhanced look at the root tells something else. The Aleph – Yod can mean island, but is better translated 'a place sought for refuge, or shelter'. The Mem – Resh, mar, means bitterness, rebellion.

Once more we must extrapolate a definition:

These names imply; 'The Light – Bearer will cause you to conceive and produce children who will wander in their uncleanness, My Father YHVH has helped, He is the place of refuge from bitterness and rebellion! 2Cor. 11:14-15. It would seem our casual, flippant relationship with the Word, may leave us prone to deception. No one would intentionally allow themselves to be deceived. However, the fact remains that we have been engaged in Pagan Idolatrous practices, which includes profaning the Sabbath and the other Holy Convocations, to name a few. This indicates we have turned away!

> **Deuteronomy 11:16** *Take heed to yourselves, that your heart be not deceived, and ye turn aside, and serve other gods, and worship them.*

His wrath is being kindled as we speak, just look at the results of Revelation during the last 3 ½ years of tribulation. This is not the wrath of Satan being poured out; this is YHVH Himself judging the Earth. We should pay closer attention to what we're hearing!

As we've shared, the Hebrew language is a picture language. Thus, when we look at the genealogy of Aarons' sons above, a hidden treasure is revealed when we look at all the letters used to write their names. *Remember these men are charged with setting in order, guarding the Lamp. If we count the letters present (12) their individual gematria totals 785, the absent letters (10) those not accounted for, watched over, visibly seen, we have a total of 710. When we subtract them we're left with 75, the gematria of H#1966, הֵילֵל heylel, another name for Lucifer, also translated – 'Light Bearer'. Though not accounted for in the picture, the counterfeit light bearer – Lucifer, as in Gen. 3 and Isaiah 14: 12 – 15 subtly waits. He is hidden. Let's look at these absent letters and their word pictures:

1. **Gimmel**, to lift, to be proud.
2. **Chet**, the fenced off place.
3. **Tet**, the Serpent.
4. **Kaf**, authority.
5. **Mem**, womb.
6. **Samech**, Sukkah.
7. **Pey**, mouth – words
8. **Qof**, the head, the One who comes at the last.
9. **Tzade**, the righteous one.
10. **Shin**, to bite or consume.

Our Extrapolated Definition

The Proud One, inside the garden the fenced off place, the Serpent, will exalt his authority over the womb in the Sukkah – dwelling place. However, with His words the Righteous One will destroy the Head of him at the last! Gen. 3:15.

> ***Isaiah 14:13*** *For thou hast said in thine heart, I will ascend into heaven; I will exalt my throne above the stars of God: I will sit also upon the mount of the congregation, in the sides of the north.*

Quite frankly, at the same time the language is being restored there are multitudes in the Believing Community returning to the celebration of the True Festivals of the Creator. This brings us to an example in the rehearsals of the Fall Festivals where we see Yahweh command the entire Congregation to assemble in order to hear the Word. It is during Yom Teruah, Yom Kippur and Sukkot, (These are just the Fall Feasts) where the Torah is read before the whole congregation during the 7-year Shemitta cycle: Again, we see connections with the Menorah and the reading of the Torah with this 7-year cycle of liberty.

There are many scholars who believe these Fall Festivals will introduce us to a Jubilee or year of release in a combination of both the Shemitta (7-year cycle) and the beginning of the 120th Jubilee (7x7=49years). If so, what can we expect? Perhaps you should look at Lev. 25:1-13, Deut. 15:1-5 and Is. 61:1-5 and its New Testament equivalent, Luke. 4:17-21.

First, let's examine the Hebrew word specific to this 'release', Shmittah:

♦ Shemitta, H#8059   שְׁמִטָּה   *shĕmittah*

A remitting or release from debt. It is from the root shamat and can infer to let go, to let drop or fall. This hints at a legal document much like in todays' court where the accused has his sentence set aside by the Judge. This is the purpose of the Shemitta year. However, without an understanding of the legalese or legal jargon that is the Torah (In Hebrew) how can one know the judgment being rendered them? If you or the lawyer representing you doesn't know or understand the court language, he will mishandle or misrepresent your case.

A peculiar twist to this definition of Shemitta can be seen in a familiar story that invites scrutiny once it is seen in the Hebrew - 2Sam. 6:6 – it is the account of Uzzah and the Ark. But what connection does this story have with the Shmittah? This should be interesting because of the Ark representing the Living Word or Light, and Uzzah who handles it inappropriately.

In verse six we see that Uzzah puts forth his hand to steady the Ark because the oxen shook – shamat it (*Note the root of Shmittah). On the surface it seems Uzzah is killed because he refused to let the Ark fall, yet, if we look at the other key words in this verse the hidden reason for Uzzah's death is seen. Uzzah was a Levitical Priest. He knew how to 'handle' the Ark and the Law it represented. He was, for all intents and purposes, a 'doctor of the law.'

> **2 Samuel 6:6** *And when they came to Nachon's threshing floor, Uzzah put forth his hand to the ark of Yahweh, and took hold of it; for the oxen shook it.*

Hmmm? Where's that reason? It can only be seen in Hebrew. So much for those who don't think you need to learn it!

♦ Nachon, H#5225   נָכוֹן   *Nakown*

Translated 'prepared'. That which is arranged, established.

♦ Threshing floor, H#1637   גֹּרֶן   *Goren*

That which is smooth, leveled, an open door or gate. The root -stem, Gimmel-Resh, ger means stranger, while the Nun indicates 'life.'

This sounds almost surreal! As if they are intentionally being brought to this place to unite the Whole House of Israel, or to begin the dispersal. This reminds of Jacob who himself was brought to the prepared 'Place' to encounter the ladder/DNA of YHVH] It hints at Ezekiel's Bones!

♦ Uzzah, H#5798   עֻזָּא   *'Uzza*

Strength. It also has the same root AZ, Ayin-Zayin, meaning goat. In biblical literature the letters Ayin-Zayin-Alef are the root of the name of Azazel and are connected to sinful impurity and rebellion. Ironically, with different vowel points, it also spells Gaza! The principal ancient stronghold of Philistia and the Nephilim! Ironically, the Ayin represents a womb, the Zayin a Seed or weapon, while the Alef indicates first, head, 'husband'. Is this again, a reference to the first occurrence of seed, word, light, from the wrong 'husband' being planted? The Gematria of Ayin-Zayin is 77! A double reference to Sheva – an oath cutting or Shabbat! Are the Shabbats prepared 'places' for an encounter? These "7's" inadvertently point once again at the 7-branched Menorah! As well as, the 7-colors of the Rainbow!

♦ Put forth, H#7971   שָׁלַח   *shalach*

To put forth, to send out or away, to put away or divorce.

♦ Ark, H #430   אָרוֹן   *'arown*

A chest, ark a place to collect or gather. However, if we break it apart, the Alef-Resh root means 'light' while the Vav-Nun suffix shows the diminutive, I.E. 'the Light in a condensed or finite form'. [It is an established fact substantiated by many great minds like Nikola Tesla that the Ark was in fact a large Leyden jar or capacitor capable of generating tremendous power or light] The Ark literally represents the "House of the Seed" or Light. It contained the "Stones of YHVH". Eben HaYHVH! It was a representation of Yahshua the Man – Ark. You are also an Ark, capable of receiving and transmitting His word!

♦ Elohiym [needs no explanation]

♦ Took Hold, H#270   אָחַז   *'achaz*

To seize or possess.

♦ Oxen, H1241   בָּקָר   *baqar*

Oxen, cattle, it is spelled the same as a word meaning to seek, enquire, to cleave open, to inspect diligently.

♦ Shook, H#8058   שָׁמַט   *shamat*

To release, loose, rest, to be made to fall.

Before we examine our extrapolated definition we must remember that the Torah was written and placed in the side of the Ark to be read by the Whole House at the conclusion of the Shmittah cycle during the festival of Sukkot! It's about restoring the Coat of Many Colors to the House!

Therefore, the timing of this incident becomes significant. How so? 2Sam. 5:4, 5 tells us the length of David's reign: 7.5 years in Hebron – 33yrs in Jerusalem. It is quite possible the Ark as mentioned with Uzzah above was being transported during a Shmittah year to Jerusalem where the Torah could be enquired of (1Chron. 13:3). Remember it (Torah) was not enquired of during Saul's reign (H#7586, שָׁאוּל Sha'uwl, to ask, desire, demand, beg, require, to consult, and to grant). Saul is the son of Kish, whose name means to bend, or snare, to lure. Kish's father is referred to by two names: Abiel (El is my father) and Ner, meaning lamp! These names prophetically declare: *Because Israel failed to enquire of YHVH they were bent or snared away from the Niyr Elohiym – The Lamp or Light of YHVH).*

The Light was contained in a box, the Hebrew is H#727, אָרוֹן, though translated 'ark or box', it comes from a root Alef, Vav, Resh – UR, which infers to gather and is also closely related to several words meaning to burn or inflame! Its gematria, (Alef=1, Vav=6, Resh=200) 207 is equal to that of another famous word – 'Meribah', H#4808, מְרִיבָה, meaning strife or contention, yet it is from the root of H#7378, riyb, to strive or contend, to conduct a legal case or suit. At the Meribah encounter (Exodus 17:1-7) Israel was camped in a unique place, Rephidim, H#7508, meaning resting places or balusters – stair rails! This was the same place where Jacob had his dream of the Ladder or DNA helix of YHVH! The root of Rephidim – raphad, means to refresh, renew, and to reinvigorate one who is weak or faint! From this same word we get the word heal, H#7495, raphe, one of the Names of YHVH (יְהוָה רֹפְאֶךָ:). YHVH had given Israel Living Water from the Rock and Manna just prior to this chapter to renew their DNA just as Jacob witnessed in his dream! They complained because they had no 'Living Water' – Word – Light, in the place of Re-phidim - Rest and Healing – Shabbat - and now YHVH has a case against them! If you're celebrating or 'worshiping' on the wrong day whether it's Sun-day instead of the Sabbath or a holi-day instead of His Holy days, you're going to be thirsty – stop complaining it's your fault! If you continue to chide with Him the result will be the same as at Meribah and just as with Uzzah - someone dies – in this case it is the Struck Rock! The Rock rep-resented Yahshua!

In our current case Uzzah suffers personally but, the Nation of Israel is also at fault because they (The Levites) failed to bear the Ark upon their shoulders (indicating taking personal responsibil-ity) while supported by wooden poles, instead it is placed upon a cart (1Chron. 15:13). Is it possible that a Union exists between the handling of Torah and Keeping Sabbath that cannot be bro-ken? Ex. 31: 14 tells us that one who defiles the Sabbath shall be put to death and cut off from among his people. I.E. have no in-heritance. The word here for defile is: H#2490, חָלַל chalal, to pro-fane or pollute ritually or sexually. To wound fatally, to pierce or bore through! The Sabbath – whether the weekly, Shmittah (eve-ry 7th year) or Yovel (every 49th year) is a season of time set aside for intimacy with the Torah – the Husband! The House of Israel has been cut off for 2730-years without an inheritance. We've been alienated from the Commonwealth of Israel. Another oppor-tunity to handle the Ark is being tendered us and we must not be fooled into mishandling it again! The Rainbow of Noah pictured a washing away of all that would have made us unclean and un-fit! A time of restoration. Just as King David (Who represents the Messiah) leads the processional into the Holy City dancing be-fore the Ark of His Presence, His Word, The Bride is also making ready!

From Genesis 3 forward the Bride of YHVH (symbolized in part by the Levitical Priesthood) was in a Niddah (unclean) condition – Tainted by blood. 7-days are required for her ritual cleansing, the same for a spiritual 'washing' as well, at the end of that 7th –

day, 7,000 year period, a ritual cleansing occurs. To contact the husband or another clean Male while in an unclean, niddah condition required both parties to be cut off from the people! Was Uzzah in fact, unclean? The Sabbaths are set aside as a harbinger of the ritual cleansing of the Bride! Thus...

To fail to assemble is an egregious, inexcusable, offense to Him! To fail to appear for the ritual cleansing is to abnegate the role of the Bride! 'Tis strong language, but true nonetheless. *Note 2Cor. 4:2 ... *nor handling the word of God deceitfully...* the word for handling is #G1389, doloo, do-lo-o. To ensnare, to catch by bait, entice, deceive. Hmmm? Doesn't that sound the same as the definitions of Saul's' Kindred's names? In fact, the following verses in Corinthians speak of letting the light shine out of darkness! Having a treasure in an earthen vessel! The cleansing Agent seems to be the Light as it is refracted through the Waters! It is powerful enough to sterilize the seed of the enemy. Take heed which side you're choosing!

Our conclusion seems to fit that of Gen. 3 *where the Rebellious One, Uzzah – Azazel – Satan, is in the "prepared place – Nachon". He will cause them to become ger – strangers, exiled from the Life of YHVH and divorced from the Ark/Light.* Like Uzzah his flesh served to ground him causing the 'light' to kill the flesh. Had Lucifer, (whose name hints at flame, light) and Adam both handled the 'light' properly, they would have understood – been illuminated properly, in the Presence of Torah – Word – Messiah! Yet each failed to inspect diligently the Shmittah or the rest period. Incidentally, the word rest is the root of Restoration! This is the sole purpose of all facets of our discussion, the language, the Sabbath, the Holy convocations, the pinnacle of which is the Sabbath – the release of YHVH planned from Creation! It is my opinion that the incident of Gen. 3 takes place during Yom Kippur, which incidentally would have been the time to announce the Yovel! Just as in Ex. 31 Adam dies and is cut off from his people! How apropos to see the approach of the 120th Jubilee season

(50-years x 120 =6000yrs.) in conjunction with the Shmittah or restoration year and the reintroduction of the Rainbow Language!

The above evidence suggests a strong connection exists between the weekly Sabbath, the 7th year of the Shmittah/release, the seven sevens of years (49) known as the Jubilee and the handling of the Ark – Torah of YHVH and the restoration of the LIGHT TO ADAM's Temple! Could the Sabbath (including festivals and Shmittah years) be a season of 'recharging' the catalyst? Restoring the Light within the Tabernacle? Aren't you and I 'Living Stones'? Restoring us to life and our inheritance? Exactly! That's the premise of Sabbath, Shmittah and Yovel!

> *Isaiah 61:1-3 The Spirit of the Lord GOD is upon me; because the LORD hath anointed me to preach good tidings unto the meek; he hath sent me to bind up the brokenhearted, to proclaim liberty to the captives, and the opening of the prison to them that are bound;*
>
> *To proclaim the acceptable year of the LORD, and the day of vengeance of our God; to comfort all that mourn;*
>
> *To appoint unto them that mourn in Zion, to give unto them beauty for ashes, the oil of joy for mourning, the garment of praise for the spirit of heaviness; that they might be called trees of righteousness, the planting of the LORD, that he might be glorified.*

Most of us have heard the old saying that every cell in the body is changed over a period of seven years; but recent investigation has uncovered facts of far more significance to us as human beings. This concerns the emotional, physical and mental changes that seem to occur in approximate seven-year intervals.

The significance of the number 7 cannot be overstated. It is visible throughout the fabric of Scripture, connecting every major thematic emblem, including that of the 7-colors of the Rainbow, and the 7-brances of the Menorah, which as we've alluded to earlier in this book represents the earliest visible 7 planets. The White light of the Menorah and the Stellar luminaries would have contained all 7-colors of the Rainbow; literally casting a kaleidoscope of rainbow colors upon the Table of Showbread in the Holy Place, representing the Bride and her Coat of Many Colors!

That said, many who study the Stars and their constellations note the natural progressive order of the Zodiac and the connection of the Menorah's number 7 to that of the '7th' House or Constellation called Libra. This is really intriguing, in particular since we've discussed the Hebrew rendering of 'Libra or Scales' as it commonly translated. In Hebrew the Name is Mozenim – defined as scales or balance. The balance hinges upon the pendulum of the center rod, like the 6-brances who cast their light to the pendulum or center Candle. The root of the word Mozenim is the same as the word for 'Ear' – ozen. If you observe upper and lower scales of the Constellation Libra *The brightest star in the lower scale is ZUBEN AL GENUBI (A) and means 'the purchase or price which is deficient'. This tells us that man is weighed in the balance and found wanting.* This connects us back again to Daniel 5:27 and the fall of Babylon – and Belshazzar: "Thou art weighed in the balance and found wanting". Surely, we can conclude the importance of the influence the Signs. These luminaries received their light from the light. Genesis 1:14. If they become more prominent in the heavens as omen of these End Times, lending their voice as a prophetic message, shouldn't we listen? Remember they represent a Great Circle – A Rainbow of Light in the heavens.

Signs in the Heavens?

Genesis 1:14 *And YHVH said, let there be lights in the firmament of the heaven to divide the day from the night; and let them be for signs, and for seasons, and for days, and years.*

Now, we must examine the Hebrew again: Let' begin with the word 'light'.

- Lights, H#3974 מאור *ma'owr*

Translated light or luminary. Note the Mem prefix indicating from or out of, the place of origin, followed by Alef-Vav-Resh, which spells 'owr'. These 'lights' are from or out of the ORIGINAL LIGHT source! Ironically, the gematria of ma'owr equals 247, the same as H#2167, Zamar, a verb meaning to play an instrument, to sing with musical accompaniment. This is seen in Job:

> **Job 38:7** *When the morning stars sang together, and all the sons of God shouted for joy?*

Do these 'Morning Stars' sing?

Astronomers at the University of Sheffield have managed to record for the first time the eerie musical harmonies produced by the magnetic field in the outer atmosphere of the sun. They found that huge magnetic loops have been observed coiling away from the outer layer of the sun's atmosphere, known as coronal loops, which vibrate like strings on a musical instrument. Another strange fact is that every galaxy has a different "song". There aren't two galaxies with the same audio signal. These indicate that each star is pulsating. You'll also note that the sound of one star will vary slightly from another. That's because the sound they make depends on their age, size and chemical composition. Measuring these sounds involves a technique called 'stellar seismology'.

How coincidental that Hebrew, the Language of YHVH-Torah-Creation, is specifically designed for singing each letter serving as a note! Thus, the entirety of the heavens are strategically arranged to form a full orchestra that sings all of Torah! What does this have to do with the Calendar? Is it possible that the calendar represents the Time signatures, (beat), the tempo (speed) and the rests, etc. that tell us the length & speed of the song, when and how long to rest, what to expect before, during and after each stanza, thus adding emphasis to the message? In effect, serving as a timepiece a CALENDAR!

In our above example the 'Morning Stars' sang: Morning, H#1242, בקר boqer, means morning, daybreak, etc. But, as a verb, it means to seek, to look for, to consider, or to investigate, as in a formal search for official documents (Ezra 4:15, 19). Now, look at the word 'Stars', H#3556, כוכב kowkab, though primarily meaning star, it serves as a metaphor indicating personification, numerous progeny. These stars represent SEED/SONS whose voices sang, H#7442, רנן ranan, to be overcome with Joy! Why? Look at the Hebrew letters: Resh = head, first, beginning, while Nun-Nun spells life. They sang of the beginning, the first birth – first born (son) of life! This word Ranan, Resh-Nun-Nun has a gematria of 300, the same as Kaphar, to cover, atone, and Ruach Elohiym, which fits the pattern of Gen. 1:2 where the Ruach – Spirit of YHVH hovered over the (birthing) waters of creation! Again, confirmation of the Message in the Heavens and the chronological order of that message revealed as a Calendar! This first hint of the 7-Festivals of YHVH (connected to the 7-branch Menorah) was revealed in the Mo'ed known as the – Day of Atonement, the Day of Covering which is typologically revealed in Gen. 3:21 where Abba covers HIS SON ADAM with the Blood or congealed light 'Skin'!

Incidentally, this same two-letter root stem, (Kaf-Bet) from Stars, kowkab, is seen in Ps. 19:1 where we're told the heavens declare, H#5608, ספר caphar, to recount, declare, to cipher – a cepher-book, the glory, H#3519, כבוד kabowd, glory, weight, importance. The heavens – stars recount [in a living book] the importance of Messiah, The Word who is the Glory of YHVH!

155

The connection of the above Stellar Luminaries with the pattern of the Menorah serve as a means to inculcate the message written in the heavens as a certifiable witness to the veracity of the Rainbow language. The restoration of this Holy Tongue will allow a more concise communication between those who have an 'Ear to hear' the Shepherd's voice and the Shepherd. Many of you have heard the most famous of all "Jewish" mantras – the Shema – a word which when translated, literally infers both to hear and obey. In Hebrew thought one cannot be separated from the other, much like attempting to separate Faith from Works. Therefore, if Father is revealing His word during this season and this word is the 'legal' jargon of His Covenant, then shouldn't a higher level of commitment or obedience be the direct result of that hearing and understanding? In addition, if He does require a higher commitment, then we should also anticipate a pronounced increase in the level of the demonstration of that word in action!

It would seem the Great Suzerain King requires a loyalty from those servants whom He empowers to act on His behalf. Simply put, "if you love me, keep my commandments". This love is not the 'touchy – feely' emotional love familiar to most. It is actually a covenant term clearly identifying this specific stipulation. Its demonstration as a matter of obedience whether one feels emotionally inclined or not, proves allegiance which results in being blessed by the King. As Co-Regent in the Earth, Adam was first charged with this demonstration of obedience. Those conditions have not changed. It is not a matter of 'he knows my heart'. In fact, the commandments were implemented because He knows our hearts and our propensity toward straying outside the boundaries! Obedience to His word is the highest form of praise! Adam is commanded to be fruitful, multiply, replenish and have dominion. He is afforded every means necessary to accomplish this task and his physical, mental and spiritual welfare provided for in the interim. With one condition that serves as a restraint: A 2nd commandment is given to enforce the first: *Stay away from that Tree*...WHY? What critical role does this 2nd commandment play? Adam heard but, will he obey? Will you?

Chapter 13

Adam's Second Commandment

There are many of you reading this book and weighing the magnitude of this information who will find yourself on the razors' edge of indecision. Looking at the evidence and comparing it to where you are now, honestly, like many skeptics you'll weigh the responsibility of becoming both a 'hearer and a doer', against the perceived need for this Rainbow Garment – The Language that stands against the status quo, against complacency and frankly, in direct confrontation with the stagnant condition the Church currently finds itself languishing in. Change is an implacable foe! You will want to assuage your fear by over-thinking this book and reconciling yourself by taking a position of scoffing at this whole idea. Peter warned us this would happen:

> *2 Peter 3:3-4 Knowing this first, that there shall come in the last days scoffers, walking after their own lusts, and saying, Where is the promise of his coming? For since the fathers fell asleep, all things continue as they were from the beginning of the creation.*

Don't fall for that! Complacency drove Adam out of the Garden. Let me remind you of the 2nd Commandment given to Mankind after being admonished to be fruitful multiply and replenish, subdue and have dominion (The First Edict). This Light, this Word is that seed necessary to accomplish the above. It must be guarded with your life. Your eternal destination hinges on whether you attempt to mollify your flesh with a fig leaf or take up this Bloody Garment! The 2nd commandment should serve as a menacing warning as we look back at Adam in hindsight. Allow me to take you back to Genesis one more time. Chapter two specifically: verses 16 and 17 in particular so that you may see this commandment.

> ***Genesis 2:16-17*** *And YHVH Elohiym commanded the man, saying, Of every tree of the garden thou mayest freely eat: But of the tree of the knowledge of good and evil, thou shalt not eat of it: for in the day that thou eatest thereof thou shalt surely die.*

The Hebraic word translated here for 'knowledge' eclipses the insipid English translation (For some reason it always does, go figure☺) leaving no doubt this wasn't a tree with "fruit" the eating of which would be conducive for ordinary learning. It comes from Strong's H#1847, דַּעַת, da'ath, properly rendered knowledge, discernment, perception, or skill. The root of da'ath comes from H#3045, yada' which indicates to learn to know, to find out and discern, and to be acquainted with: as in a carnal relationship! It includes the action of knowing both as commencing and as completed. YHVH is not mincing words here. He is warning Adam to stay away from this 'TREE'; else he'll become engaged in actions that will expose him to carnal lusts associated with what or whomever this tree represents. It seems fairly clear from Genesis 1 that each tree bore fruit that had its' seed within itself. It is also very plain that the first commandment inciting Adam to procreate sets the context for this discussion of what is good and what is evil. The mere act of intimacy itself is not inherently evil and explodes the myth that sex is bad. [Sex outside of the marriage relationship – one man, one woman crosses the boundary] What Adam is being warned of here is the 'entity' metaphorically represented by this tree, he whom had taken the act of intimacy and perverted it previously! Lucifer was familiar with and perverted the boundaries established for proper sexual intimacy. Indeed ancient texts suggest the mingling of the seed of angels and animals occurred producing the monstrosities of Greek Mythology, as well as, the known miscegenation with man which according to Genesis 6 was quite prevalent. Another clue is the dire consequence for this deed: The Death penalty was immediate! However, in the Hebrew the phrase is: מֹות תָּמוּת, muwth t'muwth, dying you shall die! Is it possible that two types of death are being emphasized? (One; to die physically, the second to die spiritually) This would seem to be confirmed by the need for the slaughter of the Lamb in Genesis 3.

There seems to be a powerful connection here regarding the keeping of His commandments. In fact, we should look at the Hebrew word for 'keep' while here: H#8104,שָׁמַר shamar, to keep, to retain (within bounds) to guard. Ironically, the first place this word is used is in Genesis 2: 15 where Adam is placed in the Garden for the express purpose of dressing it - Shamar – keeping an eye on it. This word has a gematria or numeric value of 540 (Shin-300, Mem-40, Resh-200) which happens to be the same value as that of Strong's H#4975, מָתְנַיִם mothenim, translated as 'LOINS'. How cool is that? If you just missed the connection, let me explain a bit further. You can see how the commandments are the vocalized Word-Seed-Light, which issue out of His loins, right? Therefore, in His role as Husband to guard His loins would seem to indicate faithfulness by the One espoused to Him. To guard the seed! Eden wasn't the place of Seed; it was the *womb for the seed*! It's as important to guard the womb as it is the seed. To do otherwise would seem as a compromise and expose one to spiritual and physical infidelity! Adam and Eve turned from the Tree of Life toward the Tree of Carnal Knowledge thereby, violating the Conjugal rights of the Husband! Even 1st Corinthians chapter 7 confirms that the husbands' body is not his own, in the same fashion; the wife's body belongs to her husband. It's a no brainer! If you love me – keep the terms of the Wedding Vows – i.e. keep my commandments as Yahshua so often emphasized.

Now, in view of what we've discovered, it seems when we hear the declaration in Exodus 20: 6 requiring those who love Him to keep His commandments and then we see it echoed in the Gospel accounts, particularly, in the book of John, where Yahshua makes the same declaration –If you love me, keep my commandments - that marital infidelity would be the natural result of breaking or abrogating His Word! Since these commandments comprise the Marriage contract. It is the Word, the entrance of which releases the spark of Life – and impregnates the Bride with the Light which illuminates all mankind.

> *John 1:4, 9 In him was life; and the life was the light of men. That was the true Light, which lighteth every man that cometh into the world.*

These Commandments, in my opinion, are inexorably linked to retaining possession of the Light Garment, I.E. the Word or Seed which gives physical identity to the Vocalized Word whose aura promises to shroud the Believer who keeps – Shamar's – this 'contractual agreement'. Are you beginning to understand why no other Scriptural verse serves to polarize the Judaeo / Christian / Hebrew Roots community like this one? Our allegiance to the God of Abraham, Isaac & Jacob is predicated upon this foundational Corner Stone: The Commandments of YHVH! We must keep, shamar – guard the Word or Seed, the light! I'm convinced this was exactly what Yahshua alluded to in His 'Sermon on the Mount' recorded in Matthew:

> *Matthew 5:14-15 Ye are the light of the world. A city that is set on an hill cannot be hid. Neither do men light a candle, and put it under a bushel, but on a candlestick; and it giveth light unto all that are in the house.*

You, dear Reader are this 'Light of the World'. Why hide the light? Why hide the truth? These are His commandments not ours! Thus, keeping them becomes an indicator of the intensity of the light being refracted through you! I.E. how much of the Rainbow is visible in your life?

However the argument(s) regarding the 'Keeping' of these sacred laws can vary depending upon which camp you adhere to! We will not attempt to address the various positions of each, but, instead, focus on exactly what is being said regarding the observance of these 'Laws' and what fidelity to them literally entails. We will see what relationship necessitated their existence and we will examine a preponderance of evidence peculiar to a select group. It is through their observance (The Commandments) that fealty to the King of Creation was/is/and will be: demonstrated. These are not 'suggestions'! If we are to be part of the restoration of the 'pure language', which I believe, is the Garment of Light originally worn by Adam, if true, we must face the facts: Seeing the Truth in its original language and context will expose the naked condition of the Church and its fig leaf of traditions! My goodness the silence is palpable isn't it?

As mentioned previously, our Key phrase (If you love me, keep my commandments) is seen literally in two distinct places: Ex. 20: 6 and Jn. 14:15. Additionally, various combinations of: "KEEP" and "AND" and "MY" "commandments" can be found in 20 other verses for a total of 22 occurrences. This number connects us once again, to the Alef-Bet of the Hebrew language, the legal language of the Covenant! The Language which envelopes the 'wearer' in a garment of light! It is my contention and ample proof exists, that both Old & 'New' Testaments present Ancient Near Eastern Treaty flavor and character and thus, (My opinion again) were written originally in this Hebrew 'legalese' - the purpose of which was to enable those who would bind themselves in Covenant with YHVH to demonstrate the same authority as He, without the compromise inherent in and peculiar to, every other language! {As demonstrated from the Gen. 11 Tower of Babel account forward} In every account, the Patriarchs were charged with this 'terminology', i.e. a grammar specific to YHVH alone. He duplicated Himself, by coding His DNA within these 22 letters, in effect, making them the building blocks of Creation. Our exile from the Tree of Life precipitated our limited access to this language. Here's the textural proof: In Genesis 3: 23 we see Adam relegated to 'tilling the ground'. The Hebrew phrase reveals whom this 'ground – adamah' represents: לַעֲבֹד אֶת־הָאֲדָמָה laevod ET-haadamah. *(Pay attention to the Alef-Tav) The word till, H#5647, עָבַד 'abad, indicates to work or serve, to make oneself a servant. However, there is another ancient term used for tilling – 'ear the ground' - an Old English term meaning to plow or break the ground! This gets interesting. One of the Hebrew words for plowing is H#2790, חָרַשׁ, charash, meaning to cut in, to plough. It can also mean to engrave, to be silent, dumb or deaf. It indicates cutting into or inscribing letters on a tablet! What is being said here in Genesis 3: 23? It seems Adam is being told *"if you serve the Alef-Tav (Messiah) and expect to glean anything, you must lend yourself to the plowing, hearing, engraving, speaking and inscribing of the letters!"* That's why the Apostle James fervently admonishes us to not be 'hearers' only, but 'doers' of the word as well. To put what you hear into action!

Furthermore, we would also note, this phrase, 'if you love me, keep my commandments' is attributed both to YHVH and Yahshua, which requires us to examine His (Yahshua's) assumed role as THE SON OF YHVH AND THUS, HIS MESSIAH, within the framework of Ancient Treaty language. [ATL] First things first: Many of our readers disdainfully regard the 'Old Testament' as antiquated, and are of the opinion that it has been modified by our Messiah and perhaps others who were appointed the authority to change it. Nothing could be further from the Truth! Neither YHVH nor His Word – changes! It cannot, the moment it does, the legal fabric that Creation is woven from will begin to unravel and nothing constant can be found! There will be no more light! Men support the fallacy of these purported 'changes', because it's easier on the flesh and quite honestly, men love darkness rather than light and will gravitate toward eliminating anything that supports Truth. That said; everything we've discussed hitherto must be measured correctly. That standard of measure must be the foundational documents of the Covenant – the Torah. All other books should complement, not contradict what is posited within its framework. Personally, I am of the opinion that the Prophets, the Writings, and the New Testament, when properly examined, in context, and without the interference of our traditional bias (Most give more credence to the tradition than the Truth) will say the same as the Original Text of the Torah. It takes an effort to dig the Truth out from under the burdensome load of opinion and tradition, but it can be done. Adam was told to PLOUGH the ground! Likewise, you and I should serve, hear, obey and write the vision! *See Habakkuk 2: 2, 3.

It is my position (and I take this stance with the understanding that I'll be castigated by many) the Old Testament was penned in the Language of Creation – Hebrew – this is patently undeniable: I also am convinced the New Testament was written in the same tongue as well. (The only minor difference being the Paleo script verses the Chaldean Flame letters) However, there was a concerted effort by the enemy who appealed to those camped out around the Tree of Carnal Knowledge, to pathologically launch a campaign of lies and disinformation to destroy the vestiges of the Hebrew text. In doing so, much of the Church world has been neutered; with little to no ability to demonstrate the Power once resonant in the Light, Sound and Color of His Word! Can I offer any proof? You read this and decide.

Do both 'Testaments' contain the same Covenant/Treaty Language: Is There Proof?

♦ Papias, bishop of Hierapolis, c. 150 A.D. said: "Mathew put down the words of the Lord in the Hebrew language, and others have translated them, each as best he could."

- <u>Irenaeus</u> (120-202 A.D.) Bishop of Lions, France, wrote: "Matthew, indeed, produced his Gospel written among the Hebrews in their own dialect."

- <u>Origen</u> (c. 225 A.D.) said: "The first Gospel composed in the Hebrew Language, was written by Mathew. For those who came to faith from Judaism."

- <u>Eusebius, Bishop of Caesarea</u> (c. 325 A.D.), wrote: "Matthew had first preached to the Hebrews, and when he was about to go to others also, he transmitted his Gospel in writing in his native language" (Ecclesiastical History III 24, 6).

- And Jerome, translator of the Scripture into Latin (Vulgata or Vulgate version), says the same.

- Dead Sea Scrolls depict an overwhelming number of Hebrew pages both secular and Scriptural, which again, confirm Hebrew as the language spoken and written by Yahshua and the disciples.

- Scriptural evidence itself: Jn. 19:13, 19, Luke 23:38, Acts 21:40.

- In addition, there are over 5366 manuscripts of the New Covenant in Greek, each differing from the other and containing several hundred variants. However, in each one of these manuscripts there are idioms which are almost meaningless in any language -- including Greek -- except in Hebrew! How can such a thing be explained unless it is because the original was Hebrew?

Two of the Most Common NT. Hebrew Idioms: "Son of Man" and "Peace Be Unto You"

Most scholars acknowledge that parts of the "Old Testament" follow the parameters of Ancient Near Eastern Treaty language consistent with that found among such Civilizations as the Hittites, Sumerians, Egyptians, etc. I contend however, these ancient Nations only borrowed what had already been established and in practice since Gen. 1 and can be seen throughout the entirety of the Scriptures - Genesis to Revelation. I believe in order for the Language of Creation, the Rainbow language to be transferred from one generation to the next, each succeeding generation must have one who functions in the role of 'First born' much like the role of the High Priest who orders the Lamp daily. The physical role of firstborn had to be established by YHVH Himself by the giving of Messiah as His First born. This sets the precedent. In so doing, He is able to offer a 'Treaty of Peace' to those who were estranged from Him and who will repent and turn from their wicked ways.

This is why we have to examine where our understanding of the origin of these 2 Hebraic idioms derives:

Both are terms consistent with Ancient Suzerain Language where relationship between the Great King and His Vassal subjects is framed as 'Father and Son'. As I said, the relationship originates out of what can be termed as a 'Treaty of Peace'. Our phrase "if you love me keep my commandments" serves to legally establish the boundaries for this relationship, which is seen in our 2nd witness of "If you love me..." in John 14: 13-16. It is here where the validity of the role of Messiah-Yahshua as THE SON OF YAH can be linked inexorably, to His role as Vassal Servant of Abba YHVH! The Son or Vassal was tasked with the language of the Covenant and the implementation of its terms within his realm. This Language brought light – illuminated; in other words, brought understanding to those seeking Covenant with the Great

King! Being entrusted with this Light enabled the Kingdom to be propagated, to become fruitful, multiply and replenished. It also allowed the Vassal Servant to subdue and exercise dominion over those who would oppose the King! The Sign or Seal of the Covenant took various forms, such as the Rainbow to Noah, Circumcision (Whose etymological root implies to 'encircle' to form a Circle of Blood) to Abraham and the burning Bush to Moshe – an eternal Flame like the Menorah or Tree of Life! The Restoration of this Great Seal of the Kingdom of YHVH – the Cyclical Language of Hebrew is taking place now! No greater sign exists! This is part of the legal framework of Creation and the Spirit that imbues this Ancient Holy Tongue is waiting to confirm Himself to you, by enveloping you in this Light of the World! The Scriptures are rife with confirmation if you're willing to look.

> ***Hebrews 11:6*** *But without faith it is impossible to please him: for he that cometh to YHVH must believe that He is – and that He is a rewarder of those who diligently seek Him!*

To further accentuate my colossal 'theory' there is an even more pure form of Ancient Suzerain Covenant language seen couched vividly in the description of the relationship of husband (Suzerain) and wife (Vassal) which initiates the Marriage (Treaty) shone in Gen. 1 & 2. We have the Great King – demonstrated in Adam – While the Vassal – Eve, is defined as the help meet עֵזֶר כְּנֶגְדּוֹ: Edzer K'negdo – which sports the root word neged, H#5048 - H#5046, and connotes, in front of, before, parallel to – to manifest, to tell or make known, A MESSENGER! Eve was the physical messenger for/of [representing the king] Adam: Ancient laws dictate that a messenger of the King was to be treated his equal and the message was to be sealed, until one who was worthy could open it! Often as many as 7 seals would be affixed to the scroll. The Womb of Eve was SEALED – when broken by the Serpent, the death penalty was invoked! Adam (The Husband) is the ONLY WORTHY ONE! Rev. 5: 2, 9 indicates The Lamb only is worthy to open the 7 Seals upon the Book. Breaking the Seal allows light or Seed to penetrate the womb. Just like the Light penetrated the darkness of Creation in Genesis 1 and the same example can be seen with Mary the mother of Yahshua who is overshadowed by this same Spirit! This is the Pattern and the very reason the Great Copycat, a.k.a. The Adversary in his role as deceiver appears also as a messenger of light, thereby seducing those who will not guard the womb properly!

As we continue, we find framed within this context, that our ATL documents also quite often contain a term that is used to describe intimacy between Adam and Eve (Gen. 4:1, 'Adam knew his wife...' H#3045, יָדַע yada') which infers to know one sexually, and is the same word used in Gen. 3: 7 after the fact, to describe their naked condition. This verb yada parallels Ancient Treaty language where the term 'to know' infers to recognize, to know; by seeing, hearing or experience: Ancient Near Eastern treaties repeat this verb 'to know' in the technical sense of "to recognize a legal relationship" and "to recognize treaty stipulations as binding." Eve becomes subject to Adam after the fall! Gen. 3: 16. The Wedding – Treaty documents required: (These same requirements are reflected in the "role" of Yahshua as husband and the "Ecclesia" or Believers as Bride) *Note the following:

♦ Husband to be Lord/Master. (1Pet. 3: 6)

♦ Wife to obey husband. (1Pet. 3:5,6)

♦ Wife becomes chattel of husband, she owns no property. (1Cor. 6:20)

♦ Treaties were between equals. Ketubah is between Husband and Father of the Bride! The Bride is required to marry 'up' in status! She has no light of her own. Like the Moon, she receives her light from the Sun!

This would seem to add perspective to the puzzle of Matthew 7: 23…And then will I profess unto them, I never knew you: depart from me, ye that work iniquity.

♦ Profess, Gk. #3670   *homologeo*

To agree with, to concede. Hmmm? It is evident Yahshua is NOT agreeing with those in front of Him. An obvious Non Sequitur! What is happening? This word homologeo is a compound of Homo meaning together (ONE-Echad?) and logos, word, speech. It is the generic term used throughout the NT to indicate the written word! What is being inferred is that Yahshua is in agreement with the Word – or Treaty – the Ketubah, not those in front of Him! He is both Light and Truth. If we walk in the Light, we are covenant partners.

♦ Knew, Gk. #1097   *ginosko*

To learn, come to know. It is also a Jewish idiom for sexual intercourse between a man and woman. The same as the Hebrew word Yada!

♦ Depart, Gk. #672   *apochoreo*

To go away, depart. Another compound from apo – a separation of a part from the whole, the origin of a cause & Choreo – to turn ones' self. We get our English word 'choreograph', to arrange, to direct, a blueprint, chart, and map.

♦ Iniquity, Gk. #458   *anomia*

The condition of without law, contempt and violation of law – Torah!

Yahshua is citing legal precedent! He is agreeing with the Treaty Terms, acknowledging the candidate (Those whom He addresses in this chapter) as never having sought to YADA – recognize a legal relationship, by consummation. Therefore, this origin of A JUST CAUSE AGAINST THEM stems from their willful separation from the blueprint, the frame of the Treaty, and ultimately their becoming a lawbreaker! By not keeping his law – teaching and instructions, they willfully repudiate their right to the Garment of Light and instead grope about for the fig leaf of carnality. *It feels good to the flesh, thus it must be right. He knows my heart, though my actions say otherwise.* How foolish are we? Just like the Prodigal Son who returns from self-exile, the Father watches for our return and as the Great Suzerain King is wont to do, He restores the Son. The contrite heart of the returning son allows for the restoration of the Signet Ring and the Coat of Colors! Isn't this worth the effort? What cause is worthy of a champion if not one that others find daunting? What price worth paying to have access to the vaunted Tree of Life? The Rainbow Garment of Light?

King David uses the same legal terminology when addressing Israel: "Is there not a cause" 1Sam. 17:29! [In the law of master and servant, (Treaty Language!) the term [Is there not a cause] means some substantial shortcoming on the part of the employee which is detrimental to the employer's interest and which the law and a sound public opinion recognize as a good cause for employee's dismissal . See Colaw v University civil service merit board etc., 341 N.E.2d 719, 37 Ill.App.3d 857.] This is exactly what provoked the measures taken by YHVH in Genesis 3! Being forewarned of 'dying you shall die', the compromise of Adam and Eve, left the Garden undressed – it is the same euphemistic terminology as "defiling the Father's bed". A heinous crime where one willfully allows the marriage bed to be spoiled! The Creator had just cause: They are subsequently deprived of their Light Covering!

It is this 'Just Cause' which allows for the wrath contained in the Seals of Revelation (opened by Yahshua only, in His role as Crown Prince of the Earth – Vassal Servant on behalf of YHVH – the offended Great Suzerain) to be poured out upon the earth! This wrath follows the Pattern of the judgment upon Adam and Eve, the Great Flood, and the Bitter Waters of Jealousy mentioned in Numbers chapter 5, and the Plagues of Exodus: all of which point to the Cup of Jealousy drank by Yahshua in order to liberate His Bride! Babylon the Mother of Harlots will be forced to drink of this cup as revealed in the cups, bowls and seals of Revelation!

Both the terms sons of God and "son of God" appear in Jewish literature where leaders of the people, kings and princes, were called "sons of God", and are found predating the New Testament. {The Apocrypha and Pseudepigrapha contain a few passages in which the title "son of God" is given to the Messiah {see Enoch, cv. 2; IV Esdras vii. 28-29; xiii. 32, 37, 52; xiv. 9}

Though I am convinced Yahshua is the literal, Son of Yah, from both a filial and Covenantal relationship, one does not abrogate the other! In fact, ATL seems to provide a permanent transfer of all rights and responsibilities, along with filiation to the Son, thus making the case against Yahshua being 'literal born' a moot point except for the necessity of one coming in the flesh and living without sin, in order to redeem Fallen Man from his corrupt flesh and to restore the Coat of Many Colors – the Rainbow Language! This point of contention regarding the Sonship of Yahshua usually stems from the Jewish perspective of Deut. 6: 4 and is, I believe, a direct attempt to counter the Greek bias in presenting Yahshua in the role of Jesus the Covenant Breaker! If Yahshua is a Covenant Breaker as accused, then you have no hope to attain the ancient Garment of Light – the mantle that identified the First Born Son who would also function in the role of High Priest. To expose the fallacy of any valid argument against the Coat of Many Colors rightfully belonging to Him and loaned to us as a result, we must prove the legitimacy of His right as Heir, which will open the door for your claim to an inheritance as well. Let's examine the verse in Torah most used to deny Yahshua the right to function as YHVH in the earth:

Deuteronomy 6:4

Hear, O Israel: The LORD our God is one LORD: [KJV]

שְׁמַע יִשְׂרָאֵל יְהוָה אֱלֹהֵינוּ יְהוָה אֶחָד:

Shema Israel YHVH Eloheinu YHVH echad.

What does Shema – hear and obey, have to do with acknowledging the "Oneness" of Elohiym? Surely, it indicates the hearing and obedience to His vocalized written word, specifically, the language of Creation, the tongue of Eden, the Light that was/is/and is to come as well as, the Alef through Tav of the Hebrew written letters, which by Yahshua's own declaration in Revelation 1: 8 & 11, 21: 6 and 22:13 (rendered Alpha and Omega in the Greek) are clear identifiers of Himself! The textural structure of the Book of Revelation is literally rife with Ancient Near Eastern Treaty language. Coupled with the Hebraisms embedded in the text (which cannot be translated properly outside of the Semitic language) they offer scholarly evidence, that I feel firmly indicates Hebrew as the linguistic origin of this Apocryphal Book. The many references to the Light of His Presence here also add circumstantial evidence to the Rainbow Language as the multi-faceted Sign of the Covenant promises and the curses implemented when said promises are invalidated by disobedience. It's plainly simple: If you love me, you'll keep my commandments: In doing so, you guard my word, seed, and light!

The focus is in arguing against the 'plurality' of the Godhead, specifically, Yahshua as Messiah - is always directed to the adjective 'echad' supposedly meant to infer 'one' as in – the 'only'.

Ironically, it is used here to describe the dual Noun 'YHVH Elohiym' which is a PLURAL NOUN IN HEBREW! [*Remember the Hebrew legalese, the tool used to interpret the contract:] In fact, 'echad, is a poor choice to prove 'one as in the only', when it usually infers one as in Primacy – the First! The main Hebrew word for solitary oneness, only, H#3173, יָחִיד yachiyd, is never used in reference to YHVH! And no satisfactory answer can be found (here we cite the 'law of first reference') when the noun Elohiym (plural of Eloah) is found in Gen. 1 – a total of 32 times and 1/3 (11 times) of those is seen connected to the ET – Alef-Tav, (seen a total of 28 times) while not one usage of the Singular, Personal noun – name of YHVH Himself, is found! In fact, YHVH the singular noun is NOT SEEN until Gen. 2:4 – 5 where the generations of the heavens and earth, the plants of the field before they were in the earth, and every herb of the field are declared after the Covenant is witnessed or attested to, in the prior 3 verses. It's a continued reckoning of Seed being accounted for – The Seed of His Word. The plurality of the 'Godhead' fulfills this – "seed planted equals son" – law. This is why we need to learn to plough the ground! 2 Timothy 2:15 adds emphasis!

> ***2 Timothy 2:15*** *Study to show yourselves approved workman that need not to be ashamed, rightly dividing the word of truth!*

It cannot be done outside the Hebrew language which alone is able to illuminate the Truth!

While we're here in Genesis 2, there's a peculiar Hebrew word I would like to show you.

> ***Genesis 2:6*** *But there went up a mist from the earth, and watered the whole face of the ground.*

Look at the Hebrew for mist, H#108, אֵד 'ed, translated as mist or vapor. An exhalation of breath! Science has proven that the breath for your voice comes out of your diaphragm or lungs as it

172

is compressed. When one whispers, (Like the Serpent, the Nachash defined as a 'whisperer') what is expelled comes from used breath, *breath that has already been exhaled. It is a false breath.* The word 'ed, comes from H#181, 'uwd which indicates a fire brand. Therefore, The Breath or Voice of YHVH in the Garden literally materialized as a fiery rain – perhaps cloven tongues of fire – much like that descending upon Mt. Sinai and in the Pentecostal Experience of the Book of Acts! This Breath of Fire – Light was the Shroud of Eden's Garden! To solidify my contention of a 'birthing process' indicated here in Genesis 2:4 spend a few minutes with me as we examine the word for 'Generations'.

♦ Generations, H#8435   תּוֹלְדוֹת   *towledah*

Descendants, families, races, a begetting! From H#3205, yalad, to bring forth, to beget, to declare one's birth. Curiously, this same word indicates to beget a SON! Thus, the first instance of the singular noun YHVH being used is in connection with His begetting a Son! The Tetragrammatons' – YHVH – is translated 'The Existing One', from H#1961, Hayah, to be, become, exist, come into being and can be seen when He introduces Himself to Moshe in Ex. 3:14, אֲשֶׁר אֶהְיֶה אֶהְיֶה Ehyeh, Asher Ehyeh, I AM THAT I AM! This seems clearly to declare that YHVH intended to reveal Himself in the earth in the same fashion as A Father begetting a Son, His image is transferred, revealed in, the Seed. This follows the Law of Genesis: Everything reproduces 'after its' kind'. Ironically, YHVH chooses to identify Himself with this "I AM" אֶהְיֶה שְׁלָחַנִי אֲלֵיכֶם: (I AM has sent me to you) and thus, His Son should also be recognized by the same appellation. Incidentally, one of those 'I AM' appellations is seen in John 8:12 and 9:15 where Yahshua remarks "I AM THE LIGHT OF THE WORLD" once more confirming the identity of the Light as the same as the Word or Voice who walked in the garden! The Rainbow language theory is beginning to seem more than mere conjecture! In fact, the thesis which is this book centers on this mind-bending, life changing proposition!

This ATL is consistent throughout The Tanach and NT. Where even the most ancient existing NT manuscripts concur with the above: Remember, it is our contention that Hebrew was the original language of the NT. And, the Greek manuscripts record myriads of "I AM" sayings – [EGO EIMI] attributed to Yahshua who would not have spoken Greek but, Hebrew, and would have been applying this reference to YHVH to Himself! This was such a clear indication, that even in His day one was left with only 2 choices: Either believe He was the Son of YHVH or kill Him for blasphemy! This is exactly what the Romans and the Religious Pharisaical Jews did! However, don't get to smug; you're just as guilty for your own sins against Him as well! If you believe Him to be The Son of YHVH, then you must demonstrate your loyalty to the Great King by obeying His Commandments!

Furthermore, in the above texts employing ego eimi, Yahshua did not just say "I am He," in the context of being a human Messiah, empowered by YHVH, as some allude to. History records many who believed and publicly confessed themselves as some kind of messiah or savior for Israel. The testimony of the Sanhedrin themselves in condemning Him to death attests to the fact that He was saying *"He was YHVH in the Flesh"*! He was confirming the fact that He represented the Great Suzerain King of Creation and as His representative on the earth through an Ancient Treaty established in Gen. 1 and sealed in Gen. 2; Yahshua could offer this treaty of PEACE on earth - to all men! This follows treaty guidelines where provisions were made for RENEWAL OF COVENANT – in incorporated in the text, long before it was broken. (Gen. 3) The choice is that of the one would meet the terms!

Matthew 21:33-46 *Hear another parable: There was a certain landowner who planted a vineyard and set a* *hedge around it, dug a winepress in it and built a tower and he leased it to vinedressers and went into a far country. Now when vintage-time drew near, he sent his servants to the vinedressers, that they might receive its fruit and the vinedressers took his servants, beat one, killed one and stoned another. Again he sent other servants, more than the first and they did likewise to them. Then last of all he sent his son to them, saying, 'They will respect my son.' But when the vinedressers saw the son, they said among themselves, 'This is the heir. Come, let us kill him and seize his inheritance.' So they took him and cast him out of the vineyard and killed him. "Therefore, when the owner of the vineyard comes, what will he do to those vinedressers?" They said to Him, "He will destroy those wicked men miserably and lease his vineyard to other vinedressers who will render to him the fruits in their seasons." Yahshua said to them, "Have you never read in the Scriptures: The stone which the builders rejected has become the chief cornerstone."*

The word in Hebrew for stone, is H#68, אֶבֶן 'eben; the prefixed Alef indicates future tense, 'I will'. Bet-Nun = son; i.e. 'I will Son You'. The word cornerstone, when broken down in the Greek, gives us: corner, Gk. #1137, goneia, a corner, a secret place, from Gk. #1119, gony, the knee, to kneel down, to bow the knee and used of those worshipping YHVH. The word for Chief, Gk. # 2776, kefala, means the Head, chief, Master, of a husband in relation to his wife!

Once more our Extrapolated Definition.

The Son many reject(ed) is in fact, the soon to be crowned: Vassal Servant - King of the Earth in lieu of the Great Suzerain King to whom all will bow! He is the Living Word, The Shining One, clothed with the Light of Creation!

The Apostle John introduces Yahshua as The Word who was with God (Yahweh) and instrumental in the creation of all things. He indicates Yahshua as the agent of Life, which was the Light of all men. This Light would shine amidst the darkness and the darkness would not comprehend it. This eternal struggle intensifies unto the day we find ourselves in: A day of mortal struggle between good and evil, light and darkness. We've talked a good bit about the genuine light; why not spend a few pages on the counterfeit?

Chapter 14

The Counterfeit Light

Throughout these pages we've discussed How the Creator spoke everything into existence by the release of His word in the form of Light. We've also addressed the necessity of separating The Light from The Darkness. I want to provoke you once again to think outside your pretty, painted proverbial box called "tradition". We'll begin by looking at your concept of Darkness, חֹשֶׁךְ H#2822, traditionally rendered 'darkness, obscurity, the secret place'. Variants of the spelling [same consonants, different vowel pointing] indicate: 'to hold back or to retain, to restrain', to bring confusion, or uncertainty. It may also identify something as obscure or insignificant. It hints 'to infer or to grow dim', be hidden or concealed, to be a variant. Having said that, for you to automatically associate darkness with Satan, leaves verses such as Psalm 18:11 hard to explain.

> ***Psalm 18:11*** *He (YHVH) made darkness his secret place; his pavilion round about him were dark waters and thick clouds of the skies.*

Could it be that the Original Presence or Person/Being, represented by this 'darkness' in Genesis 1, existed at one time himself, as a luminous Being, who because of his own rebellion, had the light (Word-Seed-Language) stripped from him, leaving him naked? Did the absent of that light now make him a lesser being, obscured by and insignificant to, *THE Light Being*? Was there a reason to clothe him in darkness in order to hide or conceal him? It sounds exactly like the condition of Adam! The garment of Light and the Life it formerly provided are now withheld from him. He is driven from the Presence! Could this be the reason for the antipathy displayed toward Adam who is cloaked in the Light Garment that Lucifer himself once wore while walking among the Stones of Fire in Eden? It would help explain why the Stars are referred to as Sons of the Morning, Sons of YHVH! Throughout antiquity the Stars have served to represent the Angels – both Fallen and the Elect! In fact, a dual role can be seen associated with those mythological 'heroes' of ancient texts where they are depicted as both a god-being and stellar body! Confused yet? Let's hope not, because we've much territory to cover! Look with me at Genesis 6 again!

The Nephilim

Genesis 6: 4 declares there were 'giants', (H#5303, נְפִיל nĕphiyl) in the earth and also after the flood. These were/are by genetic design a by-product of the Fallen Angels and the daughters of men. As a side note of interest; *Gesenius's Lexicon intimates that the ancient versions link this word niphelah with the "Giant in the Sky", i.e. the Constellation Orion!* In relation to what has been this book's theme [Light, Sound, Seed and Word] what connection exists here?

The Online Etymology Dictionary has: Orion a bright constellation, late 14c., from Greek Oarion, name of a giant in Greek mythology, loved by Aurora, slain by Artemis, of unknown origin, though some speculate on Akkadian Uru-anna "the Light of Heaven." Another Greek name for the constellation was Kandaon, a title of Ares, god of war, and the star pattern is represented in many cultures as a giant (such as Old Irish Caomai "the Armed King," Old Norse Orwandil, Old Saxon Ebuðrung).

Though the meaning is convoluted, others feel it may possibly be related to Greek 'οριον (horion) "boundary, limit". Hmmm? Does this sound vaguely similar to the boundary established between Light and Darkness and usurped by Satan in Genesis 3 and the Fallen Ones in Genesis 6? If Light is indeed - Seed, then Darkness must be 'seed' as well. They (The Fallen Ones) crossed the boundary established for their SEED! It is my opinion that the Powers that BE, in an effort to obviate the Message in the Heavens (So clearly visible as to leave no excuse to the Believer) began to change the Hebrew names to those counterfeited to a large extent, and therefore hidden in Arabic, Greek, Latin and English. Thus accomplished the truth becomes convoluted. As a result, in the aftermath, a grotesque picture is painted where the Fallen Ones are deified by the Mystery Religion(s).

I personally believe the Stellar Luminaries point to the redemption plan of YHVH through the work of Messiah and as such, each constellation's message should point to Him. Following this line of thought, allow me to show you the Hebrew understanding of whom is really represented by the constellation of Orion: *Orion: Known as The coming prince. Today he is called the Great Hunter which is irrelevant. The picture shows a mighty man in front of Taurus. He is obviously triumphant.* *Remember, Nimrod fashioned himself as 'the great hunter' of Greek Mythology. The Counterfeit proves the existence of the Genuine, Yahshua, He who is the Coming Prince.

The ancient Egyptian name is HAGAT meaning 'this is he who triumphs'. The name was probably spelt OARION originally, providing a variant meaning 'coming forth as light'. The Akkadian name was UR-ANA 'the light of heaven'. The name ORION appears in Job 9:9 and 38:31 and Amos 5:8. This constellation is a magnificent sight with 78 stars. As 'the coming prince' he stands with his left foot on LEPUS the enemy. His sword has the head and body of a lamb, his right hand holds a club, and his left hand holds the head and skin of a lion. Stars confirm who he is. The brightest in the right shoulder is BETELGEUZ, meaning 'the coming of the branch'. In the left foot is RIGEL or RIGOL "the foot that crusheth". In the left shoulder is BELLATRIX meaning 'quickly coming' or 'swiftly destroying'. A star in the belt AL NITAK (A) means 'the wounded one', reminding us that this deliverer was once wounded. Other unidentified but named stars relate similar meanings - 'who bruises', 'treading on', 'the branch', 'the mighty', 'the ruler,' 'the strong', 'coming forth'. So the divine star message adds detail of the coming return or Second Advent of the Messiah. [Source: E.W. Bullinger. The Witness of the Stars]

Truly, the heavens declare the glory of YHVH! The Lesser Lights in overwhelming testimony – like the extended branches of the Menorah point their light to the Center One – The Great Light who illuminates Creation; The Light which envelopes those who are 'in Him'. Allow me to show you the thoughts of the Psalmist on this very issue:

Psalm 19:1-6

Verse one begins by telling us the heavens declare, H#5608, סָפַר caphar, to score with a mark, inscribe, to tell, to speak, to narrate or recount an event, to be polished or shine. It becomes very plain their purpose is to convey in an 'illuminated' message, the glory of YHVH.

Psalm 19:2-6 Day unto day uttereth speech, and night unto night sheweth knowledge. There is no speech nor language, where their voice is not heard. Their line is gone out through all the earth, and their words to the end of the world. In them hath he set a tabernacle for the sun, which is as a bridegroom coming out of his chamber, and rejoiceth as a strong man to run a race. His going forth is from the end of the heaven, and his circuit unto the ends of it: and there is nothing hid from the heat thereof.

The Hebrew word for sun, H#8121, שֶׁמֶשׁ, shemesh, reminds us of the Niyr Elohiym – The Lamp of YHVH or Menorah! The Center candle is called the 'Shamash' or Servant, from H#8120, שְׁמַשׁ Shamash, to minister. It is used in Daniel 7:10 to describe the Ancient of Days out of whom a fiery, H#5135, נוּר nuwr, (fire, to shine, a lamp) stream (H#5103, נְהַר, nehar, a river of light flowing together as one) issues! This seems to personify the events of Genesis 1:3 where the "Ancient of Days" spoke light into creation! His word is light, it is sound, and it has the 'colors' of the Rainbow within it. It is this same picture described by the Prophet Ezekiel in chapter 1 verse 28 where he gives details of what appeared as both fire and a rainbow: There are only two places in the Old Testament where both 'bow and cloud' appear together. One of them is Genesis 9 and the Rainbow Covenant, the other is here in Ezekiel 1.

The apocryphal book of Revelation adds to this by describing the rainbow as a Levitical emerald. The Levitical tribe is a kind of human rainbow. As mediating priests, the Levites are a continuous human reminder of YHVH's promises. The Levites also stand between Israel and the throne of YHVH, to absorb the wrath of the Creator that breaks out against the wicked, just as Aaron stops a plague with his censor (Numbers 16:41-50). Aaron makes a cloud with the incense, and stands in his rainbow-colored clothing in the midst of the cloud and stops the plague. That censor was a firebox; could it perhaps serve as a portable 'LIGHT'?

The priesthood, by definition, functioned as a 'light carrier', and as such, would have resembled a human rainbow. Now that human rainbow is serving to renew the covenant as the priesthood attired in the Variegated Robe of Joseph - teaching the Hebrew Torah to the Nations. We are like an emerald lens, the green-tinted visor, surrounding Father's throne, through which He views the rest of the world. As we gather around the throne, we ourselves become the precious stones that are the memorials of Yahweh's promise, reminders to Him to keep covenant. This is seen in the Name given the first man – ADAM, which, as we've discussed can be rendered 'I will blood you'. I will clothe you with a luminescent garment, capable of absorbing and reflecting My Light – Word!

> *1 Peter 2:5 Ye also, as lively stones, are built up a spiritual house, an holy priesthood, to offer up spiritual sacrifices, acceptable to YHVH by Yahshua Mashiach.*

The Greek word for lively indicates to breathe, to live. Much like those hot, fiery, living coals Aaron used to staunch the plague. Fire literally breathes! Ask any fireman who has ever watched a house in flames! The fire fanatically draws oxygen to feed it, at times creating winds of 100mph!

This seems to be the hidden message of Isaiah 6:6 where the unclean lips of the Great Prophet are sanctified by a live coal from the altar. Lips would indicate the ability to speak, particularly, on behalf of YHVH. The Hebrew word for COAL, H# 7531, רִצְפָּה ritspah, indicates a 'glowing stone'. Its origin can be traced to the word, resheph, which indicates a flame or lightning bolt! A curious Hebrew word pun can be seen here as well. The KJV tells us a being called a Seraphim (from H#8314, שָׂרָף saraph, an angel) took the live coal. It is curious to see the above word for lightning bolt – resheph – which also comes from this same word saraph! The verse could just as have easily read: A flying lightning bolt came unto me a living coal or lightning bolt and touched my lips! That ought to change anyone's tongue! As a result, Isaiah is commissioned to tell the people they are able to hear but, don't understand, they see but can't perceive. This seems to be the condition of Isaiah before encountering the LIGHTNING BOLT of the Creators Word, the Rainbow of His Covenant which was placed on his lips, H#8193, Saphah, the lip, or language, giving him the ability to speak. The people in this last day will be healed and have their sins purged by that same Holy Tongue! Incidentally, Isaiah is translated as 'Yahweh is Salvation', a cognate form of Yahshua, who was the Living Word! Isaiah, like Yahshua, came with his lips bearing the Language of Torah! Scripture is plain the Language and thus, the Book has been sealed for a season. As we write, this seal is being broken. Based on Ancient Treaty Language only an ambassador of the King may break the seal. I.E. divulge the contents, expose what has been hidden. We cannot boast of ourselves. We are only 'somebody' to the extent that we represent the King! Anything short of that exposes our limitations. *But, we have this treasure – His Rainbow Language – in earthen vessels that the excellency of the power may be of YHVH and not of us!* 2Corinthians 4:7 Special care should be taken to grasp the full intent of this 'treasure in earthen vessels', if we're to associate it with this power of YHVH. What pray tell, does it have to do with the Ancient Language?

According to ancient documents, when title deeds were transferred there were at least three copies. One given to the participants each, another was taken and buried in an earthen vessel. Jeremiah 32: 14 gives a vivid account of such a transaction. The terms or language of the document was binding upon those participating. That's the premise of 2 Corinthians 4: 7: We have this treasure i.e. the title deed of our inheritance, the Living word of YHVH - the Language of Creation. Yet, we have been alienated from this covenant document for generations. It was intentionally hidden, sealed if you will by the Great Suzerain King until a worthy one comes who is able to break the seal. The intent of YHVH has been to conceal the language until a specific time from those who would casually search for it. At the appointed time, He would restore the Pure Language to the People! The Ordinary Believer, who is hungry and thirsty after righteousness can now be filled to the level of his hunger! The title deed is available for use. We must begin to possess what is ours and to depose those who have usurped our inheritance. Let's look behind the veil to witness the clandestine efforts of those solicited by YHVH to seal the language, i.e. burry the Ancient Treasure – title deed, until the end!

Chapter 15

Daniel Conspires to Hide the Language

In my efforts to provide to you conclusive evidence regarding the present restoration of the Rainbow Language, we have naturally touched on how this 'communication link' between the Creator and man suffered destruction in incremental stages. In particular, we've looked at the Genesis accounts of Eden, the Great Flood and also the Tower of Babel incident. It is my opinion the final effort to conceal the Tongue of Yahweh from all but the few who were initiated into its sacred care, began with the venerable Prophet Daniel! As we followed the enthralling twists and turns of this mystery we found empirical data linking Daniel to several other notable persons in Scripture, compelling us to the conclusion that his was the grandest conspiracy of the ages!

Take a deep breath here, you're going to explore a strange new world and boldly go where few men have gone before! We'll begin our Enterprise (Another bit of poetic license☺) by examining this name 'Daniel', H#1840, דָּנִיֵּאל Daniye'l, rendered 'Yah is my judge'. As a young man he is taken hostage in the first deportation to Babylon and lasts through the transition to the Persian rule. Daniel is believed to have exerted great influence upon the Babylonian – Chaldean astronomers of his day, the evidence of which is seen in the Gospel accounts of the Wise men from the East who are searching for the New King – Messiah! (Matt. 2:1) Because Daniel had been made a Eunuch he has no offspring to whom he may pass his material legacy. Many Scholars believe the gifts brought by these Chaldean astronomers were indeed, the inheritance of Daniel who became the chief among them and who reserved these treasures for Messiah. The gifts enable the financially constrained Joseph (who hasn't the means to offer an expensive sacrifice and must settle for a turtle-dove or pigeon only a short while earlier) the means to relocate his family to Egypt to escape Herod's persecution! Daniel quite frankly, is seen in some rather unusual places, which honestly, the casual search will not reveal. One of those places catenates a series of (heretofore) anonymous persons by means of their role in hiding the Rainbow language for a season. Let's start with the Scroll of Esther.

The Melilla (Scroll) of Esther has intrigued scholars for generations, primarily, because YHVH Himself is never addressed in the book. Yet, hidden within the depths of the Hebrew language a plot twists – its' tentacles connecting many of the Prophets whose works are eschatological in scope. Ezekiel, Daniel, Nehemiah, Ezra, Zechariah, Joel and Jeremiah! Let's examine the name of Esther:

♦ Esther, H#635   אסתר   *'Ecter*

It can mean, 'star', also hidden. It is cognate with H#631 - H#633, meaning to bind, obligate, imprison, a bond of abstention or agreement. What is YHVH obligating Himself in a bond of abstention to hide? And, from whom? Could it be the language? The Coat of colors? WE WILL FIND OUT! Remember the setting of this account is connected with the supposed end of the 70 years of Israel's captivity. She is also called 'Hadassah' her Hebrew name. *See earlier chapters.

The theme of Esther revolves around an ancient Hebrew festival called Purim. The purpose of this remarkable event reveals through history that Yahweh has planned the End from the Beginning and is a rehearsal depicting Esther in the role of the

Bride, who like Esther, is conspicuously hidden until a future time of great upheaval – where she will have another encounter with Haman, the Anti-Messiah. Through this testing she becomes the Chosen Bride of the King and is (along with her people Israel) vindicated. However, as we peel back the layers we find something else masked further underneath, linking us to the final revelation of the language of Torah, the Hebrew tongue, which was also to be secreted away until this final appointment of destiny, where the Bride, her husband, her kindred and her people will be revealed. Wait for it...we'll be back to visit this... For now, on to her Hebrew name which is...

♦ Hadassah, H#1919   הדסה   *Hadaccah*

Translated, myrtle. However, Klein's Etymological Dictionary of the Hebrew Language tells us its' root, Hey-Dalet-Samech, means to totter, to shuffle along, to walk with tottering steps. *Remember this! It is closely related to H#1917, haddam, a noun meaning pieces, to tear into pieces. It is used in Dan. 3:29 to refer to people, nations and tongues who speak against YHVH being TORN! Ironically, the myrtle tree branches were used to construct the Booths of Tabernacles, called, H#5521, sukkah, the root of which, H#5520, sok, means a cover, or hiding place. Not much else is revealed regarding the meaning of the myrtle tree. However, the ancients believed it held the key to immortality and had connections to a true and lasting marriage. Wouldn't the House of Israel, those 10 Northern Tribes dispersed into the Nations be torn by YHVH and themselves torn from the Covenant Language? Now you understand the significance of the Outcasts being 're-gathered' coincident with, the restoration of the Pure Tongue!

With the underlying threat of extinction on the cusp of their release from captivity here in Esther's story, the future connection is obvious! Israel is threatened with annihilation in the coming season during our day which parallels Purim and is commonly known as "Jacob's Troubles". As with Esther - though YHVH has hidden Himself, His Word for a time, causing us to shuffle along and totter having been torn from Torah –Hebrew, because of our Idolatry, He has promised to provide a future hiding place, a 'Sok'. Spelled Samech-Kaf, its value = 80 the same as the Hebrew letter Pey, meaning mouth, to speak and also the value of H#3550, kahunnah, the priesthood or office. It is the restoration or building of the Sukkah, that reminds us of a promise to restore the pure language as a hiding place, a covert in times of trouble! What was hidden now becomes the hiding place! How marvelous to remember the first Exodus and the initial stopping place: It was also named Sukkot! The place where we will Tabernacle with Him!

The Palace at Sushan!

Literary license allows an author some leeway when producing his wares for the reader to contemplate. However, you're probably wondering what in the world does what some deem as "questionable" (the practice of celebrating Purim) have to do with a book dedicated to the Hebrew language. Admittedly, it can stump the novice. However, you've hung around to this point and you know how Abba Yahweh loves to hide things for you! The word Purim is translated from the plural form of H#6332, פּוּר Puwr, inferring a 'lot' or 'piece'. It also connotes to break, crush or to bring to naught. If we dissect it a bit farther, the two-letter root is formed of the Pey-Resh, and can indicate 'the fruit of the lips'. It would seem the hidden meaning behind Purim serves to expose the efforts of the enemy to crush or bring to naught, the fruit of (YHVH's) lips. I.E. what He had declared regarding preserving a remnant of Jacob throughout history. These hints reflect backward at the prophetical declaration of Genesis 3:15 where once again, we're told the Serpent would attempt to bruise the heel, (H#6119, עָקֵב 'aqeb) of the woman's seed while his own head

(Seat of power and authority) is being crushed. *Note the connection between the word heel and Jacob! Their spelled with the same 3-letter root, Ayin-Qof-Bet

Esther 1:2 tells us this event leading to Purim occurs at Sushan, H#7800, שׁוּשַׁן Shuwshan, translated here as, lily. The Psalmist uses the word in Ps. 60:1, to describe a musical instrument, shushan eduwth, "שׁוּשַׁן עֵדוּת". The Ayin-Dalet of 'eduwth' indicates a witness, thus, this looks like 'witness of the lillies'. However, in 1Chron. 29:2 the Shin-Yod-Shin root is used to describe the white, linen material of the Tabernacle. It also is similar to the word for the number six in Hebrew. Incidentally, 6 is the gematria of the word, בַּד H#906, pronounced 'bad', a noun that describes linen! Remember, linen was the material of choice for the priestly garments and as such, could have represented the garment used to cover Adam after the fall, much like the "swaddling clothes of the baby Yahshua" replacing the garment of Pure Light - the Pure language of Torah! If we look back at Ps. 60 it deals with David (Messiah figure) when he strove with Aramnaharaim, Aram can be translated as Syrian – Assyrian and Naharim means two rivers. This is the location of ancient Babylon the place where the Tongues were confused! Seems like Babylon always shows up when the Language of Torah is in preeminence. It would seem the shushan eduwth, can also indicate witness of the linen garment, the priestly vestment. Much like the Light Mantle we've been discussing at length.

Biblical proof tells us Sushan was also the residence of both Daniel and Nehemiah during their captivity. Let's look: Neh. 1:1 & Dan. 8:2

♦ Nehemiah, H#5156　　נחמיה　　*Něchemyah*

It is translated as; 'YHVH comforts'. You'll note the 2-letter root stem, Nun-Chet, which spells Noah. He constructs and enters into a vessel (Ark) to preserve humanity from destruction! Remember its' (the ark) dimensions? 300x50x30. *Note the gematria: 300 = Ruach Elohiym רוּחַ אֱלֹהִים 50 = Jubilee, 30= Lamed, to urge toward, to teach, instruct. The Spirit of YHVH will urge you toward the teachings and instructions that will bring your jubilee! As a parallel, Nehemiah rebuilds Jerusalem, which could figuratively also be an Ark or vessel of sanctuary! Incidentally, 350 is also the gematria of the Hebrew word for Tongue – Lashon! Look here next at Nehemiah's father's name:

♦ Hachaliah, H#2446   חכליה   *Chakalyah*

It is translated, "When YHVH Enlightens", from the root of H#2447, which means to be dark, dull, as in the eyes.

♦ Daniel, H#1840   דניאל   *Daniye'l*

YHVH is my judge. It has a numeric value the same as H#5542, selah, a musical term indicating a pause or silence in the score. Hmmm? Aren't we stringed instruments and Hebrew the notes?

Remember, Daniel is made a Eunuch. Lev. 21:16-18 tells us a Eunuch cannot offer the 'bread of YHVH'. Bread and Word are synonymous. There were other blemishes that disqualified one from priestly service as well. Yet, without the word, there is no seed. We have been estranged from the Seed of His Word, vagabonds who wonder aimlessly. The absence of His seed in us caused each of us to become spiritual Eunuchs unable to reproduce without the Torah!

Most scholars believe Daniel is referred to in Esther 4: 5 as, Hatach, H#2047, התך Hathak, translated by the Strong's as; 'verily, truth'. However, it is cognate with H#2046, hittuk, (same root letters) meaning a melting, (smelting of metal). It is used in Ezek. 22:22 as a simile of how Israel will be purified of her dross. Was Hathak – Daniel involved in smelting, the Truth, that Israel might be purified of her dross? We'll connect these dots more as we go. Now, let's look at another 'Minor' Prophet who had hands-on experience with the Language of Creation!

Ezra, the Scribe

It is quite obvious that Ezra the Scribe was also a contemporary of Daniel, Nehemiah, and Esther, as was Ezekiel, and Jeremiah.

♦   Ezra, H#5830   עֶזְרָא   '*Ezra*

Translated 'help'. However, by breaking apart the Hebrew we see something additional. The Ayin can mean, an eye, or a gate, womb, or spring, well. The Zayin-Resh-Alef (Alef and Ayin are interchangeable) root – zera, meaning seed. Thus, his name could also mean the womb or eye of the seed. He was a scribe, H#5608, סֹפֵר caphar, to count, to tell, inscribe, to rehearse. By dissecting the Hebrew letters, we find the Samech infers, to uphold, to lay, to sustain, and to support in a legal sense. The 2-letter root, Pey-Resh, par, means the fruit of the mouth! Ezra was a well, a womb or repository of seed/word and his vocation allowed him to uphold and support the Fruit of the Mouth, the very words of YHVH! By the way, the Law of YHVH required the King to write his own Torah. Aren't we fond of referring to ourselves as 'Kings and Priests'? Now, on to another Prophet who we've previously seen linked to the Restored Bones of the House of Joseph, those bones representing the DNA of Joseph, who like the patriarchs before him was chosen as High Priest in the earth tasked with the oversight of the Lashon Qodesh – Holy Tongue! The bones of Joseph, like those same bones of Elisha are capable of resurrecting the body of those who come in contact with the Anointing resonant within their marrow! Talk about changing the Genome Sequence! Just touch the Word! Like the woman with the issue of blood (she was nid-dah, unclean, like the adulterous woman of Numbers 5) who encountered the Life-Altering Light, Sound, and Color of the Menorah – The Rainbow Himself!

♦ Ezekiel, H#3168   יחזקאל   *Yĕchezqe'l*

YHVH strengthens. He was the son of Buzi, H#941, בוזי Buwziy, trans. 'my shame or contempt'. Thus, out of my shame and contempt (what brought this on?) YHVH strength-ened me.

♦ Jeremiah, H#3414   ירמיה   *Yirmĕyah*

Commonly translated as; 'whom YHVH has appointed'. The suffix is Yod-Hey for YHVH. The problem of translation lies with the Resh-Mem-Hey, root, which can mean, to throw, to shoot (an arrow). As a verb it can mean to deceive, beguile. The Yod prefix shows action and personal possession. He was, is and will be doing something. Is it possible that YHVH used Jeremiah as an arrow (Torah) to beguile or deceive? Hold on, don't get fidgety! The Truth is a deception to those who are outside of Covenant! His father was Hilkiah, H#2518, חלקיה Chilqiyah 'my portion is YHVH'. This is an-other compromised definition. The root is H#2505-2512, Chet-Lamed-Qof, meaning to divide, to flatter, a mouth that spins things deceitfully!

Though Daniel was told to seal up the (words of the) Book, these men and women who themselves were hearing from YHVH would have been privy to the same and as such, became instru-ments used by YHVH much like the flaming sword in Genesis 3: 24, which turned, H#2015, הָפַךְ haphak, (to turn oneself, to change oneself, to transform, i.e. disguise) every way to prevent Adam from access to the Tree of Life in the Garden. I am convinced YHVH transformed Himself in a manner that would disguise Him from anyone but the diligent seeker until such a time as this! The Books and all they contain are now being unsealed!

Why would YHVH hide or disguise His word? What purpose would it serve?

> ***Amos 3:7** Surely the YHVH will do nothing, but he revealeth his secret unto his servants the prophets.*

Let's look at a couple of Hebrew words here: Look at the key words in this verse below.

♦ Nothing, H#1697   דבר   *dabar*

Word, speech.

♦ Revealeth, H#1540   גלה   *galah*

Reveal, to uncover (to uncover the nakedness Lev. 18:6). Also, to take into exile, a spring or bowl. As Israel goes into bondage in Egypt their nakedness, like that of Adam & Eve and Noah is uncovered! Ironically, the root Gimmel-Lamed, hints at the cup positioned at the top of the Lampstand - The Menorah, The Light of the world. The cup functioned as His seed repository – like the Language of creation, anointing those who by contact with it (Him) become themselves filled with oil – Shemen, and are ignited by His Power. *Note the root of Galgal, to roll away, a wheel, circle. It happens to be the root stem of Golgotha – the Place of the Skull, which indicates an area where polling or head counting (the common term today is a census) took place. It was here, that Yahshua rolled away the reproach of Egypt and Shemened Israel again, restoring the covering, waiting until the end of our season of bondage! It was here, outside the Tabernacle, where the writings of Daniel were kept. Being a Eunuch his works were not kept in the Sanctuary! He had no seed or lineage. To remedy that happening to you, the death of Yahshua counted your head once again, numbering you among the Thousands of Israel restoring your lineage – by changing your Bloodline.

*2 **Peter** 1:4 Whereby are given unto us exceeding great and precious promises: that by these ye might be partakers of the divine nature, having escaped the corruption that is in the world through lust.*

Divine = Theios – Godlike; nature = character. You have been transformed. A metamorphosis has taken place. Romans 12: 1-3.

♦ Secret, H#5475   סוֹד   *cowd*

Counsel. It is this word, Sod, that is used to describe a level of understanding beyond the surface, it hints at a level of confidentiality beyond casual! That's why it was necessary to hide his word to protect the confidentiality and sanctity of His Seed – which is His Bloodline! It's Noah all over again! And we will see the same conditions as in the Days of Noah in just a short time!

♦ Servants, H#5650   עֶבֶד   *'ebed*

Servant, a slave. One must note the biblical time period assigned a slave – 6 years – 6000 years. This word's root can also mean to carry out, to perform. It is the time for the Outcasts, the Slaves to implement the Word of YHVH! Common sense understanding of the Hebrew would insist that if they each were complicit in the "Sealing" of the Book, then we should also expect to hear the "unsealing" from several different sources. I.E. confirmation from many men who all concur this unsealing is taking place now!

There are 44 letters in Amos 3:7. This value is equal to H#4055, מד mad, a Hebrew word for garment. If we reverse those letters it spells Dalet-Mem, blood, the covering providing the light or word of YHVH. While here, let's look at the Name of Amos in Hebrew to see another connecting piece.

- Amos, H#5986   עמוס   *'Amowc*

To bear a burden. The book concerns words which he saw, H#2372, חזה chazah; this is a more poetic Hebrew word than ra'ah, to see. It refers to seeing YHVH or perhaps the visible Astronomical signs, etc. Amos was with the herdsmen, the Hebrew word is noqed, meaning shepherd. However, the same root Nun-Qof-Dalet, is an adjective meaning speckled, like the 'speckled' cattle of Jacob who had their DNA changed when the peeled branches were placed in their water troughs. The root stem, Nun-Qof, refers to what is white in color, pure, like Light – (seed/word). These men with Amos were from Tekoa, H#8620, תקוע Tĕqowa', translated, stockade, (a place of safety, security) it is a wordplay for 'signal'. Its root can mean a trumpet (blown to unite the people) and in its verb form, to pitch a tent, to settle. Sounds as if Amos and these others secured for a season i.e. 'sealed up the books' that were the DNA clinic until the time of the end. Perhaps a trumpet will herald this great event! Let's see if we can extract a proper definition from the above words:

Like Daniel and the others, *Amos bore the burden of the words he saw written in the heavens. With the shepherds of his day, he brought the living Torah, the Pure Light, to a place of security until the trumpet signals it is time to unite the People (Zeph. 3:9) and settle them forever!* Isn't our burden to shoulder as well? Frankly, the Priests bore the Ark of the Covenant upon their shoulders, symbolic of that responsibility. In the same fashion, the House of Joseph was also tasked with the trust of keeping the Torah. We must gird our loins accordingly, else we find ourselves unfit for the task.

One More Prophet...

Most scholars believe that Joel was also contemporary with Daniel. Few fail to acknowledge his message as pertinent to the ends days and filled with foreboding concerning the scourge that will assault the House of Israel. Let's examine his name:

◆   Joel, H#3100   יוֹאֵל   *Yow'el*

Translated as YHVH is God. However, the Hebrew cognate root, Yod-Alef-Lamed, Ya'al, can mean to determine, to undertake, to attempt to do. His father, Pethuel, H#6602, trans. 'vision of Yah', though the root, H#6601, pathach, carries the idea of opening a door. Thus, these names imply, that in the midst of the coming devastation, there will be those determined to open the door to YHVH. How? Through the language of Torah, the Hebrew. That shouldn't seem so farfetched. Even the movies are preparing you for counterfeit 'gods' who will open doors or portals and make their advent here known upon the earth! I submit, you should be prepared to do battle!

There is another foreboding possibility as well. Each Hebrew letter or word has both a blessing and curse associated with it depending on one's relationship with the Creator. The above word H#6601 pathach, can also indicate to be open-minded, easily seduced. This is seen in 1 Timothy:

1 Timothy 4:1-3 Now the Spirit speaketh expressly, that in the latter times some shall depart from the faith, giving heed to seducing spirits, and doctrines of devils; Speaking lies in hypocrisy; having their conscience seared with a hot iron; forbidding to marry, and commanding to abstain from meats, which God hath created to be received with thanksgiving of them which believe and know the truth.

Eve was seduced, Noah was seduced. King David was seduced. In each case, the enemy of YHVH attempts to slander His Torah, the result of which, leads to the consumption or destruction of the Bride whose loins are uncovered! This continued until Noah entered the Ark, which seems to correlate to the Fall Festivals where Yahshua will take His Bride into the Protected Place, while the bitter waters of judgment inundate the perverse ones.

Each of the foregoing Prophets were I believe, contemporary with the principals of the story of Esther. She is forever remembered as arriving 'for just such a time as this'. As we look forward, the day finds us living in anonymity as did Esther - The bride estranged from her family, her kindred. However, as the language of Creation is restored, Esther's role as mediator and ultimately – Queen - begins to transform her role and to identify her to the Nations! The timing could not be more significant to the deliverance of Israel as a People! Like Esther we must not allow the next Haman to seduce us. What will be the identifying markers of the kindred of Esther? Where, dear Reader are these Kindred who will rise up collectively to represent the King?

Chapter 16

Esther's Kindred Revealed?

This presents a bit of a head-scratcher to many reading this book. Surely you recall that Esther's name means hidden – not known. Thus, it seems her lineage should be in dispute as she figuratively represents the House of Israel today. Like Esther, we've been hidden, our identity kept secret until such a time as this!

Let's visit this hidden clue again.

> **Esther 2:20** *Esther had not [yet] shewed her kindred nor her people...*

♦ Shewed, H#5046   בֿגַד   *nagad*

To tell, report, to make known. The same root letters can also mean, to flow, to issue forth, like water from a stream. As a preposition, it indicates before, in front of, corresponding to and is used to indicate Eve's likeness to Adam. The next cognate word, H#5050, nagah, means to illuminate, to shine.

◆ Kindred, H#4138   מוֹלֶדֶת   *mowledeth*

Birth, family background, origin. Interestingly, the root stem, Mem-Vav-Lamed, mul, means circumcision. The Dalet-Tav suffix forms the word, H#1881, Da'at, meaning word, law, etc. Females aren't circumcised physically, so, what is being said here?

◆ People, H#5971   עַם   *'am*

This word means people. It is from H#6004, 'amam, a verb meaning to grow dim, to hide, and to lose brightness. Also, to join together, to gather, to collect.

Our extrapolated definition becomes an inducement, a source of provocation, if we heed it, as our own identity becomes apparent in the days ahead of us!

Esther had not yet made known that which issued forth from her, the living water, made her like Adam and would illuminate, as her source of circumcision, the tongue of the Law/Torah. Though captivity had caused it to be hidden, its brightness lost, at the appointed time it would GATHER THE OUTCASTS AND DELIVER THEM AGAIN!

Why would the Language of Torah be sealed until the End?

Ostensibly, the enigma that once was Esther – Spiritual Israel - is fast becoming a force to reckon with. Her foes have launched a concerted effort – though misguided - to destroy physical Israel. In their efforts, they have neglected 'Spiritual Israel'. They have yet to decipher her intent and have sorely underestimated her power. Her power lies within the Cloak of Light which, once she is enveloped in it, will cause her to be transformed from slave girl into the Queen. As Haman learned to his chagrin; this time Spiritual Israel will also not tolerate Haman in the bed chamber! Though hidden, in a role reminiscent of the Wizard of Oz, the spiritual powers that supported Haman – like YHVH – may seem as if they are invisible in this book! Far from it! The deductive powers of those who immerse themselves in His Word are able to see beyond the vail. Like the words of the Prophet Elijah to his servant, "There are far more with us, than against us". In the same fashion, the clues exposing the connections with Daniel, Ezekiel, Joel, Amos and others are conclusive: The Restoration of His Pure Language is happening as we speak. Simultaneously, the Body of Eve – The hidden Esther - is being created, informing the world once again YHVH is going to have a people who will be fruitful and multiply and replenish and who will subdue and have dominion over every facet of His Kingdom on behalf of the Great King! Rise up! Oh, Mighty One and let your enemies be scattered! HalleluYah!

Many of you who read this will think of this author as one brick short of a full load. Why or how would YHVH deliberately conceal His word and from whom? Then, at a pre-ordained season allow it to be revealed again? What prohibits the Enemy – *who as the Prince of the Air and controls most of the world's communication* - from accessing this same power and using it against those who remain skeptical?

Let me share this:

Professor Andrew Weiner, Joseph Lukens, and other team members from Purdue University's engineering department had this to say upon conclusion of exhaustive research attempting to "time cloak" secret messages by manipulating light conducted along an optical fiber, making all such information practically invisible to all but the intended recipient. *If your own body is comprised of 'congealed light' i.e. blood. Could those vessels serve as optical fibers enabling your whole body to become a condenser or a transmitter of information, much like an electrical current? The Ark of the Covenant was the prototype! The quote is as follows:*

"With this new device, we don't just limit ourselves to thinking about cloaks as a way of preventing somebody from getting information, but also as a way to enable communication," says Joseph Lukens, an electrical engineer at Purdue. "One guy sees nothing, the other guy sees everything." *What are you seeing? There are far more with us than against us! (Italics mine).*

If in fact, our vocal communication can be transferred and altered, via specific light frequencies, how feasible is it to assume that the Prince of the Air – Satan – can also intercept and 're-form' those same communiques – thereby, compromising our own personal spiritual and physical security, as well as, those entrusted to our care? It would behoove one to move at the opportune time in order to circumvent the enemy's plans for you and to speak only what the Word of YHVH says regarding specific situations. Mark 4 declares: Take heed what you hear! [All italics in the above 3 paragraphs are mine]

Perhaps the import of what you just read escaped you. Throughout this work we've shown Scriptural evidence of the latent power of light and its ability to enhance or inhibit communication. The Powers that Be, those who occupy the seat of authority as Lucifer's regents in the earth are well aware of the capability and are fully prepared to demonstrate their effective countermeasures against the Word of YHVH. These weapons are only as powerful as our ignorance and lack of effort allows. They will mask themselves as Angels of Light bringing a pseudo-message of 'Peace'. They will not fathom their own deception as the Great Suzerain King of Creation answers the "Just Cause" against them. You must acknowledge the line drawn in the sand and choose your side. Does this sound fatalistic? It is for those who oppose the King!

The Prophets have foretold that Spiritual powers will be unleashed upon the earth, beings who take on the physical forms of giants displaying lying signs and wonders after their god, Lucifer, will wreak havoc among those who avail not themselves of the

Garment of Protection. The Language, which as a weapon has no opposition. It will change your DNA and assault the throne of those powers who foolishly believe they will exalt their thrones above the stars of Yah! Recently, in a Torah study, an astounding connection was made correlating the 21st Torah portion of the year – to the 21st century. The number 21 is also the gematria of Strong's H#272 'achuzzah אחזה meaning a possession, property, inheritance; from H#270 'achaz אחז grasp, take hold, seize, take possession, to provide for; *the same number, 21, points both towards something being lost – the garment and kingdom torn apart – and to something being possessed again! Josephs' garment was torn by his brothers and frankly, the fleshly garment of our Messiah was also torn in like manner.

Sounds remarkably like the account of Genesis 1:1, 2 where the perfect Creation is set into motion. By the actions of the Rebellious One, what results is chaos – the Hebrew phrase is: 'Tohu v'bohu' meaning waste and desolate. It would set the pattern for the Genesis three rebellions and each subsequent episode where the inheritance seemed to slip from the grasp of the King's servant. Realistically, there NEVER has been a plan B! It has always been the intent of the Great Suzerain to allow free choice and then lavish His affections on those who will honor His Covenant! There never ceased to be a Remnant! She is alive and well!

So, it would seem out of our next query should naturally flow the answer that has seemed to elude generations: By what means do we possess, inherit, seize and take hold of this garment? Genesis 48:4 is a quote from Jacob on behalf of the Creator Himself to his son Joseph:

> **Genesis 48:4** *And said unto me, Behold, I will make thee fruitful, and multiply thee, and I will make of thee a multitude of people; and will give this land to thy seed after thee for an everlasting possession.*

As we saw in the previous paragraphs the Hebrew word for 'possession' is: H#272, אֲחֻזָּה. The letter Alef - א as a prefix = I will & חזה chazah (H#2372) indicates, to see, perceive, look, behold, prophesy, provide; this term often refers to seeing YHVH or astronomical observations, a prophetic vision or insight; this term becomes a declaration from Yahweh – "I will provide for Joseph to see, to perceive, and he will look upon this!" In a large part, our ability to see entails having a working knowledge of the Signs in the Heavens – the Menorah of Creation - revealing the prophetical message written in the constellations. These signs in the heavens are emblematic of the 'last days'. Simultaneous with the restoration of the language we're beginning to return to the Ancient Hebrew understanding of these Constellations provided for us by Yahweh Himself. As a result, we are now being admonished to gaze heavenward, to understand the witness in the heavens and thus, see, beholding far more than just stellar luminaries. The information thus provided, lends peculiar insight regarding the origin of the Fallen Ones and their wicked, DNA perverted offspring, the Giants, whose story is told along with that of the Conqueror Who Comes – Messiah!

Ezekiel 32:27 refers to these fallen beings as: גִּבּוֹרִים נֹפְלִים gibborim nephyilm – The Mighty Fallen Ones!

In our earlier study of Amos, we were taught his name indicated 'one who bears a burden'. In this particular instance, where we see the same word mentioned above (Chazah) used in the phrase: 'words that he saw', H#2372, חזה chazah, it would seem the burden then is the responsibility of shouldering the vision or words which he beheld, much like Joseph and Levi were tasked to shoulder the Ark containing the Torah. In his book, it seems as if Amos casually mentions a couple of Constellations: (The Seven Stars (Pleiades) and Orion. Both are in the constellation Taurus: Amos 5: 8, 9) this escapes the casual observer; you on the other hand, have begun to "see". Oh, by the way, in the days just before Moshe, the House or Sign in which the sun resided was this Taurus, i.e. 'The Bull'. At the coming of Moshe the equinox turned and the ruling sign became that of the Aries the Lamb or Shepherd. It doesn't go unnoticed that Pharaohs' name can be rendered house of the bull, while Moshe represented the Shepherd of the Lamb. Interesting isn't it?

Indulge me a bit as we peel back the covering to expose what else Amos intended.

In Aramaic culture, the later term niyphlim refers to the Constellation of Orion, and thus Nephilim are considered the offspring of Orion in mythology. Amos understood that a counterfeit – Lucifer and his Anti-Messiah, appearing as "The Hunter", would fill the role of Haman, attempting to destroy the Seed of Esther – The Hidden One. Amos 5:9 says *YHVH will* 'balag', H#1082, to *burst forth upon*, to be brilliant, to shine forth, illuminate (Light-Torah-Hebrew) upon *the spoiled*, H#7701, שׁד shod, violence, destruction. This word can also indicate a demon or devil, a 'Shade'. The name Orion was probably spelt OARION originally, providing a variant meaning 'coming forth as light'. The Akkadian name was UR-ANA 'the light of heaven'. The word Taurus, bull is spelled, Shin-Vav-Resh, Shor, in Hebrew and though it means ox, or bull, it can also mean a wall that surrounds a well. A source of protection for the Living Waters, the language of Torah! Like Esther, you are the 'hidden one'. For just such a time as this you have been called! The 'message of the luminaries' who speak of the Light Himself, the Rainbow Language, has also been occluded, sealed up along with the Books of Daniel. They are awaiting you – it is time.

Chapter 17

The Unveiling of the Heavens

Surely you recall in Genesis 15 the discussion of Abraham and YHVH regarding Abraham's offspring? In response, The Creator takes him outside and declares:

> **Genesis 15:5** *And he brought him forth abroad, and said, Look now toward heaven, and tell the stars, if thou be able to number them: and he said unto him, So shall thy seed be.*

The same Hebrew word inserted here is translated into two different English words (go figure) for both 'tell' and 'number'. It is H#5608, סָפַר caphar, to tell, recite, read, record, and cipher. It is also the root of the Hebrew word for book. Cepher! Literally, Abraham is being told to 'cipher' or read what is written in the heavens for it tells about your seed! Gal. 3 reminds us this seed was singular as in Yahshua! It was a veiled, dual reference to the whole house of Israel and Yahshua, both of whom are testified of in the stellar luminaries!

It would seem that Father is divulging His Plans: The terms of which, cannot be fathomed without the understanding which the Hebrew language provides. For verification, a witness was indeed written in the Earth – the Living Torah – and in the Heavens via the message of the Constellations. There are 12 constellations; each one representing a specific tribe of the 12 sons of Jacob, as depicted in the 12 breastplate stones. They also are found representing one of the 12 months. Ironically, the story of Esther, whose name is etymologically from the same root as the Greek word for star (Aster) provides a segue allowing us to garner a peculiar insight from what is arguably, the oldest 'written witness' attesting to the Language of Creation! Once more, without the Hebrew you will not grasp its fullness. I want to establish a connection between these Lights (Gen. 1:14 מָאוֹר ma'owr, 'from or out of the owr') and that Light of Genesis 1: 3 which we've painstakingly shown to be synonymous with Word, Seed, Sound and Color.

Yahshua warns of spectacular celestial events transpiring shortly before and at His 2nd appearing. He describes those events as "fearful". The Greek word used here hints at something hidden.

> ***Luke 21:11*** *And great earthquakes shall be in divers places, and famines, and pestilences; and fearful sights and great signs shall there be from heaven.*

♦ Sights, Gk. G#5400   *phobetron*

That which strikes a terror. However, the root here (Gk. #5401, Phobos) also implies a reverence for one's husband! Reconciling this fear with that of husbandly reverence is almost contradictory, until one understands the signs (Gk. G#4592, semeion, miracle, token, from Sema, a mark to make something known) mean separate things to those who may view them - depending upon the relationship to the Husband!

Let's examine a verse in Jeremiah regarding these celestial signs.

> ***Jeremiah 10:2*** *Thus saith the LORD, Learn not the way of the heathen, and be not dismayed at the signs of heaven; for the heathen are dismayed at them.*

Here, we are admonished to not be dismayed:

♦ Dismayed, H#2865   חתת   *chathath*

Shattered, dismayed, terrified, broke into pieces, by these signs, as the heathen are. What constant is there upon which we may throw ourselves in order to not become shattered? I contend, it is the Language of Creation, which brought these Stellar Luminaries into creation. By the same token, their daily, monthly, yearly and millennial course is also viewed as a constant, a guideline whose message has remained the same since Creation.

♦ Signs, H#226   אות   *owth*

A sign, signal, omen, warning, and a distinguishing mark. *Note the Alef-Tav, with the Vav between, connecting the two. Gen. 1:14 is the first reference to this word and we're told the significance of the shadow pictures of Genesis in Isaiah 46.

> ***Isaih 46:9-10*** *Remember the former things of old: for I am God, and there is none else; I am God, and there is none like me, Declaring the end from the beginning, and from ancient times the things that are not yet done, saying, My counsel shall stand, and I will do all my pleasure.*

These words chosen by the Ruach HaQodesh – Holy Spirit are not idle space fillers. They continue to serve as a frame of reference for the very thing we're pointing toward. Look at their Hebrew meanings:

+ Remember, #2142   זכר   *Zakar*

To mark for remembrance, to record. To observe by remembrance. It is from the root, H#2134, Zak, meaning to be pure, clean, without blemish *and is used in reference to the purity of the heavens and the stars!* What connection can be made from the sign, signal, the warning of the stars and their purity? Why, their untainted, clearly visible message! This word is also cognate to H#2138, zekur, a masc. noun for man. Strongly implying a connection regarding the message concerning the "MAN" written in the stars! This is wholeheartedly confirmed by the Psalmist in chapter 19!

+ Former, H#7223   ראשׁון   *Ri'shown*

First, (as in time) former, primary.

+ None, H#657   אפס   *eh'fes*

None. However, it can mean end, or extremity, as in a boundary. It is part of the name of the place where David met Goliath in 1 Sam. 17:1, 2, called, Ephesdammim. Literally, the boundary of blood!

Our Extrapolated Definition

YHVH is saying, "Remember, recall, observe the former things from the beginning/B're'shiyth/Genesis, for I AM the boundary, the end, the fenced in place! He continues in Verse 10 with: "Declaring", H#5046, nagad, to make conspicuous, to make known, and to announce. To manifest, to bring to the light! What light? To bring to the Stars the manifest plan, message of YHVH. He finishes the chapter declaring, "My salvation (teshuw'ahti) shall not tarry and I will place teshuw'ahti in Zion – The Grafted in

Place! His word sets the boundaries! His Word is light. To move outside the parameters of His word or light is to move into darkness! It's as if one intentionally removes the Coat of Many Colors – the attire of the Firstborn who functions as the Priest of the Family - from off the shoulders! These Stellar Signs leave us without excuse: Hence the words of Moshe: I call heaven and earth as witness against you!

Let's look at one specific sign Yahshua speaks of in Matt. 24:30.

> **Matthew 24:30** *And then shall appear the sign of the Son of man in heaven: and then shall all the tribes of the earth mourn, and they shall see the Son of man coming in the clouds of heaven with power and great glory.*

Note the word for heaven, Gk. #3772, ouranos, heaven, universe, sky. We finished the last chapter visiting this word. As a side bar, it is from this word we get the name of the Planet, Uranus. Uranus is the stellar body that rules the Sign of Aquarius, the water bearer. Luke. 22: 9-13.

Though some may reject what I'm saying, Yahshua makes reference to this very Sign when He is asked by His disciples out of concern for where will they partake of the Passover. He instructs them to look for a man bearing a pitcher of water – This is in reference to: The Man - Aquarius, the Water-Bearer. The Disciples themselves represent the United House of Israel the 2 – fish of Pisces, who are tied together, i.e. they function as one. This Union will lead them to where the Paschal Lamb – Aries - will be slain!

The Progression of the Zodiacal Ecliptic is such that the month of Pisces (the Whole House of Jacob) is followed by Aquarius the Water Bearer, who leads to the Lamb/Aries/Nissan. The 1969 hit song 'Age of Aquarius speaks of the dawning of this new 'Age of enlightenment'. Many who read these materials accuse me of delving into the occult or Kabalistic realm, simply because these groups have had insight regarding what we're just now awakening to. The enemy has taken these truths and perverted them, twisting them for his own use. How can their perversion of the message negate the inherent, powerful truths hidden in the message of the luminaries. Who do you suppose put them there? Enough said!

Numbers 24:17 gives additional insight.

> **Numbers 24:17** *I shall see him, but not now: I shall behold him, but not nigh: there shall come a Star out of Jacob, and a Scepter shall rise out of Israel, and shall smite the corners of Moab, and destroy all the children of Sheth.*

Pisces held Jupiter & Saturn, the furthermost of the planetary lights. There were only 7 visible planetary "lights" comprising the heavenly Menorah or 7-branched candle, the Sun, moon, Mercury, Mars, Venus, Jupiter, Saturn, until the discovery of Uranus in 1781. Uranus comes out of Pisces into Aquarius. Note the word for destroy: H#6979, quwr, to destroy, literally to dig, bore for water! Thus, this Sign Uranus – The Light, Water, Seed, and Word – is the source which will give water to the Water Bearer for the entire House of Jacob. Uranus' solar orbit is 84 years! Thus, it spends 7 years in each house – constellation!

An interesting picture of Uranus, is seen in how its' orbit exactly matches the Hebrew Calendar of 7-days, which pertain to 7,000 yrs. A day is as a 1000 years: 2Pet. 3:8 Ps. 90: 4.

The origin of a clock with 12 hours and 60 minutes is so ancient it has been lost in antiquity. But the pattern from which it emerged is right over our heads. While our sun serves as an hour hand that travels through 12 month-long periods (like "hours") to complete one full cycle. (Jupiter crosses one constellation per year, so it functions like an hour hand that counts years. Interestingly, Yahweh told Moses to count years by sevens and to let the land rest every seventh year (Leviticus 25:3-4). Uranus spends almost exactly one "week" of 7 years in each zodiac constellation, so that it accurately keeps time in the manner the Creator commanded). Saturn does so every 30 yrs. like the lunar cycle.

There is a bright star which traditionally is the "King" of all the stars, and which heads the four stars which represent the clock numerals 12, 3, 6, 9 in the great circle in the sky which is the path of all the planets. Regulus, the Heart of the Lion, the Constellation Leo, is the "12 o'clock" star, which marks the beginning point of the clock. Uranus, is seen in conjunction with this Clock Star at the birth & death of Adam and even more remotely by percentage because of the short tenure of Messiah's life of 33 years, it can be seen emphasizing His life in conjunction as well, at the following points: His birth, (in conjunction with Jupiter & Venus), His presentation in the Temple, the beginning of his public ministry at 30, and his transfiguration at Tabernacles 2 yrs. later. Can you grasp the significance of this Stellar Clock? Hasn't the question of the ages regarding the plan of YHVH and in particular the coming of Messiah always centered on 'WHEN'? Perhaps this is another angle in the Restoration of the Pure Language and the light it shines in order that it might illuminate us regarding where, when and how? Even the heavens echo the admonition to walk in the light as children of the light should!

We are such woebegone pilgrims, unmindful of the magnanimous gesture this Restoration is! Our past rebellion merited our being exiled and circumcised from our Hebraic Heritage (Particularly the language, Sabbath and Festivals) and as a result, most of what has been mentioned in the volume of this book, foreign to us! Conversely, the Pagans overwhelmingly understand the influence of these "Signs" in the heavens! They declare that Uranus directly influences fanaticism, terrorism, dogmatism, riots, schisms, tyranny, treason and zealotry, earthquakes and disasters! Incidentally, Uranus is said to control those that fly or flit about, bringing memories of the accusation against Yahshua of be the Lord of the Flies i.e. those that flit about! (Perhaps hinting at the

Alien issue, this by the way, doubles as the Nephyilm) And this is pointing only to the effects of the Counterfeit "Angel of Light". What more could be said regarding the influence of the Light of Creation – the Spoken Word – visibly ensconced in a kaleidoscope of colors, and spoken into the life or DNA of another person or circumstance!

The Restoration of the Pure Language, the Mantle of Anointing will surely envelope the House of Joseph, and is in lock-step with the solemn adjuration of the Creator to UNSEAL THE BOOK(s). This same message is vividly displayed in every known language in Creation right above your head!

> ***Psalm 19:3*** *There is no speech nor language, where their voice is not heard.*

These signs that will strike terror in the hearts of the heathen are displayed on the "Clock"- the Zodiacal timepiece of heaven. These Signs, convey the urgency of the hour, give direction, call the sacred assemblies of YHVH together, open the doors of heaven and close them (This occurs during the festivals of Trumpets and Yom Kippur), sound the call to the wedding ceremony (Tabernacles), announce the crowning of the King (Trumpets), the year of Jubilee (Yom Kippur), The Passover celebration & Pentecost, The introduction of Light into the world (Chanukah), The Sign of the Covenant of YHVH (Sabbath), the birth of every major figure in Torah from Adam, Abraham, Isaac, Jacob, David, John the Baptist, Yahshua, the beginning of Creation and every major event in between based on Gen. 1:14, thus I would think it should detail the events of the end as well.

We are NOT to be dismayed at these signs, they reveal to us that our Redemption draws near! Finally, the constellation Virgo or Bethulah is the only constellation containing a listing of her stars from Alpha to Omega (Greek). We prefer the Hebrew of The Alef and Tav, fulfilling the promise of Gen. 3:15 and the seed of the woman! Ironically, Zephaniah 3: 9 which prophecies of the

Restoration of the Pure Rainbow Language is pre-empted by verse 8 which has all the above letters of the Alef-Bet, Alef through Tav in it as well as a marker identifying the pure language being restored.

Many ask me "what need is there in leaning the Hebrew language, much less the necessity of attempting to regain the lost knowledge of this 'so-called' witness in the heavens" that I contend is a confirmation of the Redemption Plan of YHVH? The answer to that lies in the heart of each of you Dear Readers, and after careful consideration of all the material written thus far you have no choice but to arrive at one of two possible conclusions:

> #1. Much of what I've written may be plausible, given the addition of the scientific data, yet why should we change directions in mid-stream when we've been accustomed to learning and speaking His Word in our current language?

> #2. You've experienced a 'quickening' in your spirit, which, though you don't understand, in view of the evidence you feel a desire to at least try to learn Hebrew, if for nothing else but to assuage your own fear of inadequacy in view of the lack of results that learning and speaking His Word in our own tongue has produced.

Both positions have merit and deserve answers. Frankly, this entire work was born out of my own quest for a verifiable rejoinder, to each of the above. My studies led me through a gradual migration from the first one, through the second to where I currently stand today. I am firmly convinced He is unveiling this language to the ordinary folks like you and I for the express purpose of allowing us to have a weapon in our hands and mouths, which will tip the balance in the favor of the Believers. Without this supernatural 'creative word', the enemy will overwhelm us in a tide of counterfeit words spoken against the Most High, which we will not recognize until the Anti-Messiah is firmly entrenched against us.

An honest assessment of our current condition as a Believing community will force you to admit that we are not able as individuals to produce evidence of consistently winning in any major theater against him. Corporately, we are a mess! There is absolutely no cohesion of any sort that would allow us to function as a unified Army in the field of spiritual warfare, much less what is sure to spill over into the physical realm in the form of the manifestation of those Monsters of antiquity, the Nephyilm and their offspring! If the Creator is returning this Pure – Rainbow language, and if past history serves as an accurate guide, then a unified tongue will produce results that have not been seen since Messiah Himself walked the earth! This should allow us to arrive at the only workable, natural conclusion: This is not an accident! A decade ago the mere thought of such was relegated to the surrealistic musings of one who had one to many "encounters" and disregarded entirely. Today, empirical data is mounting; the swing of the apocalyptic pendulum is no longer in the area of 'normal'. Even the general 'non-Christian' community holds its' collective breath waiting for what is now considered inevitable. So, what will you do with this information? To whom much is given much is indeed – required! The following 'final word', will prayerfully give you a starting place.

Chapter 18

Where Do I Begin?

Dear Reader, this question rings in my ears on almost a daily basis. It was the plaintive cry of my own heart as I sought Abbas' direction many years ago. Disillusioned by the lies of tradition which I myself had fervently propagated, my wife Brenda and I grasped at what was left crumbling around us; the dusty, hollow ruins of what we once thought a solid foundation in our relationship with the Creator. As the proverbial 'dust began to settle', everything we had been taught now became suspect. I remember confessing to her late one afternoon that perhaps I should quit, as I seemed unfit at this point. Mind you, we were not engaged in sin, as some of you reading may think. We were just unsure of everything we had ever been taught or had taught, ourselves, simply because we'd uncovered lie after lie, wrapped in the trappings of doctrinal opinions and traditions. I remember reading Jeremiah:

Jeremiah 16:19 O YHVH, my strength, and my fortress, and my refuge in the day of affliction, the Gentiles shall come unto thee from the ends of the earth, and shall say, surely our fathers have inherited lies, vanity, and things wherein there is no profit.

The lies though inherited had become mine! I had discovered I was worshipping on a day men were calling the Sabbath which,

214

in fact, wasn't the Sabbath at all! It was a Sun-day! Who changed Exodus 20: 8 – Remember the Sabbath day, to keep it holy? My celebrations of other supposed 'holy convocations' the spokes of which are to be connected to the center hub of the 7th-day Sabbath were also wrong! Those Seven Holy Festivals are also depicted in the picture of the Tabernacle Menorah and its 7-branches! These feast days are regulated by the lunar cycles, which in turn, regulates the gestational cycle of the Bride! They are DIVINE APPOINTMENTS – scheduled intimate encounters with the King! How could I have been wrong? By showing up on counterfeit days, who had I been entertaining in the intimate place? I felt defiled, degraded. Like Adam without the Garment of Light, I now felt, I had been compromised and no longer believed myself a suitable candidate for a help-meet to the Great King. It could only get worse…

Was it possible that perhaps I didn't even *truly know* the One whom I had presumed to worship? Did I know His Voice? His Name? I began to hear the resounding echoes of Proverbs 30:

> **Proverbs 30:4** *Who hath ascended up into heaven, or descended? Who hath gathered the wind in his fists? Who hath bound the waters in a garment? Who hath established all the ends of the earth? What is his name, and what is his son's name, if thou canst tell?*

Do you know Him intimately enough that you can call the Name of either? They each have distinctive names that are not titles. These names have been kept hidden from us while we were led to believe we were calling upon Him. Oh, His Mercy endures forever!

As you might figure, my disconsolate state found me beseeching Him for direction. I began to pray in earnest the humble petition I opened this work with: Colossians 1: 9 – 14. I began to do what I felt I was hearing in my spirit, "Put your back against the wall (Torah) and measure everything you hear and have heard by its standard. Take nothing out of context, support each position you espouse with at least two witnesses." Thus, my journey began...

Looking back, I'm grateful that I had at least a working knowledge of some of the basic tools for study: A good biblical concordance in particular. I preferred and still do, the Strong's Biblical Concordance. I delved in earnest, into the depths of the original language, with no formal training of any sort. The computer became my friend as I searched its exhaustive recesses, working to obtain any viable information that would answer the questions that lay, unanswered in my bosom. Trust me; He will not get offended if you question Him in all sincerity. Fear is a tool to keep you ignorant! Though it hasn't been easy, it has been nothing short of exhilarating! The heights and depths of His Word await those of you who will begin to immerse yourselves in an earnest search. The words of Hebrews 11: 6 seem appropriate here:

> **Hebrews 11:6** *But without faith it is impossible to please Him: for he that cometh to YHVH must believe that He is, and that he is a rewarder of them that diligently seek Him.*

As I sit here, those same basic tools are at my hands: The Strong's Concordance, a KJV-Bible (simply because I deem it the best translation of those available and the fact Strong's is keyed to it, though there are other good translations coming) and of course, The Complete Word Study Dictionary (Old Testament). These will enable you to get started. Many of you will have excuses to avoid *attempting to learn* the Hebrew Language. I've heard them all and they're just that – excuses! Hebrew is the Language of Light – He is Light! You're children of the Light! It is, in my opinion, His DNA and thus capable of repairing any debility you may have – including memory, reading limitations, learning disorders, etc. However, it will not cure laziness! This culprit, my friend, has kept many of you in bondage till this day. Rise to the occasion! I have seen children just learning to talk, (In households who were English speakers, yet who had begun listening to the Word in Hebrew) begin to speak Hebrew. I've seen others, more advanced in age, who've never looked at the Alef-Bet, until at 80 years and older – they begin to learn the Language of Creation and I've watched their excitement as the hidden truths of His Word come alive to them!

Zephaniah 3:9 makes it very plain that Abba is returning this 'Pure Language' to a specific group: *The People*. This indicates ordinary folks just like you and I. You needn't be a Televangelist, a doctor of Theology, or even the Pope. This is for you. Together the unifying power provided by a corporate language, will enable us to become the Sons of YHVH whose manifest purpose is to loose creation from its bondage and to usher in the King! You can begin by simply learning the basic Hebrew letters and their word pictures (See chart at the end of this chapter) as you incorporate their fundamental meanings into your daily Scripture study. Remember reading and studying are two different things! When I sit down I take the first verse I look at and begin to examine key words in their original language. As you do, the word pictures of the individual letters will help you to 'see' the subtle nuances of the text that only the Hebrew can reveal. Like any skill, it takes practice, practice and more practice. When you see how the Hebrew definitions enhance the text it will begin to 'come alive' and you will see things that you have never seen before! You will get addicted to looking for the hidden revelation that His Word provides! You will be changed! You needn't worry about being grammatically correct or whether you're able to pronounce each word correctly, as I've said this will come in time. What you must do however, is GET STARTED NOW! We cannot recoup the past, but we can change where we're headed!

While we still have access to the Internet, there is no greater tool available! You can find places that will help to sharpen your Hebrew skills and you're confidence in handling the Word of Creation will begin to grow! Look for specific verses tailored to the particular need you may have at the moment (Or someone you're praying for) and use the biblical concordances or Internet tools to translate them into Hebrew for you and begin to pray out loud the Hebrew Scripture! You may not experience instant change in the Physical realm, but, I assure – actually, He assures you – change will begin in the Spirit realm immediately!

I am particularly fond of what is commonly referred to as: The Aaronic or Priestly Benediction. There are many scholars who believe this to have been the prayer used by Yahshua the Messiah when praying for those listed in the New Testament. While some Torah Police may debate whether or not the individual can pray what was a "Priestly" prayer, is in my opinion, ludicrous! You are a Kingdom of Priests! Learn to make this declaration in Hebrew and insert the name(s) of those whom you're praying for. Let me stop for a second and insert that prayer, from Numbers 6:24-27.

The Aaronic Benediction

Numbers 6:24-27 The Lord bless you and keep you. The Lord make His face to shine upon you and be gracious unto you. The Lord lift up His countenance upon you and give you peace. And they shall put my name upon the children of Israel; and I will bless them.

[If inserting the generic English 'Lord' here upsets you, I apologize, it happens to be the most familiar to many reading for the first time and I want them to see and experience the thrill of the changes provided in the Hebrew language]

Now the Hebrew translation:

$$יְבָרֶכְךָ יְהוָה וְיִשְׁמְרֶךָ:$$

Ye.va.re.khe.kha YHVH ve.yish.me.re.kha:

May the Lord bless you and keep you:

יָאֵר יְהֹוָה פָּנָיו אֵלֶיךָ וִיחֻנֶּךָּ:

Ya.er YHVH pa.nav e.ley.kha vi.chun.ne.ka:

May the Lord make His face to shine upon you
and be gracious unto you.

יִשָּׂא יְהֹוָה פָּנָיו אֵלֶיךָ וְיָשֵׂם לְךָ שָׁלוֹם:

Yi.sa YHVH pa.nav e.ley.kha ve.ya.sem le.kha sha.lom:

May the lord lift up His countenance upon you
and give you peace.

וְשָׂמוּ אֶת־שְׁמִי עַל־בְּנֵי יִשְׂרָאֵל וַאֲנִי אֲבָרֲכֵם:

U.shmu Et-smi al-be.nei Yisra'el va.ani a.va.re.chem.

And I will put my name upon the children of Israel,
and I will bless them.

There are many other great resources to help you get started learning the basic letters of The Alef – Bet. I highly recommend: 'Hebrew Word Pictures' by Dr. Frank Seekins. For more advance study I suggest the hard copy of: Ernest Klein 'A Comprehensive Etymological Dictionary of the Hebrew Language'. If you have computer access: here is another great site:
http://www.hebrew4christians.com/Online_Store/Books/books.html

If you want a wonderful Bible with references to the Person of the Alef-Tav, whom I believe is Messiah Yahshua then I recommend: http://www.alephtavscriptures.com/ by William Sanford.

There are many other wonderful resources too numerous to name. However, may I also suggest a wonderful Spanish language book; dedicated to your quest for truth, written by my good friend Manual Chavarria: *La Busqueda de la Verdad* – In search of the Truth. (English translation available shortly). You may find this book at the link below:

Finally, we have countless audio and video teachings available at: Manna from Heaven Ministries. http://livingmanna.net

Dear Reader, the hour is late and the time is shortly upon us when no man may labor. It is not an accident that you picked up this book.

> ***Jeremiah 29:11*** *For I know the thoughts that I think toward you, says the YHVH, thoughts of shalom, and not of evil, to give you hope in your latter end.* [Hebrew Names Version]

He knew where you'd be at this hour, the need in your life, and the desires of your heart. He saved you for this last event in the grandest chapter of creation's history! Ezekiel speaks of a river he is challenged to step into; first the ankles, the knees – the water begins to pull – his ability to resist diminishes. He steps further, the waist, chest and finally the waters have control. His destiny, like yours lies in the bosom of this water! Where will you be drawn? The answer alone, like the test, is yours! Don't fret, the journey's already begun, you're in the deep water now!

May YHVH bless you and keep you. May He make His face to shine upon you and be gracious unto you. May YHVH lift up His countenance upon you and give you – Shalom!

Appendix: Aleph-Bet Charts

Elef Tabernacle (Mishkan Station)	Conceptual Paleo	Hebrew Letter (Modern)	Conceptual Paleo Meaning	Num. Value	Yeshua The Messiah In The Alef Bet
		Alef	Ox head, strength, first	1	The Almighty, infinite One came from heaven to earth to be finite & visible. The Word became flesh. He is our strength.
		Bet, Vet	House, inside, body, woman	2	The Architect builds His Dwelling Place, a house for us to come into and abide in Him, set-apart from the world outside.
		Gimel	Camel, lift up, transport	3	Yeshua is our go-between with Abba. He descended to die for us and ascended to resurrect us. He is Jacob's Ladder.
		Dalet	Door, threshhold, access	4	Yeshua said "I AM The Door." He is the only Way to Abba; the Way into His house where He shuts out our enemies.
		Hey	Window, reveal, behold	5	Light of the world, Yeshua perfectly reveals the Almighty to us. His Spirit reveals His grace (5), His ways and the Word.
Red Heifer Sacrifice outside camp		Vav	Nail, hook, bridge, man	6	The Son of Man (6) was nailed to the cross to join us to Him and to secure a relationship bridged between us and Abba.
		Zayin	Weapon, hatchet, cut off	7	Abba cut off His Son outside the camp in His death, so that He could circumcise our hearts from the flesh and the world.
Big White Fence.		Chet	Fence, bor-der, enclose	8	The Good Shepherd encloses and protects us in His sheep-fold. He sets the borders of what's in & outside the Kingdom.
Blue, Purple, Scarlet, Gate.		Tet	Snake, surround, mark	9	Yeshua surrounds us with His love and claims us as His own. His Spirit marks and seals us as part of His Kingdom.
		Yod	Hand, work, create, make	10	Yeshua created all things. His right hand upon us shapes and molds us into His image; working all things for our good.
Altar of Sacrifice		Kaf	Open hand, lines, filter	20	Our Rabbi lays His hand upon us. He instructs us line upon line, precept upon precept. He filters out evil from good.
		Lamed	Staff, goad, authority	30	All authority belongs to Yeshua. The Good Shepherd's staff keeps us in His fold, chastises us and wards off the wolves.
Brazen Laver		Mem	Waters, birth, bring forth	40	By His Spirit He baptizes us; cleansing, refreshing and birthing new life in us. His Word reflects the new man inside.
		Nun	Fish darting, imparting life	50	He is the Life. Yeshua imparts the quickening life of His Spirit in us that we may live His life and do His works on earth.
Menorah		Samech	Prop, support, vine, works	60	Yeshua is the Vine & servant candle, we are His branches. He supports and lights us up. He anoints us to shine & grow.
Table of Shewbread		Ayin	Eye, discern, understand	70	Yeshua is the Judge Who discerns our hearts rightly. He gives us understanding to rightly divide the Word of Truth.
Altar of Incense		Pey	Mouth, speak, communicate	80	Yeshua is the Voice of Abba. He ever intercedes for us. By His Breath He causes open dialogue between us and Abba.
Ark Of The Covenant		Tsade	Fish-hook, righteous	90	The Righteous Branch hooks us into Him, giving us desire to live righteous. He will sit on the throne in the Holy of Holies.
Pillar of Fire / Cloud		Qoof	Back of head, behind, cover	100	Messiah is like the back side of Elohim, the manifestation Moses saw. He oversees and covers us with His glory.
		Resh	Head, exalted man, face	200	The Son of Man is the Head of the "Church", the Body of Messiah. He is exalted and is pre-eminent in all things.
		Sheen Seen	Teeth, consuming fire	300	The roaring Lion of Judah will return and destroy all enemies. He's El Shaddai, the Consuming Fire Who purifies.
		Tav	Cross, sign of the covenant	400	The Alef & the Tav, the beginning & the end, signed and secured our covenant with Abba by His work on the cross.

Artwork by Eric Bissell

Prepared by David Klug

The above chart used by permission from *Eric Bissell.*

Yahshua in the Aleph-Bet

Used with permission from *William Sanford's*

Introduction to the Aleph Tav Scriptures

א   Aleph--He will manifest His STRENGTH for us

ב   Bet--He will come in a BODY, DWELLING, (born of a woman)

ג   Gimel--He will ASCEND-DESCEND for us (He is the ultimate camel man!)

ד   Dalet--He will be the DOOR-ACCESS, the PATHWAY for us to the Father.

ה   Hey--He will REVEAL LIGHT and truth, we will BEHOLD Him.

ו   Vav--He will secure--by becoming a MAN. He will be NAILED. He will be a bridge.

ז   Zayin--He will be CUT OFF. He is a WEAPON for us.

ח   Chet--He will be a FENCE--PROTECT us--ENCLOSE us to Himself.

ט   Tet--He will SET APART--SEALS us, MARK us to Himself.

י   Yod--His hand will MAKE us, ESTABLISH us, and CONFORM us to His Image.

כ Kaph--He will COVER us by His HAND, SEPARATE us to Himself.

ל Lamed--His AUTHORITY will ENFORCE, SHEPHERD us, PROTECT us.

מ Mem--He will BRING FORTH,-WASH us, and CLEANSE us-REFRESH us.

נ Nun--He will IMPART His LIFE to us

ס Samech--He will ANOINT us, RULE over us, SUPPORT us, and PROVIDE for us. He is the VINE.

ע Ayin--He will SEE, and WEIGH-MEASURE JUDGE all His creation.

פ Pey--He will INTERCEDE- COMMUNICATE-SPEAK to us.

צ Tsade--He will HOOK, HUNT, CAPTURE us. He will make us RIGHTEOUS. (Holy of Holies)

ק Qof--He is BACKSIDE of Elohim. He will RISE UP, COVER us with His CLOUD.

ר Resh--He is the HEAD-EXALTED-FACE of Elohim.

שׁ Sheen--He is and does CONSUME us-REFINE us-FIRE.

ת Tav--He is the SIGN-He will SECURE-SEAL-COVENANTS bring JUDGMENTS.

Used with permission from William Sanford's introduction to the Messianic Aleph Tav Scriptures pp xvi-xvii CCB Publishing, 2014.

CPSIA information can be obtained at www.ICGtesting.com
Printed in the USA
LVOW07s0239191015

458804LV00022B/274/P